Strange

Pennsylvania Monsters

Schiffer Publishing Ltd

4880 Lower Valley Road, Atglen, Pennsylvania 19310

Michael Newton

Dedication

For Chad Arment

Other Schiffer Books By The Author:
Strange Indiana Monsters ISBN 0-7643-2608-2 $12.95
Strange California Monsters ISBN 978-0-7643-3336-1 $14.99
Strange Kentucky Monsters ISBN 978-0-7643-3440-5 $14.99
Strange Monsters of the Pacific Northwest ISBN 978-0-7643-3622-5 $16.99

Schiffer Books are available at special discounts for bulk purchases for sales promotions or premiums. Special editions, including personalized covers, corporate imprints, and excerpts can be created in large quantities for special needs. For more information contact the publisher:

Published by Schiffer Publishing Ltd.
4880 Lower Valley Road
Atglen, PA 19310
Phone: (610) 593-1777; Fax: (610) 593-2002
E-mail: Info@schifferbooks.com

For the largest selection of fine reference books on this and related subjects,
please visit our website at **www.schifferbooks.com**
We are always looking for people to write books on new and related subjects.
If you have an idea for a book, please contact us at
proposals@schifferbooks.com

This book may be purchased from the publisher.
Include $5.00 for shipping.
Please try your bookstore first.
You may write for a free catalog.

In Europe, Schiffer books are distributed by
Bushwood Books
6 Marksbury Ave.
Kew Gardens
Surrey TW9 4JF England
Phone: 44 (0) 20 8392 8585; Fax: 44 (0) 20 8392 9876
E-mail: info@bushwoodbooks.co.uk
Website: www.bushwoodbooks.co.uk

Designed by Mark David Bowyer
Type set in Viner Hand ITC / NewBskvll BT

ISBN: 978-0-7643-3985-1
Printed in the United States

Contents

Acknowledgments

I owe special thanks to Chad Arment, author and researcher extraordinaire; to Fortean investigator Stan Gordon (www.stangordonufo.com); to Dave Frasier, a longtime friend and colleague; and again, always, to Heather.

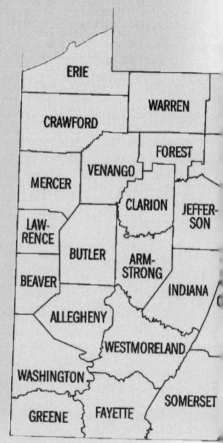

01. Map of Pennsylvania counties.
Credit: U.S. Census Bureau

Introduction
Erie Pennsylvania

Any schoolchild knows—or *should* know—that Pennsylvania ranks high among the pivotal states in American history. Italian explorer Giovanni da Verrazzano dubbed its shoreline *L'arcadia* ("wooded coast") in 1524, while Captain John Smith navigated the Susquehanna River and met local aborigines in 1608. A year later, Henry Hudson claimed Delaware Bay for Holland, though Dutch trading posts were not established until 1647. Meanwhile, Swedes established the area's first long-term settlements, in 1638. Conflict with the Dutch prompted the governor of New Netherlands to seize and annex New Sweden in 1655. Britain's Duke of York was next in line, ousting Dutch settlers from the Delaware and Hudson Rivers in 1664.[1]

In March 1681, King Charles II of England granted a tract of land in North America to William Penn, in payment of a £16,000 debt to Penn's father. Penn, a Quaker who had suffered religious discrimination in his homeland, established a colony dedicated to freedom and called it Pennsylvania—"Penn's woods," in Latin. The new colony's seat of government and primary trading center—Philadelphia, from the Greek for "brotherly love"—was founded on the Delaware River in October 1682 and incorporated as a city nine years later.[2]

Philadelphia's location and economic importance in the British colonies made it a center of revolutionary sentiment by the early 1770s. It hosted the First Continental Congress in September 1774, where delegates from twelve colonies protested passage of the Coercive Acts by Parliament, and likewise the Second Continental Congress, which convened in May 1775 and produced the Declaration of Independence fourteen months later. Once war had been declared with Britain, Pennsylvania witnessed the Battles of Brandywine (September 11, 1777) and Germantown (October 4, 1777), while providing George Washington's troops with grim winter quarters at Valley Forge.[3]

Victory over George III left Pennsylvania at the center of American democracy. When the Articles of Confederation failed to establish a workable government, Philadelphia welcomed delegates who hammered out a new U.S. Constitution between May and September 1787. Two months later, on December 12, Pennsylvania became the second state admitted to the Union (after Delaware). It also served as the nation's temporary capital from 1790 to 1800, while a new Federal City was under construction in the District of Columbia. Small wonder, then, that a gathering of Jeffersonian Republicans toasted Pennsylvania in October 1802 as "the keystone in the federal union."[4]

And so it would remain. During the Civil War, Pennsylvania suffered repeated Confederate raids. General J.E.B. Stuart invaded the Keystone State in 1862 and 1863. General John Imboden's cavalry struck the Baltimore and Ohio Railroad in Bedford County, also during 1863. In July 1863, Union and Rebel armies clashed at Gettysburg, leaving 7,863 soldiers dead, 27,224 wounded, and 11,199 captured or missing. Brigadier General John McCausland's rebel troops burned Chambersburg in July 1864.[5]

Warfare aside, Pennsylvania also stood in the forefront of America's industrial revolution. Coal mining in northeastern Pennsylvania predated the American revolution, while the discovery of "rock oil" at Titusville, in 1859, prompted construction of eight kerosene refineries between 1862 and 1868. Later, Pennsylvania witnessed some of America's earliest and most infamous labor violence, including activity by the "Molly Maguires," in the 1870s, and the police massacre of nineteen unarmed strikers at Lattimer, in September 1897.[6]

Today, with 12,604,767 residents occupying its 46,055 square miles, Pennsylvania boasts America's tenth-highest population density: 274 inhabitants per square mile of land.[7] It has been settled for nearly four centuries and is, by all accounts, completely civilized.

And yet, certain peculiarities persist.

Pennsylvania settlers reported their first encounter with an alien big cat (ABC)—a "hairy panther" resembling an African lion, shot with its mate and cubs—in 1797. The first known sighting of a giant snake unknown to science was logged in 1820. The state's premiere "gorilla" report followed in 1837. In the early 1860s, railroad workers unearthed giant humanoid remains. A flying serpent soared across the Pennsylvania sky in 1887. Five years later, witnesses logged their first sighting of a giant "thunderbird"—and a dragon with heart-shaped scales. A freshwater "sea serpent" cavorted in the Allegheny River, during 1906.[8]

And those reports are merely the tip of a frightening iceberg.

How can such things exist? More to the point, since Pennsylvania sightings have continued to the present day, where would they hide in a state where 274 persons dwell on each square mile of land?

The truth concerning Pennsylvania's modern settlement is not exactly as it seems, from government reports. For starters, the state's ten largest cities—Philadelphia, Pittsburgh, Allentown, Erie, Reading, Bethlehem, Scranton, Lancaster, Harrisburg, and Altoona, with their surrounding metropolitan areas—jam 90.4 percent of the Keystone State's total population (11,398,921 persons) into 28 percent of its total area (12,706 square miles)—leaving nearly three-fourths of the state with an actual population density of thirty-six inhabitants per square mile.[9]

But even that statistic is misleading, for rural Pennsylvania includes the Allegheny National Forest, sprawling over parts of four counties with more than 513,000 acres, and twenty state forests comprising some 2.1 million acres. Within the state forests, designated wilderness areas cover 144,943 acres. Finally, Pennsylvania boasts a total of 209 swamps large enough to rate names and notation on maps.[10]

In short, there may be room for almost anything to hide.

Strange Pennsylvania Monsters examines the full range of unknown and out-of-place creatures reported from the Keystone State between its founding and the present day. The pursuit of such mysteries beasts is dubbed *cryptozoology*—literally the study of "hidden animals"—and its subjects, while properly known as "cryptids," are frequently dubbed "monsters" for their size, peculiar form, or the frightening impact their sudden appearance may have on humans.

In broad terms, cryptids fall into four categories:

1. Animals resembling members of known species, but with striking variations in size or other aspects of appearance—"blacksnakes" many times the size of record specimens, etc.
2. Animals resembling known species, found living far from their natural range—such as tigers or "black panthers" in North America. (Some cryptozoologists dub such creatures "OOPs," for "out-of-place.")
3. Animals resembling species said to be extinct or extirpated in a given area—such as cougars found east of the Mississippi River.
4. Animals apparently unrelated to any known species, either living or extinct—such as giant bipeds that leave humanoid footprints worldwide.[11]

Strange Pennsylvania Monsters divides our survey into eight topical chapters.

Chapter 1 describes exotic invasive species reported from Pennsylvania, including some whose presence may prove unnerving.

Chapter 2 details reports of creatures listed as extinct or extirpated from the Keystone State, which still appear to modern witnesses on numerous occasions.

Chapter 3 reviews the state's long history of alien big cat (ABC) reports, spanning more than two centuries from 1797 to the present.

Chapter 4 examines lake and river monster sightings, with particular emphasis on the elusive creature known as Raytown's Ray.

Chapter 5 investigates 190 years of giant snake sightings statewide.

Chapter 6 scan the heavens in search of huge "thunderbirds," raptors the size of small aircraft, reported to menace livestock and humans.

Chapter 7 takes us in pursuit of Pennsylvania's omnipresent "ape-men," sighted hundreds of times across nearly two centuries.

Chapter 8 ties up loose ends with a collection of baffling beasts that fit none of the previous classifications—from those appearing only once, then vanishing forever, to others that haunted the state for generations.

Let the crypto-safari begin!

Chapter 1
Alien Intruders

The Keystone State is rich in wildlife. According to the latest census conducted by the nonprofit Pennsylvania Biological Survey (PABS), a total of 800 species of fish, amphibians, reptiles, birds, and mammals are recognized statewide.[1] Not all of those are native to Pennsylvania, however. And, as we shall see, the list is not complete.

Something Fishy

Surveys conducted in 1975 and 1983 counted 160 species of freshwater fish in Pennsylvania, representing either twenty-four or twenty-seven families. A more recent census identified 225 species from forty families. Of those, eighteen are identified as exotic species. The Pennsylvania Fish and Boat Commission (PFBC) lists five more invasive fish species excluded from the state's master checklist, all of which are banned by law from importation or possession within the state's borders.[2]

Exotic species recognized by the PBS include the central stoneroller (*Campostoma anomalum*); the common carp (*Cyprinus carpio*) and grass carp (*Ctenopharyngodon idellus*); brassy minnow (*Hybognathus hankinsoni*); European rudd (*Scardinius erythrophthalmus*); Amur pike (*Esox reicherti*); Atlantic salmon (*Salmo salar*); five species of Pacific salmons—the chinook (*Oncorhynchus tshawytscha*), coho (*O. kisutch*), pink (*O. gorbuscha*), and sockeye (*O. nerka*); brown trout (*Salmo trutta*) and rainbow trout (*Oncorhynchus mykiss*); eastern mosquitofish (*Gambusia holbrooki*) and western mosquitofish (*G. affinis*); blue tilapia (*Tilapia aurea*); round goby (*Neogobius melanostomus*); and northern snakehead (*Channa argus*). The PFBC list adds five more species, four of which—the bighead carp (*Hypophtalmichtys nobilis*), black carp (*Mylopharyngodon piceus*), silver carp (*H. molitrix*), and Eurasian ruffe (*Gymnocephalus cernuus*)—are not listed by the PBS as being found in Pennsylvania. A fifth invasive species, the sea lamprey (*Petromyzon marinus*), is described as a native Pennsylvania species by the PBS, although it did not reach the Great Lakes from the Atlantic Ocean until the Erie Canal was completed in 1825.[3]

Exotic species may have a disastrous impact on native flora and fauna, due in equal parts to rapid breeding and ravenous predation. The round goby, for example, feeds on native fish and invertebrates. First introduced to the Great Lakes basin in 1990, by 2002 there were 9.9 *billion* round gobies in western Lake Erie alone.[4]

Northern snakeheads rank among the more peculiar and insidious exotic species. Thus far, they have featured in four low-budget horror films, including *Night of the Snakehead Fish* (2003), *Snakehead Terror* (2004), *Frankenfish* (2004), and *Swarm of the Snakehead* (2006). But while Hollywood portrayals of giant, man-eating snakeheads are pure fantasy, the species still presents cause for concern.

Snakehead fish have inspired several horror films.
Credit: U.S. Fish & Wildlife Service

Snakeheads (Family *Channidae*) are predatory natives of Africa and Asia, where twenty-nine species are known. Their diet includes other fish, amphibians, and small mammals. An air-breathing fish, some of whose species can crawl overland, northern snakeheads build nests up to three feet in diameter, where females lay as many as 50,000 eggs at a time, "vigorously guarded by one or both parents." The young become sexually mature at two years of age, ranging from forty to sixty inches long in adulthood.[5]

The first confirmed snakehead appearance in Pennsylvania occurred in July 2004, when a fisherman hooked two at Meadow Lake (Philadelphia County). PFBC biologists then caught three more at the seventeen-acre lake, while another angler landed a sixth. Because Meadow Lake is part of a maze of interconnected embayments and tidal sloughs, the PFBC decided that there was "no practical method for eradicating snakeheads from Meadow Lake and that, given the nature of the system, snakeheads may have already accessed adjoining waters like the nearby lower Schuylkill and Delaware Rivers." State officials decided to monitor the snakeheads' progress while making "no concerted effort to eliminate the species." As PFBC spokesman Dan Tredinnick told the media, poisoning state waterways, as had been done in Maryland, "would probably do more damage than snakeheads would do themselves."[6]

Today, it is illegal to possess, import, buy, sell, or trade live snakeheads anywhere in Pennsylvania. Anglers who catch a snakehead or suspect they have caught one are urged to "dispose of it properly"—no live releases—and file a report with the PFBC.[7]

Any hopes that Pennsylvania's winter cold might eradicate snakeheads was dashed in April 2005, when six adult specimens were caught in ponds at Philadelphia's Franklin Delano Roosevelt Park. The largest was two feet long and weighed nearly five pounds. December 2005 brought news that an eight-inch northern snakehead had been captured near Philadelphia International Airport. In February 2006, PFBC spokesman Mike Kaufmann told reporters,

> We're encouraging anglers to harvest and kill all that they can. We don't know how many more there are.

The PFBC made no secret of its fears that snakeheads might damage the state's fishing industry, when earns $1.6 billion per year.[8]

Two groups of fish omitted from all lists of species found in Pennsylvania are the South American piranhas and pacus (Family *Characidae*; Subfamily *Serrasalminae*). Pacus and piranhas closely resemble each other, but while piranhas have a fierce—sometimes exaggerated—reputation for devouring any animal they meet, pacus are harmless, often advertised for sale to hobbyists as "vegetarian piranhas."[9]

The near-identical appearance of pacus and piranhas often spawns confusion when exotic fish are caught in American waters. PFBC spokesmen confidently state that any specimens hooked in Pennsylvania "are most likely pacu, and not piranha," but identification may require examination of the teeth—a risky maneuver if the captive fish is, in fact, a razor-toothed piranha.[10]

While confusion persists, reports indicate that both pacus and piranhas have been caught in Pennsylvania waters. The U.S. Geological Survey recorded the capture of an "unidentified pacu" at a Bucks County pond, near Philadelphia, in 1995. Six years later, in August 2001, Kayla Shuits hooked a thirteen-inch piranha while fishing on the Ohio River near Glasgow, Pennsylvania. The following month, Terry Schneider and John Turkovich pulled a foot-long piranha from the Ohio near Industry (Beaver County). PFBC spokesman Emil Svetahor told the Pittsburgh *Post-Gazette*,

Hollywood's treatment of piranhas exaggerates their ferocity.
Credit: Author's collection

> We're curious, but we don't make a big issue of it. We get these calls every year.

In June 2006, four-year-old James Weaver caught a fifteen-inch piranha at Leola (Lancaster County). Jim Rulli hooked a twelve-inch piranha with "big, sharp" teeth in July 2006, while fishing along the Allegheny River in Lancaster County. In each case, state authorities blamed negligent pet owners for releasing the fish, and reassured state residents that none could survive a cold winter.[11]

See You Later, Alligator!

The PABS recognizes thirty-seven species of reptiles and thirty-six species of amphibians presently inhabiting the Keystone State. Most are Pennsylvania natives, but exotic species are also recognized, including both complete outsiders and some Keystone native species found today in portions of the state outside their normal range.[12]

Italian wall lizards (*Podarcis sicula*) found their way from Europe to the streets of Philadelphia in the early 1900s, and soon established breeding populations despite the disparate climate. Observers later claimed the species had been extirpated, but occasional sightings persist to the present day.[13]

Less welcome—and listed among the PFBC's "least wanted" exotic species—is the red-eared slider (*Pseudemys scripta elegans*), a turtle commonly sold at county fairs and elsewhere until 1975, when the U.S. Food and Drug Administration banned sale of turtle eggs and specimens with a carapace length less than four inches. Violation of that rule carries a maximum penalty of one year in prison and a $1,000 fine, yet sliders have spread far beyond their native range, threatening to crowd out native turtle species. Specimens have been collected from the Lehigh River and canal system (Lehigh County), while others have been seen over consecutive years around Allentown and Bethlehem. Thus far, their spread remains unchecked.[14]

The PABS also acknowledges "numerous reports of alligators within Pennsylvania waters," while insisting that "[a]lthough some individuals might be able to survive for more than a year, the climate precludes the possibility of successful reproduction."[15] And, indeed, we find multiple reports of various crocodilians at large statewide. Such incidents include the following:

> In 1997, a common or spectacled caiman (*Caiman crocodilus*) native to Central and South America was captured in Peters Creek, south of Pittsburgh in Washington County.[16]

Caimans have been found in Pennsylvania waters.
Credit: U.S. Fish & Wildlife Service

> In June 2004 a two-foot long American alligator (*Alligator mississippiensis*) surfaced in the Allegheny River near Harmarville. PABF officers transported it to the Pittsburgh Zoo.[17]

> Another caiman was trapped at Crumb Creek, in Aston (Delaware County), in September 2005.[18]

> During 2007, no less than five alligators appeared in and around Pittsburgh. The last two specimens were caught in August—one pulled from a fountain at the downtown David L. Lawrence Convention Center, the other a four-footer snared in suburban Homewood.[19]

> Across the state, Philadelphia's suburbs produced two more reptiles in 2007. The first was seen at Haddonfield's popular Hopkins Pond in May, but eluded pursuers. A forty-two-inch

crocodile was caught in Douglas Township, in July, and packed off to an out-of-state sanctuary.[20]

Midway between Pittsburgh and Philadelphia, in Cumberland County, yet another crocodilian surfaced in August 2007. Residents of North Newton Township pulled the eighteen-inch caiman from a local creek and delivered it to officers of the State Fish and Game Commission (SFGC).[21]

Lake City firefighters captured a three-foot-long alligator in the Elk Creek Access Area, during May 2010, and subsequently gave it to an unnamed "area reptile specialist."[22]

In each case, authorities blamed unidentified pet owners for releasing the reptiles—an offense punishable by a $100 fine for each animal dumped in the wild. Thus far, none of the miscreants have been identified.

But if stray crocodilians may be hypothetically explained, what are we to make of a giant toad unknown to science? Melissa Barclay of Allegheny County described the creature in 2004, referring to an incident from 1973. Her father found the toad while uprooting tree stumps at their home in Forward Township, near Elizabeth. As Barclay later described the event:

> They were having trouble turning this one large stump over because it had some roots left that were kind of deep, but when they did, my dad uttered an expletive and I thought he got hurt. But then he called us over to look and it was pretty unbelievable. There was this huge toad that came out from between the roots of that stump. It wasn't moving at first so my grandfather slid his coal shovel under it. It was so big that it covered the whole metal part of this coal shovel (this was a coal shovel he used in the mines, it was big). That toad was about 14 inches long and a foot wide...It seemed a little sluggish, even when put on the shovel. We wanted to get something to put it in but the adults said to leave it alone... We watched it for awhile and it slowly hopped into the weeds near some trees between properties and that was the last we saw of it.[23]

The largest toad recognized by science is the cane toad (*Bufo marinus*), a native of Latin America which has been introduced from the Caribbean and southern Florida to Australia, New Guinea, and Oceania. Its record specimen measured fifteen inches long from snout to vent and weighed nearly six pounds, but most members of the species average four to six inches in length.[24] None are recognized as occupying Pennsylvania, where they would be ill suited to surviving frigid winters.

Exotic Birds

The PABS Official Pennsylvania Bird List includes 186 species that regularly nest within the state, plus others that are winter residents, transients, or "occasional visitors." Human residents—mostly hunters— have made numerous attempts to introduce exotic species, but the PABS recognizes only five success stories. At the same time, agency spokesmen grant that "[t]he high mobility and resourcefulness of birds make it difficult to make concrete classifications of species."[25]

Three species described as "abundant and widespread pests" are the European or common starling *(Sturnus vulgaris)*, house sparrow *(Passer domesticus)*, and rock dove or rock pigeon *(Columba livia)*. Doves are the oldest invaders, introduced to North America at Port Royal, Nova Scotia, in 1606. The first fifty pairs of sparrows were released in Brooklyn, New York, in 1852. All 200 million of North America's starlings are descended from sixty specimens released in New York City's Central Park by Eugene Schieffelin, a member of the misguided Acclimation Society of North America, in 1890.[26]

Pennsylvania's remaining exotic bird species are the mute swan *(Cygnus olor)* and the common or ring-necked pheasant *(Phasianus colchicus)*. Mute swans were introduced as an ornamental species in the late nineteenth century and spread swiftly, with an unfortunate impact on native waterfowl and ecosystems. A survey conducted between 1971 and 2000 found their population in the lower Great Lakes increasing by ten percent per year. The first ring-necked pheasants were released in America during 1857, ultimately thriving in the wild from the Rocky Mountains eastward, with incursions into Canada and Mexico.[27]

A pair of stranger avian invaders surfaced in Boyertown (Berks County) on March 2, 2005. That afternoon, two emus *(Dromaius novaehollandiae)*—a flightless bird, Australia's largest—suddenly appeared on Chestnut Street. When neighbors called police, one of the birds collided with a squad car, broke its leg, and later died while in the care of the Animal Rescue League. Its mate escaped, after bruising Boyertown police officer Amy Bertolette, and gave trackers the slip in the vicinity of Upper Pottsgrove. Investigators questioned a local resident known to keep emus as pets, but the man's birds were all present and accounted for. As the *Pottstown Mercury* declared:

Exactly where the two birds hail from remains a mystery.[28]

Another emu of unknown origin surfaced on the Pennsylvania Turnpike, near New Stanton (Westmoreland County), on September 1, 2008. Passing drivers called the State Police, and officers spent two hours chasing the four-foot-tall bird before shocking it with a Taser stun-gun, whereupon it dropped and died. Unnamed "animal experts" blamed the emu's death on exhaustion, rather than the shock, and officers were thus absolved. As in the prior case, local emu-farmers had no missing birds. Police surmised that the dead emu "may have escaped from a truck," whose driver failed to notice the loss of his pricey cargo.[29]

Emus of unknown origin sometimes appear in Pennsylvania.
Credit: U.S. Fish & Wildlife Service

Going Hog-Wild

Mammals comprise a relatively small portion of Pennsylvania's wildlife. The PABS recognizes seventy-one species statewide, reporting that only two—the house mouse (*Mus musculus*) and brown or Norway rat (*Rattus norvegicus*)—are exotics. Two other introduced species, the black rat (*R. rattus*) and the European or brown hare (*Lepus europaeus*), are now listed as extirpated from the state.[30]

One invader conspicuously missing from the state's official list of mammals is the wild hog (*Sus scrofa*), represented worldwide by a score of subspecies. The PABS tally makes no mention of wild hogs, although the SFGC has confirmed sightings in fifteen counties since 1993. During one recent winter, Keystone hunters killed 300 hogs statewide, while some estimates place the surviving population above 3,000.[31]

No hogs in Pennsylvania have thus far rivaled Georgia's "Hogzilla" for size—though one reared in captivity for hunting purposes reportedly grew to 10.5 feet in length, tipping the scales at 1,005 pounds—but specimens weighing 350 pounds have been confirmed. Larry Olsavsky, a wildlife conservation officer with the SFGC, told the media in 2003,

> We want them killed. They cause property damage, and a 400-pound boar is definitely a threat to human life.

However, as commission spokesman Mel Schake explained,

> This is not an easy issue. Boars are not native game animals, so they don't fall under our jurisdiction.[32]

Two years later, in August 2005, state officials confirmed hog sightings in fourteen Pennsylvania counties. In most cases, they said, no evidence of breeding was discovered, but pregnant sows and piglets were confirmed from Bedford, Bradford, Cambria, Somerset, and Wyoming Counties. In November 2006, the U.S. Department of Agriculture's Animal and Plant Inspection Service announced plans to shoot or trap wild hogs in three Pennsylvania districts, spending $60,000 to test those killed for disease. Dave Wolfgang, a veterinarian at Penn State's College of Agricultural Sciences, told reporters,

> I think everybody is concerned that we don't really know how widespread the problem is. They are most concerned about, one, some animal health issues concerned with them; two, some public health issues of a hunter type; and three, that they're a very invasive species that can cause a lot of damage.[33]

Aside from predation on native wildlife, physical property damage, and the threat of attacks on humans, wild hogs also carry diseases that jeopardize livestock. Many adults carry the pseudorabies virus, also known as Aujeszky's disease, which may cause spontaneous abortion and high mortality in piglets, while afflicting adult swine with various symptoms ranging from sneezing and fever to constipation and seizures. Swine brucellosis, an untreatable disease whose effects include spontaneous abortion, infertility, lack of sexual drive, and posterior paralysis, also threatens Pennsylvania's $241 million swine industry.[34]

Proposed solutions to the problem vary widely, from unrestricted hunting to a legal ban on shooting hogs. The latter notion—passed into law by Iowa legislators, on the theory that most wild hogs are released for the pleasure of hunters—failed to win adoption in Pennsylvania. Instead, Governor Edward Rendell issued an executive order in May 2008, permitting hunters to kill wild hogs in sixty-four counties, while hunting was banned in Bradford, Bedford, Fulton, Susquehanna, and Wyoming Counties. Rather than shooting hogs in those counties where they are known to breed, state agents preferred to try trapping them alive.[35] It remains to be seen whether that technique proves effective.

Monkey Business

Human beings are North America's only recognized "native" primates, but feral breeding colonies of rhesus macaques (*Macaca mulatta*) have existed in Florida since 1938, in South Carolina since the 1970s, and in Texas since the 1990s.[36] Warm climates encourage primate colonization, while Pennsylvania should be less hospitable, but tales of apes at large surfaced in 1987, nonetheless.

Authors Colin and Janet Bord vaguely date the first sightings from autumn, emerging from Westmoreland County's North Huntingdon Township. Within days, the action shifted 200 miles eastward to Chester County, where inhabitants reported glimpses of "an orangutan or a chimpanzee." Marlene Oatman ended the flap by shooting a "pretty big" monkey in Honey Brook Township, on November 2. State police described the creature as 2.5 feet long, weighing fifty pounds. It was covered in reddish-brown hair and sported inch-long canine teeth. Spokesmen for the University of Pennsylvania's School of Veterinary Medicine professed themselves unable to identify the species.[37]

Two years later, the Bords reported no progress in determining the ape's identity. Author Rosemary Guiley repeated that claim in 1995, while claiming that the beast was shot in October 1978. In fact, however, curators at the Philadelphia Zoo identified the monkey as a macaque,

complete with a three-digit tattoo commonly found on zoo and labora-
tory specimens.[38] There was, in short, no mystery at all.

As we shall see in later chapters, Pennsylvania's tabulation of exotic
species may not be complete. In fact, reports suggest that the Keystone
State harbors some creatures not only unnoticed by wildlife officials, but
unknown to science.

And, we find, even some species designated as extinct or extirpated
may survive to haunt those who would count them out.

Marlene Oatman shot a macaque like this one in Chester County.
Credit: U.S. Fish & Wildlife Service

Chapter 2
Going...Going...Gone?

While some exotic species find Pennsylvania's woods and waters too inviting to resist, others have given up the ghost in their conflict with humans. According to the PABS, forty of the state's known species have either been extirpated (killed off statewide) or are presently extinct (no longer living anywhere on Earth). However, through the recent work of conservationists, five of those species—including one fish and four mammals—have now been re-established in the wild.[1]

Lost Fish

Aquatic species are hardest hit in Pennsylvania, with eighteen species extirpated and only one of those re-established. Those killed off within historic times—that is, before the twentieth century—include the shovelnose sturgeon (*Scaphirhynchus platorynchus*), shortnose gar (*Lepisosteus platostomus*), blacknose shiner (*Notropis heterolepis*), popeye shiner (*N. ariommus*), northern redbelly dace (*Phoxinus eos*), bullhead minnow (*Pimephales vigilax*), blue sucker (*Cycleptus elongatus*), lake chubsucker (*Erimyzon sucetta*), blue catfish (*Ictalurus furcatus*), pirate perch (*Aphredoderus sayanus*), deepwater sculpin (*Myoxocephalus thompsoni*), spoonhead sculpin (*Cottus ricei*), blackbanded sunfish (*Enneacanthus chaetodon*), mud sunfish (*Acantharchus pomotis*), sharpnose darter (*Percina oxyrhynchus*), and swamp darter (*Etheostoma fusiforme*). A victim of recent extirpation is the silver lamprey (*Ichthyomyzon unicuspis*).[2]

Paddlefish, once extirpated from Pennsylvania, have been reintroduced.
Credit: U.S. Fish & Wildlife Service

The only happy ending for an extirpated Pennsylvania fish involves the American paddlefish (*Polyodon spathula*), also known as the Mississippi paddlefish or the spoonbill. Reaching lengths of seven feet, with a record weight of 220 pounds, the American paddlefish represents one of only two surviving species from the Family *Polyodontidae*). Its recent reintroduction to the Ohio River and various tributaries marks a victory for nature—at least in the short term—over human rapacity.

Herps Away

Amphibians and reptiles—the subjects of herpetology, commonly known as "herps"—comprise seventy-three of Pennsylvania's recognized wildlife species. Curiously, while the PABS claims that three species, one amphibian and two reptiles, have been extirpated from the state, its own website and that of the PFBC name only two extirpated species.[3]

The eastern tiger salamander (*Ambystoma tigrinum*) is Pennsylvania's lost amphibian, although the PABS admits that "occasional specimens are found (usually well outside the species' original range)." In the official view, those stray survivors are products of "bait-bucket introductions," dropped off in the wild by human captors.[4]

A curious case involves the northern cricket frog (*Acris crepitans crepitans*), whose normal range includes the southeastern quarter of Pennsylvania. Allegheny County lies far to the west of that range, near Pennsylvania's border with Ohio, but the PABS tells us that the species "no longer occurs in Allegheny County, although it was common there prior to the turn of the century."[5]

Pennsylvania's extirpated reptile is the midland smooth softshell turtle (*Apalone mutica mutica*). Once found in western Pennsylvania, along the lower Allegheny River and its tributaries, this species—whose females may sport a fourteen-inch carapace—ranks among the species wiped out by human predation and habitat desctruction.[6]

Sweeping the Skies

Pennsylvania birds have fared worse than herps in terms of extirpation and extinction. Of native species known to nest within the state, five are presumed to be extirpated as breeding species (though isolated specimens may still appear), a sixth species probably deserves inclusion on that list, and one species is deemed to be extinct worldwide. Three other species known to visit Pennsylvania in the past, though not Keystone nesters, also make the roster, with two extirpated and one presumed extinct.[7]

Extirpated native nesters include Bachman's sparrow (*Aimophila aestivalis*), Bewick's wren (*Thryomanes bewickii*), the greater prairie-chicken (*Tympanuchus cupido*), olive-sided flycatcher (*Contopus cooperi*), and piping plover (*Charadrius melodus*). A sixth native species, the common tern (*Sterna hirundo*), apparently has not nested in Pennsylvania since a failed attempt at Presque Isle during 1995. Passenger pigeons (*Ectopistes migratorius*) once swarmed across North America from the Rocky Mountains to the Eastern Seaboard, in flocks large enough to darken the sky, but mass slaughter eradicated them by the end of the nineteenth century. The last known wild specimen died in Ohio, on March 22, 1900, although unconfirmed citings continued through 1930.[8]

Of species known to visit Pennsylvania without nesting there, the brown-headed nuthatch (*Sitta pusilla*)and Eskimo curlew (*Numenius borealis*) are listed as extirpated, while the Carolina parakeet (*Conuropsis carolinensis*) has been deemed extinct in the wild since 1904 and worldwide since 1918. As with the passenger pigeon, the latter case involves some controversy, with unconfirmed sightings reported as late as 1938.[9]

Missing Mammals

At least twelve of Pennsylvania's seventy-one mammalian species have been extirpated within historic times, as have two exotic species. Of the larger native species, four have been re-established in their former habitats by modern conservationists.[10]

Native species extirpated from the Keystone State, then re-established, include:

Elk (*Cervus canadensis*), killed off by 1875 and reintroduced in 1913, presently established and managed by the SFGC in Cameron, Elk and McKean Counties.[11]

North American beavers (*Castor canadensis*), officially wiped out by 1899 and gradually reintroduced between 1917 and 1924.[12]

North American river otter (*Lontra canadensis*), trapped out of existence around 1900 and reintroduced in 1982. The Carnegie Museum of Natural History reports otter populations breeding in northeastern Pennsylvania—in Lackawana, Monroe, Pike, and Wayne Counties—with unexpected sightings farther west, in Allegheny and Crawford Counties.[13]

Fishers (*Martes pennanti*), annihilated with the river otter around 1900, reintroduced by SFGC biologists between 1994 and 1998.[14]

Four native mammalian species are listed by all available sources as extirpated throughout Pennsylvania. They include the American bison (*Bison bison*), with the last confirmed wild specimen shot in January 1801; Canadian lynx (*Lynx canadensis*), regarded by the Carnegie Museum of Natural History as a "predator temporarily expanding its range due to low prey densities further north;" moose (*Alces alces*), last known specimen killed near the Juniata River around 1790; and wolverine (*Gulo gulo*), extirpated by trappers around 1865. At least in theory, none survive within the Keystone State today.[15]

Likewise, all sources agree that one exotic species— the brown or European hare (*Lepus europaeus*)—has been extirpated statewide. Strange confusion, however surrounds the fate of two introduced rats. According the the PABS, brown or Norway rats may no longer be found within the state. Mammalogists at the Carnegie Museum disagree, listing the black rat as a victim of invasive brown rats, theoretically expelled from Pennsylvania. Even so, Carnegie spokesmen admit that "some individuals may continue to find their way to coastal seaports such as Philadelphia via incoming ships." While deeming it "unlikely that populations will be successfully re-established," the museum provides a map revealing that *R. rattus* specimens have been found in McKean and Westmoreland Counties, both far to the west of Philadelphia and separated from each other by some eighty miles.[16]

Another rodent, the native marsh rice rat (*Oryzomys palustris*), rates designation as an extirpated species by the PABS, but mammalogist Joseph Merritt left the question open in 1987, writing that "whether it persists in Pennsylvania is unclear; it probably formerly occurred in tidal marshes on the Delaware River."[17]

Nagging questions also surround the American or pine marten (*Martes americana*), a mustelid reputedly doomed by deforestation around 1900 and listed by the PABS as an extirpated species. Curiously, the Carnegie Museum contradicts that judgment published on the PABS website, claiming that "[t]he Pennsylvania Biological Survey classifies its status as undetermined at present." In support of that statement, the museum notes that "two specimens have been collected in the latter half of the century." An accompanying map places those captures in widely-separated Mercer and Wayne Counties.[18]

Even more confusion surrounds the fate of American badgers (*Taxidea taxus*) in Pennsylvania. While the PABS ignores them entirely, the American Society of Mammalogists lists them as "extinct" within the Keystone State, Wikipedia describes badgers as a "reintroduced" species thriving statewide. The Carnegie Museum reports that four badgers have been caught in Pennsylvania since 1946, "all in counties of southwestern Pennsylvania adjacent to more uniformly suitable habitat in Ohio." Curiously, the museum's accompanying map shows only one county—Fayette—which in fact lies adjacent to West Virginia.[19]

At last, we are left with the state's most controversial extirpated species.

Will the Wolf Survive?

Officially, the last gray wolf (*Canis lupus*) in Pennsylvania was killed in 1892, but are they truly gone? Folklorist Henry Shoemaker recorded farmer P.F. Conser's sighting of a "black wolf (*canis lycaon*)"—in fact, a melanistic specimen of *C. lupus*—at Meillheim (Centre County) in 1910 or 1911. The Carnegie Museum acknowledges reports of Pennsylvania wolf kills through the 1940s, but none have been substantiated. Meanwhile, an article in the *Pocono Record* claims that no wild canids of any species were seen in Pennsylvania between 1900 and 1930.[20]

Some wolves *do* live in Pennsylvania, but they are ostensibly confined to a sanctuary operated for over two decades by the Darlington family of Lititz (Lancaster County), in the heart of Pennsylvania Dutch country. Forty-odd wolves occupy the twenty-two acre preserve, favored with food, shelter, and veterinary care by a nonprofit organization. None are listed as escapees to the wild.[21]

One of the Speedwell wolves from the Wolf Sanctuary. *Credit: Dinah Roseberry*

Proposed reintroduction of wolves is a sore point with state officials and farmers alike. In February 2006, SFGC spokesmen asked the public to furnish information about a "person or persons who may have illegally released a pair of gray or timber wolves or wolf-hybrids that have appeared in Straban Township, Adams County, in recent days." One of the beasts, a 120-pound male, was shot on February 19, three days after the reported wolf-mauling of a Straban Township resident's collie. No further information on that wolf-hunt was forthcoming, but two weeks later the *Pittsburgh Post-Gazette* advised its readers to ignore rumors that wolves had been reintroduced to Penn's Woods.[22]

Coyotes were unknown in Pennsylvania before 1930.
Credit: U.S. Fish & Wildlife Service

Two of my in-laws reported a wolf sighting in April 2004, somewhere along Interstate 90 between Erie and the New York border. The briefly-glimpsed canid had a "golden" sheen in full sunlight, and rivaled their adult Labrador retriever in size. It was, they said, "definitely not a coyote, much too large." In fact, coyotes (*Canis latrans*) were officially unknown in Pennsylvania until 1930, when a hunter killed the first verified specimen. Today, estimates of the Keystone coyote population range upward from 20,000. More to the point, a DNA study of 700 coyote skulls collected from Pennsylvania and New York, completed in January 2010, confirms that modern specimens are coyote-wolf hybrids, superior in size to coyotes found in the western United States.[23]

Cat Tales

No recognized mammalian species in North America inspires more controversy than the eastern cougar (*Puma concolor couguar*), also known as the catamount, catawampus, mountain lion, panther, and puma. Officially extirpated from every state east of the Mississippi River by the early twentieth century, surviving eastern cougars are recognized only in Florida, where the subspecies *P. c. coryi* clings to tenuous life in the shrinking Everglades.[24] Still, as we shall see, a vast chasm lies between official extirpation and actual disappearance.

Conflicting reports claim that Pennsylvania's last wild cougar was killed in 1856, 1874, or 1891. Henry Shoemaker writes that the last state bounty for a cougar kill was paid in 1871.[25] Whatever the actual date, Keystone cougars continue to behave as if reports of their demise were grossly exaggerated.

French naturalist Georges-Louis Leclerc, Comte de Buffon, published the first description of a Pennsylvania "couguar [*sic*]" in 1766, writing:

> The Jaguar, as well as the Couguar, inhabit the warmest regions of South America. But there is another species of Couguar (of which we have given a figure) found in the temperate climates of North America, as on the mountains of Carolina, Georgia, Pensylvania [*sic*], and the adjacent provinces. The drawing of this couguar was sent me from England by the late Mr. Colinson, with the following description: If it is exact, this couguar must differ greatly from the common kind.
>
> "The Couguar of Pensylvania [*sic*]," says Mr. Colinson, "differs much from the couguar of Cayenne [French Guiana]. His limbs are shorter, his body much longer, and his tail is also three or four inches longer. But, in the colour of the hair, and the form of the head and ears, they have a perfect resemblance to each other.
>
> "The couguar of Pensylvania [*sic*]," adds Mr. Colinson, "is an animal remarkable for thinness and length of body, shortness of legs, and length of tail. The length of the body, from the muzzle to the anus, is five feet four inches; and that of the tail is two feet six inches. The fore-legs are one foot long, and the hind-legs one foot three inches. The height of the body before is one foot nine inches, and one foot ten inches behind. The circumference of the thickest part of the body is two feet three inches."[26]

Pennsylvania lawmakers placed a bounty on cougars in 1807, and hunters did their best to cash in. Some accounts claim that the state's last cougar—dubbed the "Nittany Lion"—was shot in Susquehanna County by Samuel Brush, sometime in 1856. Stuffed and mounted, it resides today in the Pattee Library at Pennsylvania State University. Nonetheless, Henry Shoemaker reported that the last state bounty on a cougar was paid out in 1871.[27]

The Nittany lion, shot in 1856.
Credit: Author's collection

And still, the big cats would not rest in peace. In 1874, a cougar disturbed lumbermen in Albany Township (Berks County), until Thomas Anson tracked the cat and gunned it down at a site now called Panther Springs. Like the Nittany Lion, this one was mounted and finally found its way into storage at the State Museum of Pennsylvania in Harrisburg. Meanwhile, a timeline prepared by the nonprofit Mountain Lion Foundation dates the killing of Pennsylvania's last cougar from 1891, providing no further details.[28]

Despite cessation of bounty payments, and their supposed extirpation, killings of Keystone cougars continued into the twentieth century. Henry Shoemaker reports that Delbert Reynolds found a cougar caught in a Tioga County trap, in 1901, and promptly shot it. The following year, a "very old cougar" was killed, Shoemaker says, while trying to steal hams from a logging camp "on Scootac." (There is a Scootac Road in Clinton County's Bald Eagle Township. The next closest real-life location is Tangascootack Creek, also in Clinton County.) Earl Monaghan reportedly shot another "Scootac" cougar in 1903. Shoemaker logs another cougar kill in 1905, from Clearfield County, while the late Charles Thomas claimed that his relatives shot yet another cougar in Centre County, between Monument and Orviston, sometime in the early 1900s.[29]

Reports continued during the century's second decade. Shoemaker recorded a cougar sighting by hunters at Detwiler in November 1912, surmising that the cat in question was the mate of another shot and killed in Stone Valley (Huntingdon County) three months later. The *Lewisburg Journal* claimed that another cat was killed at Paddy Mountain (Union County) in 1914. Writing in 1917, Shoemaker cited two unconfirmed cougar kills from the previous year, in Mifflin County, then omitted them from another report he published twenty-six years later. According to reports filed with the Eastern Cougar Foundation, a niece of one William Smoyer also saw the skin of a cougar shot by her uncle in 1918. Long after the fact, Henry Masker claimed to have shot a "young panther" in 1921, speculating that it escaped from a traveling circus.[30]

Meanwhile, January 1921 produced a claim that "a huge wildcat or mountain lion...as big as a two-months-old calf, with a yell that curdles the blood in one's veins," had pursued three sons of Peter Saylor along Brush Creek, near Berlin (Somerset County). The cat had "eyes shining like balls of fire," and while the three boys fled, they later organized a hunting party with World War veteran Alvey Marsh. Marsh also saw the cat and fired two shots at it, but it escaped and vanished from the area.[31]

A quarter-century hiatus then ensued, broken by Robert Frazier's claim that a carload of hunters passed him somewhere between Renovo (Clinton County) and Snow Shoe (Centre County) during deer season of 1946, with a six-foot-long cougar tied to their fender. A second case, vaguely dated from the "late 1940s," involved game warden Theodore Carlson, who shot a cougar in Elk County and showed its skin to a co-worker. A third cat killed in the same decade was a "pet" that escaped from its owner in Kane (McKean County) and was shot soon afterward by a policeman.[32]

In March 1954, writing for the *Saturday Evening Post,* Herbert Ravenel Sass reported that in Pennsylvania "stories of panthers seen in the woods are a regular accompaniment of each hunting season." Two years later, U.S. Air Force Captain Warren Aikens claimed that any cougars seen in Pennsylvania were the offspring of cats kept by a family of Mexican migrant workers in Seneca County, Ohio, during 1948. Those cats, a mated pair, allegedly produced three cubs which were released into the wild. Aikens himself saw one of the cubs at Tiffin, Ohio, in 1949, reporting that a trapper hired to catch them during 1950 found no trace of cougars. In April 1956, Aikens wrote to Pennsylvania's *Centre Daily Times,* declaring that he "felt certain one or more of the cougars migrated to the hills of central Pennsylvania" from Ohio. Perhaps, but since 1956 produced sightings of an adult "black panther" in Centre County (see Chapter 3), Aiken's theory proved nothing.[33]

Hunter John Gallant shot a young female cougar near Edinboro (Crawford County) on October 28, 1967. The cat weighed forty-eight pounds and was accompanied, said Gallant, by another that escaped. Stuffed and mounted for the Carnegie Museum, the cat was later found to possess DNA from a South American cougar subspecies. How it arrived in Crawford County with a traveling companion is anyone's guess. State wildlife authorities presume both cats were "pets" released by a negligent owner.[34]

The cougar shot by John Gallant in 1967.
Credit: Author's collection

Residents of Tarentum (Allegheny County) began reporting cougar sightings and characteristic screams from the forest in July 1979. Three years later—on June 1, 1982—a television crew from Pittsburgh caught one of the cats on videotape, prowling on property owned by Ruth O'Brien. On July 25, 1984, Stan Gordon—director of the Pennsylvania Association for the Study of the Unexplained—discovered a short trail of curious pawprints in Armstrong County's South Buffalo Township. He cast one print in plaster, later claiming that several unnamed wildlife experts had identified it as a cougar's track, but a decomposed "cougar" carcass found the same year proved to be a dead dog. Overall, Pennsylvania witnesses reported 135 cougar sightings between 1983 and 1989.[35]

Cast of a cougar paw print made by researcher Stan Gordon.
Credit: Stan Gordon Productions

Reports continued unabated through the 1990s. According to the Eastern Puma Research Network (EPRN), more than half of its 435 cougar sightings for 1993 came from Pennsylvania. The group's tabulation from July 1, 1983, through December 31, 2000, includes 920 cougar sightings statewide, eighty-three of them describing adult cats with cubs.[36]

Typical sightings during that decade include the following:

In autumn 1996 a bowhunter met a cougar near Bailey Run (five Keystone counties boast creeks of that name), estimating its weight at 150 pounds. Other sightings were logged by campers at Bush Hill and Wrights (McKean County), while a fuzzy photo and track casts emerged from Potter County.[37]

During summer 1997 a motorist and his wife watched a cougar cross a road near Hunts Run—a name shared by streams in three counties. Later, in deer season, hunter Jim Howlett met two cats near Cameron (a name shared by populated sites in three counties).[38]

In summer 1999 a group of tourists met a cougar while hiking on the Susquehannock Trail, near Potter County's Patterson State Park.[39]

In June 2000 a retired biology teacher, Jim Baker of Cameron (Cameron County) found two sets of feline paw prints in his garden. Plaster casts examined by experts identified the trespassers as cougars, possibly an adult with a juvenile companion.[40]

Cougar sightings and the controversy they inspire continue in the twenty-first century, more than 150 years after the last official slaying of a wild cat in Penn's Woods. On August 8, 2003, witness Ian Schouten and three friends met a big cat on Sinnemahoning Creek, near Driftwood (Cameron County), as they prepared for a backpacking expedition. Schouten "immediately noticed how large the legs and paws were, with a long thick tail that seemed to touch the ground and then curl up some."[41]

On February 14, 2004, motorist Ralph Brumbley saw a cat "[a]bout the size of a small deer, but with a 3-foot-long tail" cross Route 472 near Lewisville. Brumbley was certain that he saw a cougar, but Professor Gary San Julian at Penn State's School of Forest Resources had doubts. "In recent history," he said, "I haven't seen any definitive proof. There may be one out there, but I haven't seen any proof of it. I'd love to see some scat or see some hair." Kerry Gyekis, boss of Gyekis Forest Management and the administrator of a website that tracks cougar sightings in Pennsylvania, opined that "very few of them are wild cougars," then seemed to contradict himself by adding that cougars are "actually coming east like the coyote did, though it's not the same situation as the coyote. Habitat is the key. We've got more rain and we've got more game." Two months later, *Pittsburgh Post-Gazette* columnist Dr. Scott Shalaway agreed that it was "not a stretch to imagine that in the next 20 years lions will recolonize portions of the East."[42]

July 2004 brought a cougar report from the Larrabee Y ranch, near Eldred (McKean County). Owners Jake and Joyce Jacobs had mounted a motion-triggered camera on one of their game trails, hoping to capture photos of a sow bear and her cubs known to roam the property, but instead they snapped a cat identified by one biologist as a juvenile eastern cougar. Seven months later, stories circulated that an Amish farmer in Cumberland County had told SFGC officers that a cougar was killing his sheep. The state agents advised him, "Sir, you don't have a mountain lion." A week later, the farmer allegedly shot and killed the predator, which was indeed a cougar—reportedly wearing an SFGC ear tag. Thus far, the incident remains undocumented.[43]

The cougar debate continued in 2006, as EPRN founder John Lutz asked Pennsylvania hunters to report any sightings of cougars, their tracks, or suspected droppings. "It's so hard to pin anything down," Lutz acknowledged. "A cougar or puma is like a UFO with four feet." Mark Dowling, a Connecticut resident and co-founder of the Cougar Network, told reporters, "We've probably looked into this as closely as anyone has. I think what we would say is that there is no credible evidence right now of a mountain lion population in Pennsylvania."[44]

Nay-sayers dominated the media front in the latter months of 2006. Christian Berg spoke first, for the Allentown *Morning Call*, lamenting that "the overwhelming absence of proof [for cougar survival] has done little to discourage residents from submitting dozens of mountain lion sightings to the Pennsylvania Game Commission each year." In fact, Cal DuBrock—director of the SFGC's Bureau of Wildlife Management—told Berg, "I can't recall a time when we've had more. Yet we don't have a carcass in hand or any tangible evidence. We're not looking for more accounts. We're looking for more credible accounts. There are some who are attempting to perpetuate a hoax, but there are many people of high integrity who are seeing something." No cougar-hoaxers were identified, but Mark Dowling agreed with DuBrock, telling journalist Megan McKeever, "There is no such thing as a credible observer" where cougars are concerned. An anonymous December editorial in the *Clarion News* derided "conspiracy theories" involving reintroduction of cougars to Pennsylvania, ridiculing witnesses and claiming that maps of Pennsylvania reveal "a pile of concrete and asphalt stitched across the state," making cougar survival virtually impossible. Still, the *News* allowed for a possible "teeny-weeny flicker of flame underneath all the smoke," blaming reckless individuals who release pet cougars into the wild.[45]

We might ask whether 920 witnesses imagined or fabricated cougar sightings between 1983 and 2000, including the embellishment of eighty-three cases with cubs, but no amount of anecdotal evidence can sway committed debunkers.

Reports of cougars at large continue throughout Pennsylvania.
Credit: U.S. Fish & Wildlife Service

On March 1, 2007, the U.S. Fish and Wildlife Service announced commencement of a program to "review scientific and commercial information to determine the status of the endangered eastern cougar." Reports of personal encounters were invited, with a deadline of March 30 established for submissions. The study's range spanned states from Maine to South Carolina and westward from Michigan to Tennessee, where any surviving cats are protected under the Endangered Species Act of 1973. The feds took pains to reassure Keystone residents that the study presaged no reintroduction of cougars to Pennsylvania, where private possession is banned by state law without special permits. That review was still in progress during December 2008, and no findings have yet been announced.[46]

In early June 2008 a hoax email circulated through Pennsylvania, presenting two photos of an unidentified man with a dead cougar in his garage, the text claiming that it was struck and killed by a car near Altoona. In fact, the incident occurred in Arizona, prompting columnist Walt Young to write, for the *Altoona Mirror*:

> Enough, already. There are no mountain lions (aka cougars, pumas, or panthers) in Pennsylvania or anywhere else in the Northeast, nor have there been for at least 100 years or more. I know some folks like to cling to some warped romantic notion that these big cats still skulk about Penn's Woods and do so almost completely undetected by the mere 12 million or so of us humans who live here. Get over it; that just isn't so.[47]

Young clearly holds a strong opinion on the subject, but his claim that Pennsylvania cougars pass "almost completely undetected" is uninformed at best. In fact, as we have seen, between July 1993 and December 2000 cougar sightings were logged on an average of one every three days.

Another supposed cougar photo surfaced in late September 2008, snapped by a trail camera near Plummer (Fayette County). Its subject seems to be a cat of some kind, walking past saplings and ferns, but its size is difficult to estimate. Days later, on October 10, state officials announced their investigation of an alleged "big cat" attack in southern Lancaster County. Amish farmer Samuel Fisher claimed he saw three cougars near his Sadsbury Township home the previous night, shot one, and pursued it into the woods, where he was jumped and mauled, defending himself with a knife. Investigators from the Pennsylvania State Police concluded that the incident was a hoax, reporting that Fisher's knife revealed traces of human blood and deer hair, but no evidence of contact with a cougar.[48]

That said, John Lutz of the EPRN reported ongoing cougar sightings throughout Pennsylvania, including a rash of reports from Nottingham (Chester County)—next-door to Lancaster—since July 23. He referred specifically to "an apparent pet cougar seen roaming the southeastern Lancaster County countryside for months."[49]

Another hoax photo made the Internet rounds in September 2009, this one depicting a cougar dragging a deer it had killed, allegedly crossing a highway near Farmington (Fayette County). Alas, the photo—while genuine enough—had been snapped west of the Rockies, then cropped to delete a protein feeder erected for whitetail deer, where the buck was ambushed and killed. There was no highway, and no link to Pennsylvania.[50]

A month later, questioned by reporter Mike Kuhns for the *Pocono Record*, government spokesmen said the SFGC "is always open to review evidence, but to date only hoaxes have crossed the PGC." Again, that statement is erroneous, since none of the 920 sightings logged during 1993-2000 were labeled deliberate hoaxes. Chris Kross, a ranger employed at the 68,714-acre Delaware Water Gap National Recreation Area, told Kuhns he had seen a cougar in Worthington State Forest, sometime in the late 1990s, and "it made a believer out of him."[51]

Mayor Armand Martinelli of East Stroudsburg disagreed, insisting that "if there were mountain lions in Pennsylvania, there would be more sightings of them." More than one sighting every three days? In fact, sightings were not enough for the mayor. He demanded "reports from farmers and people with pets that there were attacks on their animals. They're getting a lot of that out west. I haven't seen any reports like that." The difference might be explained by Pennsylvania's wealth of deer—an average of fourteen per square mile throughout ten state forests, according to an aerial infrared survey conducted in 2005, with twenty-four per square mile in Promised Land State Park and twenty per mile in Denton Hill State Park—plus countless specimens of seventy smaller mammalian species in the wild.[52]

His first article on Keystone cougars brought Mike Kuhns a flurry of emails from readers who claimed big cat sightings. Charlie McCarthy of Bushkill reported an autumn 2007 incident, wherein he and his wife saw a cougar "bound in two leaps" across a road near Pocono Mountain Lake Estates. The cat was "medium brown, about 100 pounds, [and] had a tail about two feet long." Tina Dieckman of Long Pond described her highway sighting of a cougar on Route 314 near Pocono Manor, on September 27, 2007. Henryville's John Phillips saw a cougar on Camelback Mountain (Monroe County) in September 1999, while training for a marathon. From Shawnee (Mifflin County), jogger Dana Williams-Whitby recalled a close encounter on Mosier's Knob Road, date unknown. Ed Johnson claimed two separate sightings of different cats (judged by size) around Porter Township, advising Kuhns that his Pike County neighbors included "many believers that have seen mountain lions."[53]

None of which convinced state spokesmen. In January 2010, SFGC press secretary Jerry Feaser told Harrisburg's *Patriot News*, "The overwhelming majority of cases we investigate are proven to be mistaken identity based on examination of tracks, photos, or other physical evidence. Some cases are inconclusive. And, while some believe mountain lions exist in the wilds of Pennsylvania, we have no conclusive evidence to support such views. If someone does encounter a mountain lion, the most logical explanation would be that the animal escaped from or was released by someone who either legally or illegally brought the animal into Pennsylvania." *Patriot News* reporter Marcus Schneck compared Keystone cougar reports to Bigfoot sightings, perhaps unaware that his state has produced more than 500 reports of hairy ape-like creatures since 1837.[54] (See Chapter 7)

Cryptozoologist and author Loren Coleman held a contrary opinion. Based on modern statistics, he dubbed Pennsylvania "one of the better states" for sightings of what he called "mystery cats." Why not "cougars?" Coleman balked at using a specific label "until we identify what they are." He told Schneck:

> There's certainly some kind of large cats in your state that haven't been identified yet. It's going to take a lot of evidence. It's a political issue, as well as a zoological issue.[55]

As we shall see in the next chapter, Coleman's explanation for Keystone mystery cats requires a greater leap of faith than any claim of relict eastern cougars.

Meanwhile, Pennsylvania scholar Chad Arment—a prolific author of scientific and speculative works, including the first (and only) textbook on cryptozoology—posed a question each of us should keep in mind as we proceed:

> Is there stuff out there that hasn't been discovered because no one's really looking for it?[56]

Is there, indeed?

Chapter 3
The ABCs
(Alien Big Cats)

In strict scientific terms, all "big cats" are members of the Genus *Panthera*, including the lion (*Panthera leo*), tiger (*P. tigris*), jaguar (*P. onca*), and leopard (*P. pardus*). These cats are distinguished from all others by a specially adapted larynx and hyoid apparatus, which permit them to roar. While some authors count cougars, cheetahs (*Acinonyx jubatus*), and snow leopards (*Uncia uncia*) as big cats based on size, none can roar, and thus they are excluded from purely scientific discussions of "big cats."[1]

Cryptozoologists, on the other hand, normally *do* include cougars in any discussion of "alien big cats"—or "ABCs"—defined as any large cat seen, caught, or killed in a location far from its normal range. Thus, a cougar found in England or Australia, for example, would qualify for ABC status, as would a lion found in Canada or a tiger seen in Brazil. Discussion of ABCs—or "mystery cats," as some authors prefer—also includes reports of large felids whose descriptions match no species known to science.

Lions at Large?

Pennsylvania's first known ABC report dates from 1797, a mere ten years after the U.S. Constitution was drafted in Philadelphia. Author Henry Shoemaker considered the cat an unusual "panther"—i.e., cougar—although its description bears little resemblance to any known specimen of *Puma concolor*. Shoemaker prefaced his tale with a statement that "[o]n very rare occasions panthers with manes were taken; one of the last such was killed in the Bald Eagle Mountains by the celebrated frontiersman, Peter Pentz," in 1797.[2]

According to Shoemaker, the incident occurred in a "bare place" on Bald Eagle Mountain, between Castanea and McElhattan (Clinton County). Early farmers in the region lost livestock to cougars, including "one panther which gave no end of trouble for six years."

Shoemaker wrote:

> Those who saw him at close range, for he was very bold, and would carry off a sheep out of a barnyard stated that he had a tawney, matted mane like a lion. If he were seen today he would be classed as an "escaped lion from a circus," but as there were no circuses in this country in those days he couldn't have been that.
>
> Experimental zoologists would have ticketed him as a hybrid between a panther and a shepherd dog. But he was in most probability a particularly masculine panther, a veritable *Felis Couguar Rex*.[3]

Cougars, of course, do not sprout manes, regardless of their age or personal virility. If indeed this particular cat was maned and had not escaped from a mythical circus, it must represent some unrecognized species.

After multiple attempts to slay the creature, local residents enlisted "the redoubtable Peter Pentz." In a lull between battles with Indian tribesmen, Pentz visited a friend named Isaac Dougherty in present-day Clinton County, and was sitting down to dinner when a commotion arose from the barnyard. Grabbing guns, they rushed outside, where five young steers were huddled in a mass in one corner, lowing pitifully. A full panel of the slab fence was down, and around it were several pools of blood. There was a bloody path three feet wide leading from the barn into the woods, looking as if every inch of the way had been contested in some fierce combat. The men were good runners and soon overtook the warring elements... In the semi-darkness they made out the prostrate form of a red and white spotted steer; on it was crouched a huge yellowish animal with a long hood of matted hair like a lion.

Nearby lay the two hounds, panting and occasionally giving vent to howls of pain. "Felis Couguar Rex" was clearly master of the situation. When he saw the two hunters he gritted his teeth so audibly that they heard it plainly twenty yards away. Then he buried his head in a hole he had ripped in the carcass of the steer, taking a last long drink of its blood, and turned and bounded off in the direction of the steep face of the mountain.[4]

Both Pentz and Dougherty missed with their first shots, then pursued the cat to a cave, where they built a fire at the entrance. Reloading both single-shot muskets, Pentz crawled into the cave, leaving Dougherty outside. Soon, two shots echoed from below ground, and Dougherty entered the cave with torch and knife in hand. As described by Shoemaker:

When he came to the bend in the passage he called "Peter, Peter, are you alive?" Immediately came the cheery answer, "Yes, yes, Isaac, but I had to kill two of them."

Dougherty hurried his "snail's pace" as best he could, until by the wavering light of his torch he could see the outlines of Peter Pentz and his victims. They lay one behind the other in the narrow gallery, but the foremost one was *Felis Couguar Rex* with a bullet hole through his mustard colored skull. The second was a female; she, too, had been shot through the head.[5]

Farther back in the cave, Pentz and Dougherty found three cubs, which they took home as pets. Before leaving, Pentz "scalped the male carcass, and hung the trophy, with its matted mane, to his belt." No account has survived of the cubs, or what they became upon reaching maturity, if in fact they survived.[6]

No other reports of maned lions have surfaced from Pennsylvania, and we are left to speculate on the species of cats shot by Pentz.

On the Spot

French polymath Constantine Samuel Rafinesque described another unusual Keystone cat in an 1832 issue of his periodical, the *Atlantic Journal and Friend of Knowledge*. Seen in Pennsylvania's Allegheny Mountains, the beast was ten feet long and spotted on the sides, with a black stripe down the middle of its back. While it vaguely resembled an ocelot (*Leopardus pardalis*), Rafinesque noted that the cat was "very different from *Felis pardalis,* by size four times larger."[7]

That is an exaggeration, since the record adult ocelot measured four feet nine inches (including an eighteen-inch tail), but they are relatively slender animals, normally tipping the scales at fifteen to twenty pounds when mature. Indeed, the cat described by Rafinesque rivals the largest jaguar on record for size, if jaguars had ever ranged so far north.[8]

Mention of jaguars brings us forward to September 2003, when La-Gene Morris saw a large spotted cat stalking a bird outside her Allison Avenue home in Washington (Washington County). "It was huge," she later told the local *Observer-Reporter*. "Its head must have been 12 to 14 inches long. I tried calling 911 and police, but I couldn't get anyone to listen to me." Neighbors were likewise skeptical, until a resident of nearby Windsor Highlands, in South Strabane Township, reported a "mountain lion" prowling along Dodd Drive. Police belatedly appeared, but found nothing.[9]

Based on personal research, Morris thought the cat—with its solid-gray head and spotted body—was a jaguar. "I know they hunt at night," she said. "I figure it must have been hungry to risk coming out during the day." While reporter Kathie Warco opined that "it was certainly not a jaguar...and it likely was not a mountain lion or cougar," police sergeant Walter Alrutz nominated a bobcat. Then, in the next breath, he admitted, "Bobcats aren't that big. They look like a big house cat. But bobcats are very, very rarely seen anywhere but the mountains. I've never heard of one migrating this far south." SFGC officers declined to comment or investigate, leaving Morris worried. "I'm just concerned the animal could attack someone," she said. "Every day it is out there."[10]

LaGene Morris reported a jaguar sighting from Washington County, in 2003.
Credit: U.S. Fish & Wildlife Service

Felis Catus

We owe the earliest accounts of Pennsylvania's next mystery cat to C.H. Shearer, an artist born in Berks County in 1846. He later wrote:

> When I was a boy the long-tailed wild cat inhabited the range of mountains which culminates at Mount Penn, above Reading. I have caught three of them in Irish Gap [i.e., Irish Mountain], say about 1857 or 1858, two by a hind foot, and one by a front foot. I always dreaded to get them in my traps as they fought so fiercely and were hard to kill. They were larger than the biggest domestic cats, their winter coats very fluffy, their faces were broad and the tails were beautifully ringed. I was never sure if they were a native wild animal, or were brought over by early Colonists from Europe, or else were tame house cats gone wild, in the third or fourth generation. I have sketched them and remember their appearance as clearly as if it were yesterday.[11]

Chauncey Logue—a trapper born in Clinton County during 1870, renowned as "probably the leading bob cat hunter of his generation"—recalled that:

> [t]he older people where I was brought up, it was a wild region up to twenty years ago, always gave me to understand there was a fourth species of the cat family in Pennsylvania, a long-tailed wild cat. As a small boy I saw the carcasses of several that had been killed by hunters, and my recollection is clearly that they were not like house cats that took to the woods.[12]

Another Clinton County hunter, Emmanuel Harman, born in 1832, reported that:

> [y]oung panthers were sometimes found in the woods by the early settlers and because of their long tails, called 'wild cats,' but there was also a true wild cat in the Pennsylvania mountains, with a long tail, clearly marked and barred; these I have seen and helped kill several times when I was a boy.[13]

George Betzer, a state game protector born in 1862, wrote that:

> As a boy in Snyder County, in the mountains I always heard the old hunters say that there were still a few long-tailed wild cats left, of a race fairly plentiful when the first settlers came in,

but quickly killed off and driven away. Once while on a hunt I helped kill a magnificent long-tailed wild cat; it ran up a tree and out on a limb, and we shot it. I examined it closely, and it was anything but like a domestic cat that becomes wild. I have seen many domestic cats that took to the woods, they are great game destroyers, and I have killed them, but there are differences about the size of the head and body which allow no mistakes being made by a careful observer.[14]

Bucks County also had its share of wildcats. According to the Bucks County *News,* an "authenticated" individual was shot on Spruce Hill "fifteen or twenty years before the Civil War"—i.e., sometime between 1841 and 1846—followed by two more reported kills in 1920, both cats being slain by a son of Daniel Trouts.[15] The final capture of a documented specimen occurred the following year.

On January 16, 1922, teenage hunter Tunis Brady trapped and shot a male wildcat, while reportedly missing its mate. The *News* described that incident as occurring "on the edge of the State Auxiliary game preserve in the Tinicum Swamp," but no swamp with that name exists in modern Bucks County. The same article refers to Brady's prize as "the Nockamixon cat," presumably referring to Nockamixon Township in northern Bucks County. Immediately to the east lies Tinicum Township, where George Eberhart reports the cat was slain—perhaps in the area of modern-day John Heinz National Wildlife Refuge, established in 1972 adjacent to Philadelphia International Airport.[16]

In any case, all accounts agree that Brady delivered the dead cat to game warden Warren Fretz in Doylestown, who said that local residents had been plagued by nocturnal "unearthly howls" for the past three years, prompting Brady and others to lay traps for the prowlers. Brady's cat weighed 8.5 pounds and stood 13 inches tall at the shoulder. Its other measurements remain ambiguous: the *News* claimed that its body measured 20 inches from the tip of its nose to the base of its tail, then added an 11-inch tail for a reported total of 30 inches. Where the lost inch went is anyone's guess.[17]

The cat was photographed in black-and-white, but we must trust the *News* for a description of its coat,

> ...the fur being a sandy gray, with some yellow or huffy marks [*sic*] the buff colore being particularly noticeable on the body under the hind legs. A dark line extends from the shoulders along the spine to the end of the tail. The black stripes extend entirely around the body and hind legs. On the front legs the black bands

run into black patches on the underside. The top of the head is black, and the face grey, marked with regular black lines.[18]

Consulting *Illustrated Natural History,* published by John George Wood in 1853, the *News* concluded that the Bucks County cat's markings were "precisely those" of the European wildcat (*Felis silvestris silvestris*), theoretically introduced at some point by immigrants to North America. While logical enough, that case remains unproved. Henry Shoemaker, writing in 1922, accepted the claim but curiously dubbed the creature *Felis catus,* the scientific name for the domestic house cat. Eight years later, George Eberhart speculated that it may have been a jaguarundi (*Puma yagouaroundi*), a medium-sized wildcat whose normal range extends from southern Texas to northern Argentina.[19]

By any name, the cat qualified as an ABC—but what is its status today? Tunis Brady acknowledged missing one specimen, said to be female, and Bucks County naturalist Eilzabeth Cox penned an article for the *News* in January 1922, contending that in distant Fayette County "these long-tailed wild cats are by no means uncommon." Carriage drivers in that district carried raw meat to distract the cats, and pistols to defend themselves, although her unnamed witness "never knew them to attack anyone."[20]

The European wildcat: a possible New World transplant.
Credit: U.S. Fish & Wildlife Service

The next report of an unidentified Keystone wildcat was logged twelve years later. Hunters at Foley Draft, eight miles from Driftwood, shot the male animal later described in the *Pennsylvania Game News* for June 1934. Judged to be a "wildcat" or a "tame cat gone wild," it weighed thirteen pounds and measured thirty-seven inches from its nose to the tip of its tail. According to the article,

> The head was large, the face was flat and blunt, with long whiskers, protruding tusks, and sharply pointed ears, which had long black tufts on their tips. The shoulders were broad, the body stout, the tail long. The markings were light yellowish brown on his stomach, with dark spots. The back was dark brownish tan, with dark stripes. The tail was eight inches long, dark brown with black rings.[21]

Two more decades passed between that incident and the next recorded slaying of a Pennsylvania wildcat, in October 1955. Coon-hunting brothers Bob, Earl, and Jack Anderson shot the cat after it battled with their dogs for fifteen minutes, leaving the hounds "chewed up pretty good." They noted the felid's foul odor and described it to the Titusville *Herald* as "32 inches long, [with] striped legs and a long tail[;] it was much larger than a domestic cat, which it resembled quite a bit in appearance."[22]

There the matter rests, at least for now, with no record of any wildcats killed or captured in the past eight decades. Whether they are gone for good, or simply well concealed, remains unknown.

Hold That Tiger!

On November 2, 1883, the *Daily News* of Lebanon, Pennsylvania, reported sightings of "a strange wild animal supposed to be a tiger" on Terrace Mountain (Huntingdon County). Local hunters had pursued the beast in vain, while it "commuted [*sic*] serious depredations among the poultry and stock of the farmers in that locality." According to the newspaper, "The supposition is that it has escaped from some traveling menagerie."[23]

Three and a half years later, in July 1887, witness William Howell met a similar cat in the woods near Ebensburg (Cambria County). He described it to the Connellsville *Keystone Courier* as "about two feet high and five long, of reddish brown color, with stripes on the sides." Howell surmised that the cat was "an American lion that has escaped from some menagerie."[24]

Since no menagerie was located in either case, we are at liberty to question that conclusion. Furthermore, since cougars are the only living "American lions" recognized by science, and none with striped coats have been found to date, Howell's identification of the cat remains suspect.

Large cats resembling tigers have been seen in Pennsylvania since 1883.
Credit: U.S. Fish & Wildlife Service

Famed Pennsylvania trapper John Swope logged another tiger report, albeit second-hand, in his journal for November 1909. There, he wrote:

> A man told me that he had two other men and some dogs treed a large cat 9 feet long from the nose to the tip of the tail, and he said it was striped like a tiger and [had] rings around its tail like a coon. I told him that I would have liked to have seen it as I never saw one like that before. It was as large as a panther, and that they had killed it with the first shot, that the ball went right through its head and it fell down dead, and the dogs would not go near as they were afraid of it.[25]

Fourteen years elapsed before the next Keystone tiger report, in February 1924. Early in that month, Game Protector James Geary of Allentown shot a peculiar animal on Blue Mountain, described in press reports as an eighteen-pound "Maine tiger cat, said to be a cross between an Angora cat and a raccoon." Ignoring that absurdity, it may be that Geary shot a Maine coon—a distinctive breed of domestic cat honored today as the official state cat of Maine. They bear no resemblance to tigers, and precious little to raccoons. This particular specimen's capital offense was dining on a pheasant as a game warden approached.[26]

Pennsylvania's last tiger sighting, so far, was logged in summer 1986. On July 27, Carl Eastwood of Nicholson reported seeing a large striped cat in some woods along the border between Susquehanna and Wyoming Counties, prompting a search by police. Officers in a helicopter spotted the beast, described as "a small tiger, about 200 to 300 pounds," then lost it again in the forest. Sightings continued for the next two days, some witnesses describing a typical tiger, while others thought they had seen a cougar. The search was canceled, without result, on July 29. The tiger, presumably, remains at large.[27]

Missing Lynx

In mid-November 1902, while traveling in Tioga County from Tiadaghton to Wellsboro, James Kerr met a cat which he compared to "a large panther or lynx." It shadowed him for a time, unimpressed by the stones Kerr lobbed in its direction, giving him a chance to study it by moonlight. Kerr later told the Wellsboro *Agitator* that the animal "was from four to five feet long, about the size of a big dog, and was spotted."[28]

The cougar (or panther) and lynx are not easily confused. Cougars cubs are spotted, but do not attain the size claimed by Kerr. The Canada lynx may have a spotted coat, and is closer in size to Kerr's cat, with a record height of twenty-two inches and length of forty-one inches. Unfortunately, Kerr did not describe the creature's tail, which in the lynx is a mere stub and could never be mistaken for a cougar's.[29]

Black Panthers

The remainder of Pennsylvania's ABCs are commonly described as "black panthers," a phrase devoid of any scientific meaning. All documented "black panthers" are, in fact, either jaguars or leopards with melanistic coats, in which an excess of the pigment melanin obscures the animal's normal spots or rosettes. "White panthers" also exist, products of albinism, leucism, or the chinchilla mutation. Despite various eyewitness reports throughout history, no melanistic cougars, lions, or tigers have yet been acknowledged by science.[30]

Pennsylvania's first black panther appeared at Jobs Corners (Tioga County), sometime in 1934, but it crept under the media radar until February 1936. On February 18, Joseph Shuckwood saw the beast on O.J. Furman's farm, reporting that it was "the size of a lion, black, with a long tail curled up in that fashion." His report brought F.N. Garrison forward with a sighting from 1934, while farmers Furman, Austin Prutsman, and Myrt Scott all blamed the cat for killing their cattle and sheep during summer 1935. Other stories, undated, referred to a black panther trapped in a farmer's shed near Coryland (Bradford County) after killing a pig, and another that terrorized a female traveler south of Ralston (Lycoming County) "a few years ago."[31]

In April 1938, the *McKean County Democrat* reported that a "phantom panther" had roamed through Potter and Tioga Counties "for several years." Locals deemed it an evil spirit until unnamed "reliable sportsmen" met the beast and described it as a flesh-and-blood creature "the size of a big police dog. It has a long tail and its body is almost black." Game warden Leslie Wood vouched for the latest pair of witnesses, who saw the cat near Gaines (Tioga County). Woods set the tone for future cases, opining that the panther "was either imported for a pet when it was a cub and later released or that it escaped from a zoo or a circus."[32] Precisely *which* zoo or circus was never disclosed.

November 1944 brought a report from Gettysburg's *Star and Sentinel* that "[a] good-sized menagerie could be assembled if all the wild animals reported running loose in this section of the country were captured." Early in the month, rumors circulated that a black panther had escaped from a circus train at Westminster, afterward mauling both cattle and humans around Carroll County. The story—and livestock attacks—soon spread to Maryland, where game warden Lee LeCompte blamed cattle-killings on a pack of wild dogs. Back in Pennsylvania, meanwhile, authorities dismissed the panther story as "a lot of hokum."[33]

The same could not be said on August 22, 1945, when a panther surfaced in Titusville, surprising Judy Walters and her children in the backyard of their home on North Dillon Drive. Viewing the cat from a distance of twenty feet, Mrs. Walters told the Titusville *Herald,* "It was shiny and jet black. The sun was glistening on him and he had a pretty coat." The cat fled eastward, dodging armed neighbors, later appearing to a child (who called it "a big black bear") and two adults on West Elm Street. Subsequent reports backdated sightings of the panther to the previous week, adding three more witnesses to the list.[34]

While police searched in vain for the Titusville panther, local gossips worked overtime. Without providing details or documentation, they claimed that two panthers had bolted from "a wrecked carnival" somewhere in New York state, during 1942 or 1943, later surfacing at Corry

(Erie County). One was alledgedly shot there—although no record of such an event has survived—but not before they mated to produce the Titusville cat.[35]

A pair of altar boys from St. Elizabeth's Church, brothers Arthur and Edward Giacoma, met the Titusville panther on September 1, 1945, prowling the south side of town after six o'clock mass. Police rolled out again to hunt the cat, without result. A month later, the *Herald* published a "theory" that the panther was, in fact, a black dog of "ferocious appearance," owned by one Charles Foss of Pleasantville, but the paper's unnamed informant offered no proof.[36]

Black panther reports from Pennsylvania number in the hundreds.
Credit: U.S. Fish & Wildlife Service

On October 11, 1945, the *Herald* reported "a definite wave of panther fear" in Ringgold (Jefferson County), where locals armed themselves despite snide comments from the SFPG. "You can kid all you want about it," one Ringgold resident said. "To us, its mighty real. When the snows come, we're going to track it down and kill it. We figure we'll have something to show that might surprise you."[37]

November 1945 saw the panther panic spread to Pottstown (Montgomery County), where posses spent five days tracking "The Thing of Sheep's Hill"—a beast variously described as a black panther, cougar, bear, black fox, or "a wild chow dog." Two teenagers suffered wounds from trigger-happy hunters, but The Thing escaped unscathed, after feasting on chickens and turkeys.[38]

Perhaps discouraged by the promiscuous gunfire, the panther or its twin appeared on Route 277, a mile outside Corry, on July 29, 1946. J.E. Fitch lobbed a rock at the beast and it fled—and turned white, according to Chester and Harry Fisher of Allison Township, who saw a large albino cat leaping across their property on August 1. Residents of Bear Lake (Warren County) cheered a black panther's demise on August 9, but the animal killed by a passing car proved to be a child's tomcat. Panther sightings continued from Warren County through October 1946, while resuming at Corry and Titusville.[39]

Pennsylvania's panther crossed the border into neighboring Chautauqua County, New York, during winter 1947, then returned for an appearance at Corry in mid-February 1947. Merle Dodd's wife saw it amble out of a swamp there, presumably headed southwestward to Allegheny County, where Orville Earl and Alfred Carlson saw the beast around Bloomfield, in July. The panther sighting came as no surprise to Earl, who told reporters he had "seen them before." September brought the action back to Warren County, after Ida Bronson saw a "coal black beast" leap over a fence near her home. Sheriff Ralph Millikin declared that "the beast killed a calf Wednesday night [September 12] on a neighboring farm and carried most of the carcass away," but deputies beat the bushes in vain.[40]

Thirteen months elapsed before the next panther sighting in Erie County, on October 9, 1948. Young William Dunnewold saw the cat first, six miles north of Corry, and his parents caught it stalking their cattle a short time later. The panther fled when Ernest Dunnewold ran to fetch his rifle, and resurfaced near Pottsville in mid-November, where witnesses included Chief of Police Daniel Guldin. Locals surmised it was the same beast that prowled their woods in 1945.[41]

All was quiet until January 1951, when a cat dubbed "The Thing" caused a stir in southwestern Pennsylvania's Washington County. The Charleroi *Mail* described it as "[a] varmint mountain lion, at least some kind of large animal ...described as a large, sleek, black beast, about three feet long, weighing about 175 pounds, with a long tail." While certain unnamed farmers reckoned that it was a dog—"possibly a crossbreed of German shepherd and Doberman Pinscher"—three witnesses named in the *News* report were adamant about the creature's feline characteristics. So was Harold Cain, who saw The Thing at Marianna, days later. He told the *Mail*,

> I don't know what kind of an animal it is but it doesn't look like any police dog I ever saw. It is black and huge and has short ears.[42]

Another police chief, Peter Orsini of Clairton (Allegheny County), was among the witnesses to the Keystone panther's next appearance, in February 1951. Orsini estimated the black cat's length at four feet, discounting its "long tail." Seven months later, Paul Olsen and son Grant spied a black cat "bigger than a large dog" near Titusville, noting its tracks and "terrifying cry."[43]

Three hundred Crawford County residents turned out with guns in early April 1952, to stalk a panther that had killed two deer near Coons Corners. Wesley Sliter's wife saw the cat in her backyard, telling reporters that it was "so black it shone." West Branch (Cambria County) suffered a panther scare in September 1952, while November brought sightings from Pioneer (Venango County). An unnamed local hunter claimed that he has shot the beast twice on November 14, then saw it escape. "I don't believe in panthers," he declared. "But I don't know what sort of animal this was."[44]

Residents of English Center and environs (Lycoming County) reported multiple sightings of a "large, shiny, black cat" in June 1953. Despite that consensus, an unnamed "well-known sportsman" opined that the beast "could be a lion, tiger, leopard, or panther" that had escaped from some unspecified traveling circus. On July 19, Duke Bradley and Harold Knight saw a panther near Riceville (Crawford County), describing it as "larger than any dog and very shiny black." Teenager Phillip Reynolds claimed that "a black, shiny animal with a long tail" attacked him in Hasson Heights (Venango County) on August 27, but searchers found nothing.[45]

On September 13, 1953, a Lehigh County motorist saw a "cold-black animal with back as high as the top strand of the guard rails" on Route 8, north of Centreville. Besides its "catlike walk," the beast had "greenish eyes, pointed ears and a long body, much longer than a dog's. It looked like the panthers in the zoo." On October 21, an unnamed witness saw a large catlike creature "blacker'n heck" on a logging road between Jerusalem Corners and Shamburg. Corlena Simpson of Chambersburg (Franklin County) watched a "black mountain lion" through binoculars in mid-November. Aside from its green eyes, she said the cat was "about 30 inches high, [and] had a body three feet long plus a long tail."[46]

January 1954 brought Lycoming County hunters out in force to stalk "The Critter of Cogan House Township" around Bobst Mountain. Judge Charles Williams organized the dragnet after the first panther sighting, on January 17, but The Critter escaped, leaving only a common red fox in the bag by January 31. Mrs. Arden Bennett had no better luck on October 30, when she fired her shotgun at a panther on Sanford Road, near Spartansburg (Crawford County). She described the cat as four feet long, plus a thirty-inch tail. "It was just coal black," she said, "with not a mark on it, and it was built just like a leopard."[47]

The first panther sighting of 1955 was logged in mid-January, at Valley View, west of Bellefonte (Centre County). Three weeks later, Dean Probst and two companions saw the cat cross in front of his car near Lock Haven (Clinton County). Josephine Irwin saw a panther at her parents' farm, near Frizzleburg (Lawrence County) on February 25, while residents of nearby Pulaski reported "weird howls" in the night. Ohio trucker Frank Steiner told police that a panther "leaped at him" on March 1, while he checked his truck's lights outside New Castle. Police searched in vain for that cat, which left Steiner unmarked, while game warden Calvin Hooper speculated that the trucker may have seen "a grey wolf or a lost, black coon dog."[48] Speculation of a wolf at large was startling in itself, since the last known specimen of *Canis lupus* in the Keystone State was slain six decades earlier.

Meanwhile, the *Record-Eagle* of Traverse City, Michigan, reported a "reign of terror" in Pittsburgh's Mount Washington district, inspired by reports of a "fercoious wild beast...four feet long with black hair." Policemen shot a common tomcat, blaming workmen at a local trucking company who supposedly found "an overgrown Angora" on a truck brought in from Indiana, using it to "scare the day shift."[49]

Centre County produced a new round of panther sightings in April 1956, explained after a fashion to the Penn State *Daily Collegian* by Air Force Captain Warren Akins. According to Akins, a tribe of Mexican migrants brought two black cougars to Seneca County, Ohio, while harvesting sugar beets in 1948. The cats produced three cubs, which eluded hunters during 1949 and 1950, hypothetically finding their way into Pennsylvania years later.[50] With all respect to Captain Akins, no part of his tale is verifiable today—and, again, most zoologists deny the existence of melanistic cougars.

Patrolman D.S. Mancuso was cruising past Connellsville's Sandusky Lumber Yard on August 6, 1957, when he stopped to visit brother-in-law Guy DeLuca. As described to his superiors and to reporters from the Connellsville *Daily Courier,* DeLuca "pointed to the hill side behind Sandusky's and there, as big as you please, was a black panther. We both could hardly believe what we saw, but there it was. It was a real beauty, walking there on the hill side. We watched it for at least a minute before it disappeared on the other side of the hill."[51]

Authors Colin and Janet Bord report that an unnamed boy glimpsed a panther sometime during 1958, while target-shooting at "Flat Rock, near Renova," but they provide no further details. Eight Pennsylvania counties have locations named Flat Rock, but it has no town called Renova. *Renovo*, Pennsylvania, may be found in Clinton County—but Clinton has no Flat Rock. The mystery remains unsolved.[52]

Twenty-four months elapsed before the next panther sightings, around Glen Richey (Clearfield County). Game Warden Victor Hollopeter was among the early witnesses in October 1959, drawn by the creature's sounds while stalking poachers. Facing staunch denials from the SFGC, Hollopeter had to speak in guarded terms. "I certainly would not want to say there is a panther around here," he told the Clearfield *Progress,* "because from everything I've read it isn't possible." Still, he admitted, "It certainly looked like a panther—with low body, heavy muscular legs and a rope-like tail. It wasn't a bear, a dog, or a bobcat."[53]

Nor was it an illusion, according to Robert Brown, proprietor of nearby Browncrest Farms, who said the cat was "worrying" his cattle. Neighboring farmer James Moriarty reported the same beast prowling around his livestock, though none had been killed. Other witnesses also described the same cat, weighing "between 65 and 70 pounds," notable for its "heavy long black tail resembling a rope."[54]

Steve Szalewicz, a reporter for the Titusville *Herald,* saw a possible panther on October 1, 1962, while hunting deer near Oleopolis (Venango County), but tried to talk himself out of it. Reporting the incident to his readers on April 4, 1963, he wrote: "That was a funny looking animal. We know that it was black, it was too large for a house cat, yet it had a long tail, too long for a dog. It did run like a dog but seemed to lope along the road and bound....Certainly this was not a black bear ... nor a dog ... nor a cat ... but then what was it?" The title of his column—"Imagination Unlimited"—suggested that the whole thing was a fantasy.[55]

And yet, two months after Szalewicz's experiment in self-deprecation, Bruce Krepp, his son, and two other companions saw a panther twice, two miles west of Cooperstown, on June 2. They blazed away at it with rifles, but failed to bring it down. John Clites of Hyndman (Bedford County) had slightly better luck on December 16, wounding a "black cat of the hills" that had killed five pigs "and drained their blood" over the past month. Clites followed the injured cat's blood trail, but finally lost it. He described the "coal black" cat as five feet in length, with a tail at least two feet long.[56]

Pigs were on the menu once again, at New Stanton (Westmoreland County) in January 1969, where one witness described the predator as a panther, "not a large dog or black kitty." Game wardens, unimpressed, insisted that a dog was probably to blame. The following month, in Henderson Township (Jefferson County), residents claimed that a "black mountain lion" *and* a pack of wild dogs were slaughtering deer.[57]

Fast-forward to April 1983, when a pair of black panthers were sighted by several witnesses around Tyrone in (Blair County). A local mechanic reported a "60 pound" cat leaping over a twelve-foot fence with "something small" in its mouth, but police once again blamed "large dogs roaming the neighborhood."[58]

Police officers should be reliable witnesses, but two from Nockamixon Township seemingly failed that test in July 1987 when they reported "a large black cat" crossing Route 611. Staffers dispatched from the Philadelphia Zoo found tracks near the scene, which they identified as canine, but a theoretical argument could be made that the paw prints were left by a different animal.[59]

Pennsylvania panther sightings accelerated in the 1990s. John and Linda Lutz, reporting for the Eastern Puma Research Network, logged 282 sightings of large black cats statewide, between July 1, 1983, and December 31, 2000. They treat those cats as melanistic cougars, in defiance of prevailing zoological opinion, but we are concerned with the statistics here, rather than the interpretation.[60]

Large black cats continue to haunt Penn's Woods in the twenty-first century. On March 9, 2003, Wendy Broome and Eileen Smith saw a panther behind their home on Skinner Creek, near Port Allegany (McKean County). Fascinated, they watched the cat through binoculars for nearly an hour. "He was cleaning himself just like any cat you've ever seen," Smith said. "He continued to do that the whole time until he left." In parting, the panther left a paw print measuring five inches wide. Unfortunately, while the women also snapped a photo of their feline visitor, their camera lacked a zoom lens and the picture provided no details.[61]

Retired forester Kerry Gyekis examined that cat's paw print, declaring it the track of a large male cougar. Based on twenty years of tracking Pennsylvania cougar sightings, Gyekis opined that rare black specimens exist. He offered no supporting evidence to contradict the view of most zoologists, but noted two sightings of normal tawny-colored cougars near Port Allegany "more than a year ago."[62]

Seven months later, on October 12, Ronald and Brenda Graham were fishing for salmon at Elk Creek, in Girard Borough Park (Erie County), when they saw a "pure black" cat which they referred to as "a mountain lion." As Brenda told the Erie Times-News, "He just stopped and looked at me. It was definitely a cat—pure black. It should have been scary, but we didn't even think to be scared." In fact, they videotaped the forest prowler and produced still photos from the tape. Researcher Chad Arment writes that "[s]till images from the video clearly show a housecat profile," but Brenda Graham remains unconvinced, insisting that the beast weighed at least 100 pounds—some twenty-five pounds heavier than her Labrador retriever.[63]

A few weeks later, in late October or early November 2003, Jeanne McGinnis saw a large black cat that "appeared to be a mountain lion" at the Holiday Mobile Home Park in Cherry Ridge (Wayne County). She kept the sighting secret until May 7, 2004, encouraged to go public when a resident of nearby White Mills reported seeing the panther or one of its kin. Eight days later, on May 15, George Chaplauske glimpsed the "biggest black cat he had ever seen" at Lake Cadjaw in Cherry Ridge Township. He described the animal as "four feet long, two feet high, with a long tail that touched the ground, about two feet long, round and thick."[64]

Something Else?

One more report of a mystery cat completes our list, at least for the present, but it is vague and sadly confused by association with the "Jersey Devil," discussed more fully in Chapter 8. We owe the tale to authors James McCloy and Robert Miller Jr., who include it in the appendix to their 1998 book, *Phantom of the Pines.*

As described therein, the case dates from March 1973, when "a huge cat-like creature, suspected by some of being the Jersey Devil, reportedly kill[ed] chickens and rabbits" in Upper Pottsgrove Township (Montgomery County). Sadly, without further details, the incident defies analysis.[65]

Irish author Ronan Coghlan compounds the confusion, citing McCloy and Miller as his source for a second vague sighting from "Berkeley Township (PA)" in summer 1979, but that site—more specifically, the Robert Miller Air Park—is actually situated in New Jersey.[66]

What's Going On?

The most common explanation for North American "black panthers," offered by sources ranging from Kerry Gyekis to spokesmen for the EPRN, claims that the cats are melanistic cougars. Gyekis calls them rare, but the EPRN's list of 282 panther sightings between July 1983 and December 2000—i.e., one incident every three weeks, spanning seventeen years—might argue otherwise.

Sightings of black cougars have been claimed since the eighteenth century, at least, when Georges-Louis Leclerc's *Natural History* described a "black couguar" or "black tiger" reported from South America. His witness, a physician at Cayenne, French Guiana, clearly distinguished the "black couguar" from jaguars and cougars (called "red tigers"), but Leclerc concluded that the beast in question might be either a jaguar or jaguarette.[67]

Another eighteenth-century author, Welsh naturalist Thomas Pennant, referred to black cougars in his 1771 *Synopsis of Quadrupeds.* He described a:

> ...black tiger, or cat, with the head black, sides, fore part of the legs, and the tail, covered with short and very glossy hairs, of a dusky colour, sometimes spotted with black, but generally plain: Upper lips white: At the corner of the mouth a black spot: Long hairs above each eye, and long whiskers on the upper lip:

Lower lip, throat, belly, and the inside of the legs, whitish, or very pale ash-colour: Paws white: Ears pointed: Grows to the size of a heifer of a year old: Has vast strength in its limbs.—Inhabits Brasil and Guiana: Is a cruel and fierce beast; much dreaded by the Indians; but happily is a scarce species.[68]

Again, he was probably referring to a melanistic jaguar.

Dr. Karl Shuker cites one "officially confirmed case" of a black cougar, shot near Brazil's Carandahy River in 1843, but since the pelt was not preserved, said confirmation must remain debatable. Other claims of melanistic cougars shot in Colorado, Costa Rica, Nicaragua and Panama lack any supporting physical evidence.[69]

Sixty-seven years after that reported lucky shot in South America, British naturalist Richard Lydekker described variant types of cougar found in Latin America:

> In addition to these local races of puma, individuals of a brown colour, and others nearly, if not quite, black, are sometimes met with. Other specimens may be nearly white; but the statement that albino pumas have been found in the Allegheny Mountains and New Mexico are not authentic.[70]

Henry Shoemaker proposed a startling solution for some Pennsylvania mystery cats in 1917, which authors Mark Hall and Loren Coleman later adapted to cover a wider range of unidentified felids. Specifically addressing the "panthers" shot by Peter Pentz in 1798, Shoemaker wrote: "Perhaps the earliest form of the panther [cougar] possessed maned males. They may be a modification of the prehistoric lions which Prof. [Joseph] Leidy called *felis atrox* [now *Panthera leo atrox*], and which ranged parts of the continent."[71]

America's prehistoric lion,
Panthera leo atrox.
Credit: Author's collection

Panthera leo atrox, the American "cave lion," was larger than modern *P. leo* and *P. tigris* at eleven to thirteen feet long, standing five feet tall at the shoulder. Approximately 100 specimens have been retrieved from the La Brea Tar Pits in Los Angeles, California, but none so far reveal manes. Paleontologists say these cats lived during the Pleistocene epoch and presumably became extinct around 11,000 years ago—in short, some 8,990 years before Peter Pentz recorded his thrilling encounter.[72]

Undeterred by that majority opinion, Hall and Coleman suggest that *P. l. atrox* not only survived into modern times with maned adult males, but that sexual dimorphism within the species may produce melanistic females, thereby explaining reports of "black panthers" at large across North America. Basing that theory on studies of fossilized cave lion molars, Coleman opines that "[t]he sex-linked differences in the cats is the key to the lock that opens the mystery of the phantom feline question." And before dismissing the thought out of hand, we must consider multiple eyewitness sightings of tawny maned males traveling with "black panthers" through Illinois and Indiana, recorded in 1948, 1958 and 1964. If not related in some way, why would a lion and a "panther" live together?[73]

Mike Grayson, writing to *Fortean Times* in 1982, raised multiple objections to the survival of *P. l. atrox,* subsequently amplified by Karl Shuker in his classic work, *Mystery Cats of the World.* Simply stated, Grayson opined that the radical difference in pelage suggested for males and females is unprecedented in nature; that no American lion prides have been sighted in modern times; and that anomalous "black panthers" appear worldwide, in locations where *P. l. atrox* never lived. Shuker adds the observation that *P. l. atrox* was once classified as a jaguar (thus, no mane), and that some authorities still regard it as distinct and separate from *P. leo*.[74]

Coleman responded in 2001, chiefly addressing the issue of prides. "The simple answer," Coleman wrote, "is while *Panthera atrox,* the Pleistocene American lion, may have been social, it did not exist in prides." To buttress that view, he cites paleontologist George Jefferson, who deems it "highly improbable that *P. l. atrox* lived in lion-like prides or cooperatively hunted in social groups."[75]

Whatever the explanation for Pennsylvania's ABCs, they continue to appear and startle modern witnesses, sublimely unimpressed by all official claims that they belong solely to myth or urban legend.

Chapter 4
Unidentified Swimming Objects

Worldwide, some 900 freshwater lakes and rivers allegedly harbor large creatures unrecognized by science.[1] The more famous include Scotland's Loch Ness (home of "Nessie"), New England's Lake Champlain (with "Champ"), and British Columbia's Lake Okanagan (home of "Ogopogo"). Some U.S. states lay claim to a dozen or more "monster" lakes, but Pennsylvania's roster is more modest, with only two on file.

The reason for that cryptid shortage is unclear. Certainly, the Keystone State is "wet" enough for any self-respecting beast, with 1,829 lakes and reservoirs, plus 7,027 rivers and streams large enough to rate names.[2] Even so, history records only two aquatic Pennsylvania cryptids, and one of those has not been seen for 124 years.

Wolf Pond

Wolf Pond is, in fact, a lake. It lies in Dauphin County, southeast of Elizabethville, but is not large enough to rate a mention on the PFBC's interactive map of lakes statewide.[3] It's once-resident creature may belong more properly to Chapter 5, but since it has been sighted only in the lake, and not on land, it is included here.

We owe our sole description of the creature to Charles Montgomery Skinner (1852-1907), a New York writer who divided his time between editing the *Brooklyn Eagle* and compiling tales from American folklore. In 1896, he summarized the story of Wolf Pond.

> A snake haunts Wolf Pond, Pennsylvania, that is an alleged relic of the Silurian age. It was last seen in September, 1887, when it unrolled thirty feet of itself before the eyes of an alarmed spectator—again a fisherman. The beholder struck him with a pole, and in revenge the serpent capsized his boat; but he forbore to eat his enemy, and, diving to the bottom, disappeared.

The creature had a black body, about six inches thick, ringed with dingy-yellow bands, and a mottled-green head, long and pointed, like a pike's.[4]

Might the beast, in fact, have been a pike? These freshwater fish, of the Genus *Esox*, include four North American species and one confined to Asia. Some are olive green with yellow spots or stripes, and three species are recognized in Pennsylvania: the chain pickerel (*Esox niger*), muskellunge or "muskie" (*E. masquinongy*), and northern pike (*E. lucius*). Size is a problem, however, since the largest pike on record measured six feet long and weighed seventy-seven pounds. Pennsylvania's record musky tipped the scales at fifty-four pounds, three ounces, while the record northern pike weighed in at thirty-five pounds and the largest chain pickerel fell two ounces short of nine pounds.[5]

None are large enough to tip a boat without assistance from its occupants, and only the most imaginative fisherman could inflate a six-foot pike into a thirty-foot reptile. On balance, it seems likely that the encounter of 1887—if not pure fiction—involved one of the snakes from our next chapter, going for a swim.

But Pennsylvania's *other* USO is something else, entirely.

Raystown Ray

Raystown Lake, in the heart of Huntingdon County, is a man-made reservoir initially created by the U.S. Army Corps of Engineers between 1907 and 1912, with construction of a hydroelectric dam on the Raystown Branch Juniata River. The present 8,300-acre lake—Pennsylvania's largest contained entirely within the state's borders—was completed in 1973. It measures twenty-eight miles long, with a maximum depth of 200 feet.[6]

Raystown Lake, alleged home of an unknown creature.
Credit: U.S. National Oceanic and Atmospheric Administration

What are the prospects for a monster dwelling in a modern man-made lake? Raystown Lake is fully stocked with fish—including four species of bass and three species of trout, plus Atlantic salmon, bluegill, carp, catfish, crappy, muskellunge, perch, smelt, and walleye[7]—so a resident beast would have plenty to eat, but where would it come from? How and when did it arrive?

A press release issued by the Huntingdon County Visitor's Bureau in April 2006 declared that sightings of Raystown Lake's monster—logically called "Ray"—have been recorded "for decades." Dwight Beall, the reservoir's managing director, said:

> We've known it's been in there a while now. It's a private creature, but it comes out around this time of year. Call it Raystown's own Punxatawny Phil.

A website devoted to Ray includes two undated photos of shadowy forms submerged in the lake and a third, allegedly snapped from the Visitor's Bureau Center itself, depicting a long-necked unknown swimming close to Seven Points Marina.[8]

The 2006 press release includes speculation on Ray's identity from one Jeff Krause, identified as a local wildlife biologist. He told the article's anonymous author:

A patch celebrating Raystown Ray.
Credit: Author's collection

> I believe it must be a vegetarian. We have not seen any evidence of this animal taking fish, geese, otters, or ducks. So I would suggest that our swimmers and boaters are very safe. It appears this animal's habits are similar to Manatees, which are completely herbivorous and gentle. The increase of weed beds around the lake is probably providing more food in the shallows for herbivores and that would increase sightings.[9]

Perhaps, but Dwight Beall added that "Ray has been known to scare off fifty-pound striped bass." That may be true, since Pennsylvania's record landlocked bass was caught by Robert Price of Huntingdon at Raystown Lake in 1994 weighing almost fifty-four pounds, but as with the photos of Ray, Beall provides no dates or other specifics.[10]

For a monster of such venerable age—"decades" old by 2006—Ray boasts a paucity of documented sightings. The website dedicated to its history lists only eight, with the first logged by Pittsburgh resident John Pendel in July 1994. Pendel, his wife, and four friends were cruising on Raystown Lake at 9 a.m., when they noted "ripples in the water, a long dark somewhat shiny black object that surfaced to the top of the water, then it seemed to spin and turn over and then submersed [*sic*] and disappeared." Comparing the beast to their nineteen-foot boat, the witnesses estimated its length at ten to twelve feet.[11]

Twelve years passed before witness "John" reported the next Ray sighting, on May 14, 2006. John was fishing with an unnamed friend at 2 a.m., when "something large and dark slowly appear[ed] in the water" at a range of forty yards. It was eight to twelve feet long, by John's hasty estimate, and sank immediately when he pinned it with a flashlight's beam. "There were no noticeable features such as a head or humps," John recalled.[12]

Two months later, on June 16, Ray startled a group of tourists identified only as "Lee, Lea & Family." The visitors were sitting in a boat near Panther Cove, when they saw a "figure" passing some 100 yards away, disappearing behind Marty's Island. They gave no estimate of size, nor any details of the beast's description, if in fact it was an animal.[13]

Fisherman "Walter G." logged the next Ray encounter near Seven Points Marina at 6:00 A.M. on June 20, 2006. Nearby, something three or four feet long rose from the water, snatched a floating stick, and then submerged. Walter G. first thought it was a muskellunge, then revised that judgment to describe the object as "a large leg." Back at home, the witness "joked and said that I would have liked to seen the rest of it," but after viewing Ray's website he changed his mind. "Now I think that maybe I didn't need to see the rest," Walter wrote. "But [what] could it have been?[14]

A T-shirt promoting "Ray" as a tourist attraction.
Credit: Author's collection

Another two years passed before Ray showed itself to Mike Sieber, his girlfriend and parents on August 3 2008. The two couples were dragging their Jet Skis out of the lake at Seven Points Marina when Sieber's girlfriend called out, "Look! It's Raystown Ray!"[15] Sieber goes on to write—

> I looked to see what she was talking about and saw a neck and a head sticking about 3 to 4 feet out of the water and it was striding toward a boat that was coming into the no wake zone at the 7 Points. We watched it for about 3 minutes. We saw a wake in the water from its neck and about 15 to 20 feet behind that wake was another wake, but we couldn't see what was causing that wake. It disappeared the closer it got to the boat. My mom, dad, girlfriend and I all saw this thing. If it wasn't Raystown Ray, I would like to know what it was![16]

Witness Penny Foor offers another Ray sighting from late August 2008. Fishing near Seven Points with a companion, close to midnight, Foor was startled by "this whooshing sound" from somewhere near the middle of the lake. Her partner turned a spotlight toward the noise, and together they watched a large, nondescript object pass within thirty feet of their boat, raising a wake that rocked the boat "enough to almost push us to shore." Foor later wrote, "There are no fish that act like that that are native to the lake. Not even eels break the water like that. And definitely none that big. We know fish at the lake can get huge, but they lay at the bottom, they don't even hunt at the surface."[17]

March 2009 brought the first dated photo of Ray, allegedly snapped near the dam. Ray's website quotes the anonymous photographer as saying, "We could see something in the distance that kept coming to the surface. As we got closer, it looked to be at least 20 ft. long. It surfaced about 6-7 times and we were able to get one good photo."[18]

Witness "Bill" reported the last known sighting of Ray—at least, so far—on August 29, 2009. While fishing with his son near Snydertown, around 6:45 P.M., Bill saw something that "looked like a large, thick black snake with a huge head that bobbed in and out of the water...The body was moving in coils or humps up and down in the water. The creature had no fins like a fish and the head was diamond shaped. The weirdest feature was that the eyes (which were dark, somewhat small and slanted) were not set on the side of the head...but placed forward. I got an excellent look through the binoculars (I'd say it was about 50 yards from us) when it raised up, it's head moved side to side. It made no sound. I'd say it was at least 20 feet long."[19]

Bill's son added one further detail, specifically "lighter colored 'whiskers' or rays on the chin and face" seen while watching the beast through binoculars. Bill tried to snap a photo with his cell phone, "but it just blended in with the water and was not discernible."[20]

And there, in the proverbial nutshell, we have the full history of Raystown Ray. Does the creature exist? And if so, does it represent a new species unrecognized by science?

Another theory, raised by skeptics in regard to Nessie and her kin worldwide, suggests that Ray may simply be a figment of imagination, drafted in the twenty-first century as a boon to local tourism. Raystown Lake draws some two million visitors per year, and while some may come looking for a monster, local merchants leave no room for disappointment. As biologist Jeff Krause reminds prospective tourists, "Even if a visitor does not get a chance to see 'Ray' while at the lake, there is an excellent chance to see nesting bald eagles and recently re-introduced osprey and river otters, which were not present just a few years ago."[21]

The rest is silence, at least from Raystown Ray.

Chapter 5
Snakes in the Grass

Wildlife biologists in Pennsylvania recognize twenty-one native species of snakes. Large species, by North American standards, include the black rat snake (*Elaphe obsoleta*), with a record length of 8.4 feet; eastern king snake (*Lampropeltis getula*), at 8.2 feet; and northern black racer, (*Coluber constrictor constrictor*), at 5.9 feet. The state's largest venomous snake is the timber rattler (*Crotalus horridus*), with a record length of 6.2 feet.[1]

While all of those are large enough to panic a die-hard ophidiophobe, reports of much larger serpents have circulated throughout Pennsylvania since the early nineteenth century, suggesting that true reptilian giants may still be at large in Penn's Woods.

Some modern reports of large snakes are explained by the exotic pet trade. Three cases from 2010 include a seven-foot Burmese python (*Python molurus bivittatus*) found in February, in the basement of a Lancaster home; a dead four-foot python recovered from a rental car in Allentown, in May; and a nine-foot python caught alive in Annville Township, in July. In each case, police logically surmised that the snakes were lost or released by negligent, still-unidentified owners.[2]

Pythons are popular in the exotic pet trade.
Credit: U.S. Fish & Wildlife Service

But what of the other reports, filed long before eBay or pet stores existed, even before the first traveling circus appeared?

Antebellum Serpents

Pennsylvania's first accounts of giant snakes come from the neighborhood of Turkey Hill (Bucks County), around 1818, although the incidents were not reported in the press until October 1898. The reptile in question was said to be "nearly 20 feet long and as big around as a telegraph pole." Local resident John Carter told the *Bucks County Gazette* that:

> This huge snake was first seen on the hill about 80 years ago, and has been seen about every 5 or 6 years since that time. Where it stays during the time between its periodical visits is a mystery.[3]

Two years after the Turkey Hill reptile's first appearance, a farmer at Gettysburg killed a black snake that measured eleven feet nine inches long, found choking to death on another snake it had partially swallowed. The still-living meal measured five feet three inches. Gettysburg's *Republican Compiler* claimed that "[t]his great snake was long the terror of the cow-hunters in the neighborhood," but no date was provided for its first appearance.[4]

Much will be said about black snakes—or "blacksnakes" —in subsequent reports from Pennsylvania, which requires clarification here. As with "black panthers," science recognizes no specific "blacksnake" species. The term is commonly applied to black racers, but may also describe the larger black rat snake, which does not officially exceed eight feet four inches long. "Blacksnakes" beyond that record length thus qualify as cryptids, and may represent a species still unclassified.

George Eberhart reports that Pennsylvania's next giant snake sighting occurred in April 1833, on Big Round Top, a hill near Gettysburg. In fact, the actual report, published in 1875, simply describes "one sunny day in 1833" on "Round Top"—which might refer either to Big Round Top or neighboring Little Round Top, both scenes of bloody carnage in the Battle of Gettysburg thirty years later.[5]

In any case, the story—told by Emanuel Bushman to the *Baltimore Sun*—describes seven youths, one of them Bushman's brother, who met a "monster snake" sunning itself on the hillside. Five boys fled, while two remained to pelt the snake with stones and watch it flee into its den. According to Bushman:

They described it as a black snake, apparently turning gray with age... They estimated its length to be from fifteen to twenty feet, and the thickness of an ordinary man's waist.

Another local, Michael Fry, claimed a sighting of the same huge snake in 1845.[6]

A fifteen-foot snake reportedly took up residence at Schuylkill Haven (Schuylkill County), following completion of the Lower Tumbling Run Dam in 1833. Despite repeated sightings and determined efforts to catch it, however, the reptile eluded pursuers for years, before taking its leave.[7]

In July 1859, while driving a mail coach from Cumberland to Bedford, Samuel Bagley and companion A.B. Cramer found "a large snake of a dirty black color" lying across the road. They first ran over it, then leapt from the wagon to pound it with a wooden rail and a thirty-pound stone, neither of which had any effect. Frustrated, the would-be serpent slayers watched their prey "slide across the fields at the rate of 2:40" and disappear. Both men said the snake "was as thick as a man's leg, and from 10 to 15 feet in length."[8]

August 1860 brought two reports of giant snakes from neighboring counties. The first incident, from Westmoreland County, involved a party of berry-pickers who met a monstrous serpent near the Youghiogheny River. The group's leader, a Mr. Guffrey, described the snake as thirty to thirty-five feet long, with a body as thick as a man's torso. No color was mentioned, aside from a white ring around the snake's neck. A $3,000 reward for the reptile's capture, or $1,000 for its carcass, remained unclaimed.[9]

Days later, and a few miles to the north in Indiana County, J.M. Taylor claimed a frightening encounter with a giant snake near Jacksonville. Taylor was driving a wagon when he saw twelve feet of the serpent protruding beneath a roadside fence and decided to kill it. While casting about for a club, however, he noted the monster's true size—thirty feet, with a body six inches in diameter—and decided that discretion was the better part of valor. Again, the serpent's color passed unmentioned.[10]

The Devil's Den

On July 1, 1863, Confederate and Union soldiers met at Gettysburg for the pivotal engagement of the Civil War. Over three days, 7,863 men were killed and another 27,224 wounded, with 11,189 captured or reported missing. Fighting raged at Big and Little Round Top, and at nearby Devil's Den, a heap of giant stones where Union snipers decimated Major General John Bell Hood's Texas Brigade and 3rd Arkansas Infantry.[11]

While some historians believe that Devil's Den earned its name on July 2, 1863, as nearby Plum Run Valley was christened the "Valley of Death," others disagree. Salome Myers Stewart, a Gettysburg resident and volunteer battlefield nurse, told reporters in 1913 that the rock pile earned its sinister name much earlier. She recalled that—

> As a child, I have heard [my uncle] tell of the snakes which infested the country, and had their "den" among the huge rocks. Parties of men were organized to rid the neighborhood of these dangerous reptiles. One big old snake persistently eluded them. They could never kill or capture him, and they called him "The Devil." He finally disappeared, and it was supposed that he died in his "Den." So, to Gettysburgers, that has always been "Devil's Den."[12]

Devil's Den, alleged home of giant snakes at Gettysburg.
Credit: U.S. National Oceanic and Atmospheric Administration

Post-War Perils

Five years after the conclusion of the Civil War, Lehigh County suffered a rash of serpent sightings. The "monster black snake" measured twenty-five to thirty feet in length, and was "the thickness of a common stove pipe." On its first appearance, in September 1870, it was observed crossing a field near Lehigh Gap with a rooster in its mouth. Sometime later, a hunter from South Bethlehem found the constrictor strangling a cat and was so frightened that he fled without firing a shot. In August 1871 the reptile pursued an itinerant lighting-rod salesman. According to the *Allentown Democrat,*

> One of her favorite amusements was coiling her tail around a limb of a tree and swing[ing] to and fro like a large pendulum, darting her tongue in and out, snapping her jaws, and emitting a sound between a hiss and a groan.[13]

Another "blacksnake" made its debut along Mercer County's Mill Creek during 1870 or 1871, although its presence first made headlines in July 1906. That belated article claimed that the snake had been seen "for more than 35 years," leaving only shed skins for the hunters who sought it.[14]

September 1874 brought a dramatic report from York County's Windsor Township, where young Franklin Rubright found himself pursued by a "monster black snake" fifteen feet long and four or five inches thick. Defending himself with a handy club, Rubright stunned the reptile and tried to drag it home, but the snake revived for another round of battle, then escaped. The *McKean County Miner* told its readers that the serpent "has been seen at different times in the neighborhood within the last twenty or twenty-five years," but always eluded hunters.[15]

Three weeks after that report, on September 30, the Williamsport *Sun-Gazette* offered the tale of another monstrous snake lurking around Morgantown, in Berks County. The reporter was clearly suspicious, explaining that:

> During the summer the scourge of the neighborhood is a large serpent, varying in length from fifteen to thirty feet, and whose chief delight seems to be to frighten women and children away from the blackberry and whortleberry patches for which that vicinity is noted. The snake story is a very good one, and serves a very good purpose in keeping timid people out of the woods, and thus permitting the professional berry gatherers to reap the harvest unmolested by juvenile competition.[16]

A report from southeastern Pennsylvania, published in August 1882, described two giant-snake encounters occurring "five or six years ago," i.e., in 1875 or 1876. The first involved John Appel of Cumberland (Adams County), who met a "blacksnake" twenty-five to thirty feet long and nine inches in diameter. Soon afterward, and farther east, Perry Morgan saw a similar reptile sunning itself on a road in Lancaster County's Colerain Township.[17]

Another oversized reptile, described as "a huge black or blue racer," allegedly died at the hands of stagecoach driver William Drake, near Kittanning (Armstrong County), on May 22, 1880. Drake hauled the fourteen-foot carcass to nearby Dayton, where it was viewed, we are told, by "hundreds of excited people."[18] As previously noted, black racers do not officially reach six feet in length, much less fourteen. The related blue racer (*Coluber constrictor foxii*) is slightly larger, with a record length of six feet exactly.

Ten weeks after William Drake's encounter at Kittanning, the Williamsport *Daily Gazette and Bulletin* reported a thirteen-foot snake "roaming around" Salford Township (Montgomery County). Local residents calculated its length from a shed skin found in 1879, which measured twelve feet six inches long.[19]

July 1882 produced a pair of serpent reports from Juniata Township (Bedford County). John Hardy was first to report the reptile, on July 28, describing it as twenty-five feet long and "as thick as a man's leg at the thigh." Later that day, L.P. Bruner saw the huge snake's track on a dirt road, accompanied by trails of four smaller companions. A three-man hunting party searched the woods on August 1, missing their giant prize but reportedly killing "one of the smaller snakes."[20]

A full year later, in July 1883, Solomon Smith found "the hide of what must have been a huge black snake" in York County's Codorus Township. The report, from Gettysburg's *Compiler*, probably refers to a shed skin, which Smith "accurately measured" at fourteen feet three inches long and one foot seven inches wide. Skeptics were invited to view the relic at his father's farm.[21]

Elias Moser of Lynn Township (Lehigh County) killed an even larger snake in June 1887. According to the *New York Times*, the reptile measured sixteen feet six inches long, and was "pronounced a king snake by local naturalists." According to the *Times:*

> The head was long and flat. The upper part of the body was a bluish black, except two broad white bands around its neck. The belly was yellowish white.

Those colors do not coincide with Pennsylvania's eastern kingsnake (*Lampropeltis getula*), whose record length is barely half that of Moser's mystery serpent.[22]

Our last report from the 1880s was filed by blacksmith Charles Woelfling and an unnamed companion on July 13, 1888. While passing through Potter County's Black Forest (now Ole Bull State Park) on that unlucky Friday the 13th, they saw a "black snake resembling a medium-sized tree in bulk and length" cross the path before them. While his companion fled, Woelfling grabbed a convenient bludgeon and killed the snake in a "pretty tough struggle," then dragged it to nearby Gaelton. Locals there measured the dead reptile at "fourteen feet and inches [*sic*] in length," prompting the *Democrat* of Olean, New York, to call it "the largest snake ever killed in the state."[23]

Gay Nineties Giants

Sometime in 1890, a "monster snake" revealed itself to residents of Greensburg (Westmoreland County). Witnesses pegged the serpent's length anywhere between eight and fifteen feet, but offered no further description. Newspapers ignored those events until June 12, 1891, when local resident Ida Robinson rescued one of her cows from strangulation by an "immense" snake ten feet long or more, four inches in diameter.[24]

Three or four days later, strolling near Jeannette (Westmoreland County), Mary Hook and Maggie Conley saw a nondescript large snake coiled beside the road. As described in newspaper reports, both women "procured clubs"—which seem to be ubiquitous in Pennsylvania's countryside—and beat the snake to death. Conley then severed its tail with a penknife she carried, before hauling the carcass into town. Bystanders measured it at ten feet six inches, but reporters were more interested in the "first case on record in which women did not run from a snake."[25]

Around the same time, a "black snake" twelve to sixteen feet long led hunters on a merry chase around Fertig Station (now Fertigs, Venango County). The Oil City *Blizzard* claimed that the reptile "could have been killed on several occasions, it is stated, but for the reason that it was desired to capture it alive, and no one in the vicinity was equal to the task." They remained inept when it returned in May 1892, when "a delegation of expert snakists" once more failed to bag the serpent.[26]

The next report, published on May 3, 1894, by the *Herald and Torch Light* of Hagerstown, Maryland, is clearly fiction. According to that article, one Al Palmer of Derry Township (Dauphin County) was passing a neighbor's barn on April 27, when he saw a snake fourteen feet long and six inches thick sucking milk from a hapless cow's udder. The reptile fled when Palmer showered it with stones, and a survey of the farmer's herd allegedly revealed five cows with bite marks on their teets![27]

A more plausible tale emerged from York County in August 1894. Bark-peelers James Meyers and James Zepp were working near the Maryland border on August 5, when they noticed a track resembling that of a single six-inch-wide wheel. Following the trail, they came upon "an enormous black snake" as it swallowed a pheasant. Meyers and Zepp withdrew to arm themselves with clubs, then caught up with the snake and found it swallowing a rabbit.[28]

Thoroughly intimidated now, the pair sought reinforcements and recruited huntsman Andy Flite, who had a gun and tracking dog. Resuming their pursuit, the party soon found *two* snakes gorged with recent meals. According to a newspaper report:

> They were as black as coal or they could easily have been mistaken for chestnut saplings lying on the ground.

Flite shot both snakes, measuring one at fourteen feet, the other at fourteen feet nine and one half inches.

According to the *Evening Times* of Monroe, Wisconsin, both were "larger by four or five feet than blacksnakes usually found in that neighborhood."[29]

October 1898 brought fresh reports from Turkey Hill, where large snakes had been seen at five- or six-year intervals over the past eight decades. Now, the *Bucks County Gazette* reported, "a number of smaller snakes measuring eight to ten feet in length have recently been killed in Patterson's meadow adjoining the base of the hill."[30]

One final item from this era comes to us undated, culled from the Gettysburg *Compiler*'s clipping file by tireless researcher Chad Arment and pegged as a turn-of-the-century tale. In fact, it is a letter to the editor from one "L.F.," recounting a story told by a Gettysburg resident "some years ago." The tale involved a group of pheasant hunters who were frightened off their game by a snake thirteen or fourteen feet long "and about the size of a stove pipe through." Though armed, they turned and fled for home.[31]

Good Years, Great Snakes

Historian Walter Lord once labeled the era from 1900 to 1914 as America's "good years," before global conflicts, Cold War, and a nuclear arms race endangered all life on the planet. Those years were also good for snake-spotters in Pennsylvania, though few of them appreciated the experience.

On August 9, 1901, three youths found a python on Presque Isle, in Lake Erie, and "killed" it, then took it home to Erie, where it suddenly revived. They displayed it at a local bicycle shop, where one E.L. Moseley measured it on August 29. Writing to *Science* magazine, Moseley described the snake as seven feet four inches long, eleven and one-half inches in diameter, and weighing seventeen pounds. It was, he thought, an African rock python (*Python sebae natalensis*). The reptile escaped from its cage on October 14 and was seen no more.[32]

Presque Isle, site of a python capture in 1901.
Credit: U.S. National Oceanic and Atmospheric Administration

Another odd—some might say preposterous—tale emerged from Indiana County in August 1902. According to the local *Weekly Messenger,* employees of Blairsville's Columbia Plate Glass factory had suffered "terrible consternation" over a snake that lurked in a swamp near the plant. And small wonder, since the reptile was described as fifteen feet long, six inches thick, with "horns two feet long" and a hiss reminiscent of "a locomotive blowing off." Despite the terror it inspired, factory hands still flocked to the marsh for a glimpse of the beast—which, the *Messenger* surmised, was actually "shaped like a pint bottle."[33]

Lewis Dersheimer's wife was cold sober in September 1902, when she took her husband's place in the driver's seat of a stage traveling from

Beaumont to Tunkhannock (Wyoming County). Along the way, in Eaton Township, she met a "blacksnake" coiled beside the road, its head raised four feet in the air. Mrs. Dersheimer killed it with a shotgun blast and measured the remains at eleven feet one inch.[34]

Details are sparse concerning the "monster snake" that appeared near Ray's Cove (Bedford County) in 1904. A short newspaper article from July 1907 says the serpent had been seen "several times in the past three years, most recently by witnesses Francis Foor and Howard Rhodes. All who had glimpsed it claimed the snake was fifteen feet long and at least six inches in diameter.[35]

Mercer County's venerable "blacksnake" made its latest appearance at New Lebanon, in July 1906, to Sunday school superintendent Jacob Crouser. Locals placed a twenty-dollar bounty on its glossy head, but the money went unclaimed.[36]

One month later, in Lawrence County's Slippery Rock Township, hunter M.C. Gallagher claimed the prize of a lifetime, when he spied a bald eagle soaring overhead with a large snake clutched in its talons. Blazing away with his shotgun, Gallagher dropped bird and snake together, but the eagle was merely stunned, battling fiercely until he knocked it unconscious with the usual handy club. A boy then arrived to warn Gallagher that the "blacksnake" was getting away, and another fight ensued, with Gallagher capturing the seventeen-foot-long reptile. Both specimens allegedly were given to the Pittsburgh Zoo, but no record of their arrival exists.[37]

In November 1906, residents of Somerset County shot a "blacksnake" twelve feet long and "33.5 inches in circumference" near a church in Brothersvalley Township. Witnesses surmised that "his snakeship is one of the South American and Indian serpents that escaped from a circus several years ago."[38]

Bedford County's serpent of Ray's Cove made its last recorded appearance in July 1907, but the year's real excitement occurred at Rose Point (Lawrence County) three months later. Farmhand John Johnson was cutting timber on a local judge's property when a "monster snake" reared its head from the brush and frightened him off. Johnson described the snake as black and twenty-five feet long.[39]

Edward Bates was picking huckleberries near Latrobe (Westmoreland County), when a "blacksnake" reportedly dropped from a tree overhead and whipped its coils around his body. Two friends ran to his aid and killed the reptile, which measured nine feet ten inches long.[40]

Bedford County's *Gazette* reported the next slaying of a giant snake on May 28, 1909. According to the article, one George Calhoun was walking on a knoll called Boher's Hill, on May 24, when a "monster blacksnake"—described as a "venomous reptile"—blocked his path. Calhoun stood his ground and stoned the snake to death, then measured it at eleven feet two inches, "verified by Pardy Gilchrist."[41]

On June 16, 1909, the Wellsboro *Agitator* reported Dennis Navle's claim that a giant snake had chased him through a nearby forest. Daniel Callahan of Williamsport (Lycoming County) saw the same snake or another like it at his farm on several occasions, before a freight train killed one of the monsters near Utceter, on June 26. Callahan collected the three pieces of its carcass, reassembled them, and measured the remains at fourteen feet seven inches.[42]

The snake seen along Whiskey Run (Delaware County) in April 1910 was only twelve feet long, but it still frightened locals with its "peculiarly large head and a body of great girth." Unnamed old-timers in Springfield Township claimed they had known of the serpent "for years and believe this is the same one." New witnesses Robert Lacy and George Sullivan saw the snake crawl into a hollow tree, but surveillance failed to result in its capture.[43]

Around the same time, a black serpent twelve to fifteen feet long and "as thick as an ordinary fire hose" turned up at Mont Alto (Franklin County). It returned in May 1911 to frighten witness George Shaffer and spark speculation that it was "the same snake for which John Robison's circus men hunted for a week about 30 years ago."[44] That claim offers the first link between Pennsylvania's giant snakes and a particular traveling circus, but it cannot be verified today.

John Corcoran reportedly killed a smaller "blacksnake" in May 1911, at his farm in Riverview (Beaver County). After a "terrific battle," Corcoran beat the snake to death and measured it at nine feet four inches—still thirteen inches longer than the record size of any native Pennsylvania species.[45]

Harry Guist of Westmoreland County had nothing to show for his hour-long struggle with another large "blacksnake," in July 1912. He claimed the snake was ten feet ten inches long, but failed to produce it, leaving the Monessen *Daily Independent* to mock him as "a brave man, a modern hero, a martyr."[46]

Boa constrictors do not reach the length claimed by witness Fred Greeley in 1913.
Credit: U.S. Fish & Wildlife Service

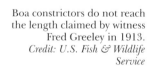

Damascus Township (Wayne County) suffered reptilian nightmares in August 1913, after Fred Greeley—"a reliable and truthful man"—met "a monster snake or Boa Constrictor" between Galilee and Tyler Hill. The serpent was twenty-five to thirty feet long, Greeley said, and "as big around as an ordinary stove-pipe." Its passing left at trail "just the same as though a large log had been dragged along the ground." Once again, old-timers spoke of vague sightings from bygone days, while newspapers referred to a traveling circus that "had a small wreck" and lost some of its snakes in 1899. No one ventured to explain how an exotic reptile might survive fifteen winters in northwest Pennsylvania.[47]

Giant Snakes in War and Peace

While World War I engulfed the Eastern Hemisphere and isolationist America attempted to ignore the carnage abroad, oversized snakes continued to surface in Pennsylvania. In July 1915, Roy Lettle shot a "monster black snake" on Hugh Neal's farm, near Punxsutawney (Jefferson County). The carcass measured nine feet two inches in length and eight inches in circumference.[48]

On April 28, 1917, while Congress debated provisions of a new Selective Service Act for military conscription, the Gettysburg *Star and Sentinel* reported sightings of two more ophidian "whoppers" from Round Top—once again failing to distinguish between Big and Little. The latest witness— Sol Pittenturfh, "whose truthfulness we do not doubt"— described a fourteen-foot "blacksnake" seen on the hill's eastern slope. The same article noted that John Rosensteel had killed an eleven-foot snake near the same location, "some time back."[49]

Reports from the Western Front eclipsed snake sightings until August 1919, when G.K. Johnston of Millbank encountered a large one near Loyalhanna Creek (Westmoreland County). A twenty-minute battle ensued, with Johnston wielding a five-foot cudgel against his black, scaly adversary, finally crushing its skull. The carcass measured "within a fraction of twelve feet in length," and was "the thickness of a man's arm."[50]

Reports from the 1920s are tantalizing, but generally vague. Sometime during the decade, an unnamed coal miner walking near Langdondale (Bedford County) saw a snake rise from a nearby thicket to face him at eye-level. In August 1927, another anonymous witness was hiking over Bedford County's Saxton Mountain when he met a serpent eighteen to twenty feet long, "gray in color with yellow markings on its face." The following year, another large snake was seen crossing a forestry road near Paradise Furnace (Huntingdon County).[51]

More large snakes enlivened the Great Depression in Pennsylvania. In September 1931, construction workers cutting a road through Franklin County's Mont Alto State Forest reported sightings, but forest rangers dismissed them with reference to a pet python lost by its unnamed owner at Pen Mar, Maryland.[52]

Two more reports emerged from 1933. The first, undated and anonymous, vaguely described another sighting of a giant snake on Saxton Mountain. The second, reported by Clint Carroll of New Castle, proved to be a false alarm. Carroll thought he had seen a snake with a head "the size of a teacup," but it proved to be a common eastern garter snake (*Thamnophis sirtalis sirtalis*) engaged in swallowing a toad.[53]

In early April 1935, Lee Erdman caught a large snake at a garbage dump north of Shamokin (Northumberland County). The New Castle *News* described it as eleven feet long, five to six inches in diameter, and weighing sixty-four pounds. Erdman thought it was probably "a cobra which had escaped from a circus or carnival." As usual, no traveling show was identified, no expert confirmed the snake's species, and its final disposition is unknown.[54]

Earth's largest cobra, and the only one known to reach eleven feet in length, is Asia's king cobra (*Ophiophagus hannah*). The largest specimen on record measured 18.8 feet, but even very large specimens rarely exceed twenty pounds in weight.[55] Shamokin's scaly visitor remains shrouded in mystery.

Three months later, young Marjorie Packer found a much smaller but "odd-looking" snake near her home in Canton (Bradford County). She tied a piece of string around it and dragged the snake home, to her parents' chagrin. The Clearfield *Progress* told its readers that the reptile "is not native to Pennsylvania and neighbors said it evidently escaped from a circus," but no further details were forthcoming.[56]

Two last cases remain for the period under discussion, both culled from undated reports by author Chad Arment. The first involves three fishermen whom a giant snake frightened at Roaring Run, between Riddlesburg and Saxton (Bedford County). In 2000, Arment dated the incident from "probably" 1940s of 1950s, but he revised that estimate in 2008, pegging the date closer to 1933. No other details are available.[57]

Finally, we have an incident from Carbon Township (Huntingdon County), dated by Arment as happening sometime "prior to 1940." Two witnesses en route to draw water from Six Mile Run saw a snake stretched across two sets of railroad tracks "plus the right of way between them." One observer estimated the reptiles length at twenty feet, with a diameter of eight to ten inches.[58]

Nightmares of the Nuclear Age

The 1950s and early 1960s spawned a rash of horror films inspired by speculation on the impact of nuclear radiation. Gigantic mutant animals and humans lurched across movie screens from Hollywood to Tokyo and London, impervious to gunfire. Meanwhile, peculiar reptiles slithered to and fro in Pennsylvania, as they had done for generations.

The first specimen on record, from August 1951, was neither huge nor particularly frightening. According to the *McKean County Democrat*, it measured barely three feet long and was slain without a fight by mail carrier Jack Hinckley at Backus. Curiously, it remained unidentified beyond a description as being "dark colored, with scales like a rattlesnake and a flat head." With no herpetologist handy, locals opined that the snake "had been 'imported' in some unknown manner."[59]

Strip-mining operations reached Bedford County in 1956, centered in the neighborhood of Hickory Hill and Saxton Mountain. The environmental disruption soon produced giant-snake sightings at Finleyville and Hickory Hill, spreading to Little Valley and Paradise Furnace in Huntingdon County, and to Spruce Hill in Juniata County. None of the serpents were captured or killed.[60]

Strip mining increased giant snake sightings in the 1950s.
Credit: U.S. National Oceanic and Atmospheric Administration

Bedford County produced three incidents in 1957, otherwise un-dated. A Coaldale resident, walking his dog, was frightened when a large snake emerged from a briar patch. Near Riddlesburg, a group of mushroom hunters saw a snake stretched over a six-foot-wide rock, with "several feet more" of its body on either side, the head and tale concealed in brush. At Hickory Hill, two miners tried to kill a serpent "as large as an 825 tire," but it escaped into a hollow log. When they returned next day, with axes, the log was empty.[61]

In 1959, while picking berries near Bedford County's Duvalls Cem-etery, a father and son heard stones rolling down a nearby strip-mine pile and saw a snake thirty-five to forty feet long. The same man and his wife reported a second sighting from the same vicinity, in summer 1960.[62]

Two final sightings from the 1950s, logged without specific dates, both come from Huntingdon County. In one case, a motorist driving from Robertsdale to Cooks at sundown ran over a "log," then watched it crawl away. Two men driving near Coalmont were more cautious, swerv-ing off-road to miss a "tree" that blocked their path, then recognized it as a snake at least twenty-five feet long.[63]

Our sole report from 1967 is sadly devoid of details. An unnamed ginseng hunter saw "something black" moving through woods near the untraceable "Old Heck Mine" and fled the area, fearing that it might be a bear with cubs. Returning the next day, he found a slate dump worn smooth without footprints, and nearby a trail of flattened grass "as if the snake may have passed."[64]

Sightings were sparse in the 1970s. A woodcutter glimpsed a large serpent near Paradise Furnace, sometime in 1971. Eight years later, a family bound for the Weaver Falls boat ramp in Huntingdon County ran over a "log" in the road, then saw it crawl away, apparently unscathed. A final rash of sightings from the "late 1970s or early 1980s" offer no locations and few other details. Two unnamed motorists reported a twenty-foot snake crossing some unspecified road at different times on one day, while anonymous hunters allegedly saw a huge serpent trying to swallow a fawn.[65]

Broad Top Township, in Bedford County, produced two sightings in the 1980s. The first, in late November 1983, involved a hunter who saw a twenty-foot snake devouring a rabbit. The reptile was "a dirty tan color with variegated markings." The second incident involved a female motorist driving near Lake Groundhog, sometime between 1985 and 1989. She saw "a huge snake" slither down a hill and cross the road, recalling its color as "very pale tan" with no discernible pattern. "It was thick around," she told Chad Arment, "like a boa or python."[66]

A lone report from the 1990s involves a woman from Everett who saw a "giant snake" on the bank of Raystown Lake. She offered no description, leaving us to wonder if she glimpsed a snake in fact, or whether she met Raystown Ray.[67]

Our last reported sighting dates from August 2000, when three men on their way to work saw a slate-gray snake with white markings crossing Enid Mountain Road, in Bedford County. As in other incidents, they first mistook the reptile for a log and never saw its head, concealed in roadside grass. Returning later with a tape measure, they found the road was seventeen feet wide, making the snake considerably longer.[68]

Florida harbors breeding populations of pythons.
Credit: U.S. Fish & Wildlife Service

It is known that Burmese pythons have colonized southern Florida since the late 1970s, at least, and reports of other exotic snake species at large have flourished since Hurricane Andrew in 1992.[69] Some observers fear that dangerous reptiles may spread throughout the Deep South states, but Pennsylvania's frosty winters should eradicate all tropical invaders. If, in fact, large snakes unrecognized by science have been breeding in the Keystone State for generations, their identity and point of origin remains a mystery.

Chapter 6
Thunderbirds Are Go!

Long before the first European "discovered" a New World in the Western Hemisphere, aboriginal tribes lived in awe—and fear—of huge winged predators known generically as "thunderbirds." In 1673, French explorer Jacques Marquette found a hybrid monster known as the Piasa carved by Illini artists on a limestone bluff at the site of present-day Alton, Illinois. From the Great Lakes to the southwestern deserts and Pacific coast, other tribes carved thunderbirds on totem poles or painted them on drums. Wherever they were found, the flying terrors were believed to feed on human beings and other large mammals, up to and including whales.[1]

The Piasa carving: a stylized thunderbird.
Credit: Author's collection

In Pennsylvania, prehistoric tales of thunderbirds came chiefly from the Black Forest, once a massive woodland sprawling over the present-day counties of Cameron, Clinton, Elk, Lycoming, McKean, Potter, Tioga, and Warren. As late as the 1920s, naturalist John Harshberger described the Black Forest as "3,000 square miles of coniferous (hemlock) and hardwood forest covering hilly country," but its days were already numbered by clear-cut logging, agriculture, and construction.[2]

Even with the wheels of progress crushing Mother Nature, though, substantial remnants of the Black Forest remain. Today, we find them in the Allegheny National Forest (512,988 acres) and five state forests: the Elk (200,000 acres), Sproul (280,000 acres), Susquehannock (264,000 acres), Tiadaghton (215,500 acres, including the forty-two-mile Black Forest Trail), and Tioga (160,000 acres).[3]

We have already seen some of those counties yield reports of giant snakes. The same is true for tales of living thunderbirds.

Nineteenth-Century Raptors

Three authors are responsible for most of our latter-day thunderbird knowledge. Hiram Cranmer of Hammersley Fork (Clinton County) laid the groundwork with a series of letters to *Fate* magazine, beginning in December 1950. Pennsylvania folklorist Robert Lyman Sr. published more tales in 1973, while cryptozoologist Mark Hall has continued research into the twenty-first century.[4] Their combined efforts allow us to trace a series of thunderbird sightings spanning more than 160 years.

The earliest white settler's report on record comes from Elvira Ellis Coats, who claimed thunderbird sightings from the Black Forest during the 1840s. Half a century later, in 1892, Lyman reports that "flocks" of birds resembling giant vultures were seen around Dent's Run, in Elk County. A.P. Akely, former superintendent of Potter County's schools, saw a gray bird four to six feet tall that "stood upright." At Centerville (Crawford County), a farmer saw a huge bird dining on one of his cows. Other birds of prey, with sixteen-foot wingspans, visited Fred Murray's logging camp at Westfield (Cumberland County). The news lured an unnamed ornithologist from Pittsburgh, who told Murray that "similar birds had been seen in remote parts of West Virginia and Kentucky."[5]

Our next report, from August 1897, was not publicized until November 1956, when Hiram Cranmer broke the story in *Fate*. According to Cranmer, nineteen-year-old Thomas Eggleton left his home to mail a letter from Hammersley Fork, then vanished forever. Searchers traced his footsteps to a bridge spanning Kettle Creek, where they ended abruptly. Cranmer claimed that locals blamed a thunderbird for snatching Eggleton, and that local schools closed for two weeks as a safety precaution, while children stayed close to home. "I was one of them," Cranmer wrote, "and many times I ran headlong into the house when I saw a large bird in the sky."[6]

Kettle Creek, scene of multiple thunderbird sightings.
Credit: U.S. National Oceanic and Atmospheric Administration

Sometime in 1898, Arch Akeley allegedly captured a thunderbird at his home in Centerville. He later described it to Robert Lyman as gray in color, more than four feet tall, but by then no trace of the carcass remained.[7]

Modern Monsters

Despite a quarter-century of fearful sky-watching, Hiram Cranmer did not glimpse his first thunderbird until April 1922, and even then he kept the sighting secret until August 1957. In his letter to *Fate*, Cranmer described the bird soaring past his home at dusk. Based on dimensions of the nearby trees, he pegged its wingspan at thirty-five feet.[8]

In a subsequent letter to *Fate*, published in March 1966, Cranmer blamed a thunderbird for killing a four-year-old girl in McKean County, allegedly snatched while her family was picking berries in 1937. He offered no further details, and inquiries to local reporters proved fruitless.[9]

Robert Lyman Sr. logged his own first thunderbird sighting in 1940, two miles north of Coudersport (Potter County). At first sight, it stood in the middle of Sheldon Road. Lyman noted that the bird was three to four feet tall and resembled "a very large vulture." As he approached, it spread wings equal to the road's width—no less than twenty feet—and flew into the nearby woods, negotiating dense second-growth timber with "no trouble." Despite its great wingspan, Lyman estimated that the bird's wing feathers were no more than twelve inches long.[10]

A year later, according to Hiram Cranmer (writing to *Fate* in March 1966), a thunderbird killed and devoured septuagenarian Barney Pluff. Unfortunately, Cranmer offered no more details, and no trace of Pluff remains in available records, including the Social Security Death Index.[11]

America was still celebrating its victory over Japan in late August 1945, when young Helen Erway stepped off of her school bus near the entrance to Ole Bull State Park. After walking some distance toward home, she saw a shadow on the road and raised her eyes to see a great bird overhead. "It was not an eagle," she later insisted. "The wings were straight out. It made a high pitch noise. The shadow on the road was about 30 feet [wide]."[12]

Terrified of being snatched, Erway ran until she met a neighbor who drove her home. Despite her fear, Helen later told another story suggesting that thunderbirds were benevolent. In that tale, one Albert Schoonover was bitten by a rattlesnake and might have died, but for a huge bird circling above him to mark the spot until rescuers arrived. Taken another way, the bird may have been looking for an easy meal, assuming that the incident ever occurred at all. In fact, it seems almost to be a garbled version of another sighting logged in 1969, detailed below.[13]

A final report from the 1940s, otherwise undated, involves witness Herb Nesman and several anonymous companions who allegedly saw "small flocks" of thunderbirds near Hammersley Fork sometime during that decade. Nesman speculated that the birds might represent a prehistoric condor species (Genus *Gymnogyps*) which ranged as far eastward as Florida during the Pleistocene epoch, but mainstream science rejects any notion of surviving "eastern condors."[14]

Flocks of thunderbirds were seen at Hammersley Fork in the 1940s.
Credit: U.S. National Oceanic and Atmospheric Administration

Spring 1957 brought three weeks of thunderbird sightings in Clinton County. Hiram Cranmer was the first to claim an avian encounter, at Hammersley Fork on March 27 or 28, followed by reports from other witnesses at Renovo, Shintown, and Westport. Estimates of the creature's wingspan ranged from twenty-five to thirty feet. Cranmer detailed the reports in more letters to *Fate,* published in April 1958 and September 1963.[15]

We can only speculate on Hollywood's possible contribution to thunderbird lore, but the fact remains that June 1957 witnessed the premiere of *The Giant Claw,* a low-budget horror film sometimes ranked among the worst movies of all time. Its somewhat muddled plot involves a huge bird resembling a condor or vulture, unleashed on modern America either from an "antimatter galaxy" or the year 17 million B.C.E. Before its swan song, the monstrous puppet-bird destroys U.S. Air Force planes and roosts awkwardly atop the Empire State Building (perhaps hoping to snack on King Kong).[16]

Sightings from the Sixties

Hiram Cranmer was among the witnesses who saw the next visiting thunderbird in Clinton County, on July 4, 1962. Belatedly disclosed to *Fate* in September 1963, the reports described a huge bird flying along local creeks, including Halls Run, Hevner Run, and Shintown Run.[17]

Two years later, in the latter part of May 1964, a group of road workers, including Charlie Passell, saw a large bird perched in a hemlock tree, at a strip mine near Alvin R. Bush Dam, fifteen miles above Renovo on Kettle Creek. Russell described the bird as follows:

> Where the wing meets the body was thick, longer neck than a hawk's but not as long as a stork or crane, bigger beak than an eagle. Definitely no eagle. Larger than a buzzard, real large.

Familiar with the local tales of thunderbirds, he said:

> That's what we must've seen because it wasn't like any bird we were familiar with.[18]

Thunderbird reports for 1968 and 1969 are regrettably mired in confusion. Multiple sources claim that Clinton County Sheriff John Boyle and his wife saw a huge bird on two occasions, once in each year, but details are sparse. The second encounter allegedly occurred on

Little Pine Creek, where Mrs. Boyle said the bird's wingspan equaled the width of the creek—a stupendous seventy-five feet! Unfortunately, Clinton County has no Little Pine Creek, although four other streams of that name do exist in Pennsylvania: Columbia and Lycoming Counties each have one, while Allegheny County boasts two.[19]

The confusion continues, surrounding a second incident from 1969, occurring in the summer or "around the same time" as the second Boyle sighting. In this case, Albert Schoonover and two companions allegedly saw a huge bird grab a fifteen-pound fawn along Kettle Creek, near Alvin R. Bush Dam and its eponymous lake. Internet author Gerald Musinsky apparently confused this event with the Passell sighting, five years earlier. It may be pure coincidence that Schoonover shares the same name as a snake-bitten hiker allegedly rescued by a benevolent thunderbird three decades earlier.[20]

The 1970s

Judith Dingler was the new decade's first thunderbird witness. On October 28, 1970, while driving along Route 220, west of Jersey Shore (Lycoming County), she saw a "gigantic winged creature soaring towards Jersey Shore. It was dark colored, and its wingspread was almost like [that of] an airplane." Assuming that she meant one of the smallest private planes available, it is worth noting that the Piper J3 Cub boasted a thirty-five-foot wingspan, while the competing Cessna 140's wings measured thirty-three feet.[21]

Less than two weeks after Dingler's sighting, Clyde and Anna Mincer saw a large bird twice on successive days, around their home in Jersey Shore. As later explained to Mark Hall, Clyde was painting his down-spouts on November 9, when Anna called out, "Look at the funny air-plane." Turning from his work, Clyde saw a bird with an estimated twenty-two-foot wingspan "riding a jet stream" overhead. "While I watched," he told Hall, "it got off the stream, flopped its wings a few times very slow, and it was back on the jet stream again." The same performance was repeated on November 10.[22]

Nor was that the end of the adventure for the Mincers. In 1977, Clyde wrote to Hall, "My wife and I have sighted twenty-five to thirty of these birds between November 1970 and December 13, 1973. None since. Three times we saw two in the air at the same time. We are on the West Branch of the Susquehanna River and see lots of bog birds but no more in the twenty-foot range."[23]

On June 8, 1971, Linda Edwards and Debbie Kraft were strolling along Cement Hollow Road, east of Jersey Shore, when they saw a large bird eating a dead opossum. It flew off as they approached, the women noting that "its wings covered the tops of four trees which was 18 feet."[24]

Two months later, still in Lycoming County, Wilson Fredericks and Clair Koons saw another giant bird flying over Larry's Creek, in Piatt Township. The incident occurred on August 7, but not further details were reported.[25]

When thunderbirds next surfaced, they were back in Clinton County. Gerald Musinsky dates the incidents from sometime "after the Agnes Flood of 1973," but Hurricane Agnes actually ravaged the Eastern Seaboard during June 21-25, 1972, claiming 119 lives in eight U.S. states. Fifty of the dead were Pennsylvanians, and Wilkes-Barre suffered some of the storm's worst damage. As flood waters were receding, a Renovo librarian saw two apparent aircraft circling over Hyner, realizing in a moment that "they were not airplanes, but birds the size of planes high in the air. No plane could fly like that." Another Hyner resident was hanging laundry in her backyard, with her infant in a basket at her feet, when a bird "bigger than an eagle" passed within thirty feet of her home. She grabbed her child and rushed indoors, keeping the incident secret for years afterward.[26]

The huge raptors returned to Jersey Shore in September 1972, appearing first to Mary Missimer and her son on September 23. They watched a helicopter fly overhead, with a dark bird the size of a Piper Cub keeping pace at high altitude. Mary subsequently told her friend Clyde Mincer that the bird "appeared to be skillfully riding air currents." The same bird, or its twin, flew past the Missimer home again on September 25, at 3:10 P.M. Clyde Mincer was present with Mary Missimer three days later, for a third sighting at 11:30 A.M.[27]

Six months later, on March 31, 1973, Joseph Kaye and his wife met a thunderbird on Route 287, near Oregon Hill (Lycoming County). The bird was standing on the highway's shoulder, then took wing and flew over their car as they approached.[28] As Wanda Kaye described it, in a letter to Mark Hall:

> Its wings were so big it had trouble getting off the ground... The one wing swept our windshield as it rose very slowly. I could see white feathers on the head and on the feet—body appeared to be black—rather like a bald eagle—as it came even with my side car window. It seemed too heavy to get off the ground. Then we were past it and it disappeared over the trees.[29]

On the evening of August 7, 1973, Inez Bull and her mother had a frightening encounter with a giant bird near Sunderlinville (Potter

County). They were returning from a dinner party when they saw the bird lift off from roadside, spreading wings that spanned the two-lane blacktop. "It flew against the side of the vehicle," Inez reported, "swiped at the front end and tried to attack it." Her mother later said, "I thought it was going to eat us."[30]

Gerald Musinsky reports another sighting from summer 1973, this one from Luzerne County. Witness Mike Floryshak Sr. was driving near Huntsville when he saw an apparent low-flying airplane skimming over a roadside field. A second look revealed that the object was, in fact, a "dirty brown" bird "gliding about six to ten feet above the ground beside the car. I didn't think it possible. The wings appeared to be twenty feet wide." The giant did not flap its wings, but wheeled "on edge" and vanished in some nearby woods, leaving Floryshak with an impression of its large, hooked beak.[31]

On October 14, 1973, Robert Lyman Jr. camped with his wife and son on Cross Fork Creek (Potter County). At 1 p.m., Lyman and his wife saw two huge birds fly over their camp. They were still discussing the incident when nine friends arrived to hear the news. Bill Good and another new arrival scaled a nearby mountain, carrying a walkie-talkie, and reported seeing a lone gray bird with fifteen-foot wings flap past them at the summit. (Gerald Musinsky later misplaced the event at Kettle Creek, in Clinton County, near Rattlesnake Mountain.)[32]

Those sightings prompted Robert Lyman Sr. to declare, before year's end, that:

> Thunderbirds are not a thing of the past. They are with us today, but few will believe it except those who see them. Their present home is in the southern edge of the Black Forest, north of the Susquehanna River, between Pine Creek at the east and Kettle Creek at the west. All reports for the past 20 years have come from that area.[33]

In fact, that range is too restrictive, since sightings recorded from Cameron, Centre and Clearfield Counties all fall outside of its boundaries.

As if spooked by Lyman's announcement, the great birds vanished for three and a half years, returning in the spring of 1977. Sue Howell and Debbie Wright, two teachers from Curwensville (Clearfield County), were driving on Route 219 at 7:30 a.m. Approaching Drocker's Woods, nine miles south of Du Bois, the road is bordered by the Moshannon State Forest and State Game Lands No. 87. Suddenly, a bird "wider than the car" appeared and flew directly toward them, veering off at the last second. Howell described it as "big, black or very dark brown with a huge beak." Wright agreed that "It was horrible, big, black and ugly. I'll never forget that. It was frightening!"[34]

Another teacher, science instructor Terry McCormick, was hiking along the Doughnut Hole Trail in Clinton County's Sproul State Forest in August 1977, when he glimpsed what he thought was "an airplane in trouble because of how low and silent it flew, as if the engine had cut out." Seconds later, he discovered that "it was a bird when it flapped its wings once and flew out of sight." McCormick described the bird as dark grayish-brown, with a prominent beak, and larger than any known eagle. "At least not one I've ever seen before," he added. "How big is a Piper Cub? Because that's how big it looked."[35]

The decade's last thunderbird witness, Herb Nesman, shared that opinion of the bird he saw near Snow Shoe during May or June 1978. Nesman was working on an oil derrick when he paused to watch a small plane pass, then saw the living creature flap its wings. He estimated that their span exceeded eighteen feet.[36]

The 1980s

After Nesman's sighting, Pennsylvania's thunderbirds took an eleven-year hiatus, before reappearing twice in 1989. The first incident is both anonymous and undated beyond the year, reported by a camper from Cameron County's Sinnemahoning State Park. The witness later told researcher Paul Johnson that he had seen "a huge bird with a 'funny-looking' beak sitting in a tree. It was between four and five feet in height and completely brown-colored."[37]

The year's—and the decade's—last sighting occurred on Thanksgiving Day, November 23. Pennsylvania State University librarian Shannon Breiner was visiting her grandmother's farm near Barbours (Lycoming County) when she saw what she thought was a deer in a nearby pasture. Approaching for a closer look, she saw the creature rise on two legs and run for cover in an adjoining marsh. Breiner, herself an avid bird-watcher, recognized it as "a large eagle-like bird. Not a stork or heron, it had a shorter and thicker neck, and broad chest and shoulders. Not a frail bird."[38]

Winging Through the Nineties

Gerald Musinsky lists the new decade's first thunderbird observer as an unnamed store clerk from Clearfield. The anonymous witness reported two daylight sightings, in early autumn 1991 and in October 1992, while driving to work in Curwensville along Route 879. Both times, she saw a large charcoal-gray bird perched on a roadside boulder. It stood on one leg, with its head turned around, beak tucked into its feathers. The witness said that its legs were "thick like an ostrich [sic] and it appeared to be sleeping." She flatly rejected a suggestion that it may have been a great blue heron (*Ardea herodias*), known to reach 4.5 feet in height and breed in Pennsylvania.[39]

One afternoon in late September 1992, Kim Foley and her two-year-old son were driving past Mount Zion Church in southern Lycoming County, near North White Deer Ridge and State Game Lands No. 252, when young Jayson called out, "Mommy, look at the puppy!" Following his gaze, she later said, "I expected to see a dog, but it was a very big bird eating a dead deer. It was huge and dark brown, almost black, [with] an ugly beak. Looked right at us in the car, it was that tall."[40]

After the fact, while perusing a field guide to birds, Kim compared it to a normal bald eagle (*Haliaeetus leucocephalus*) and golden eagle (*Aquila chrysaetos*), but declared her bird "more powerful, [with a] bigger chest and shoulders, and a big, ugly beak." She finally said it was "something like" Steller's sea eagle (*H. pelagicus*), an Asian fish-eater with a record wingspan of seven feet eleven inches, but insisted it was "not that one. It was much bigger."[41]

Kim Foley compared Lycoming County's thunderbird to Steller's sea eagle.
Credit: U.S. Fish & Wildlife Service

Two weeks later, in October, Dave Sims and his two sons saw a bird that outpaced their pickup truck on a highway near Hyner. Sims said:

> It flew ahead of the truck and disappeared in the trees. I know the hawks around here, but I never saw this one before. I've heard 'thunderbird' stories but chalked that up to regional folklore. I don't know if this was [one] or not, but it was a big, dark gray bird, and flew faster than 55 miles per hour.[42]

Our last traceable case for the Nineties dates from July 1993, when Shane Fisher and his parents saw a thunderbird over their property near Larry's Creek, a 22.9-mile tributary of the West Branch Susquehanna River. Shane said the bird "looked just like a Piper Cub. You could hear the air rush through the wings." It resembled an oversized eagle, with large black eyes, a large beak, and wings "wider than a cross bar on a telephone pole." Convinced, despite its size, that it "had to be some kind of eagle," Shane's father searched reference books without finding a raptor to match. Shane's mother opined that the bird was "large enough to carry one of us away."[43]

Twenty-First-Century Titans

Pennsylvania thunderbird sightings in the new century's first decade already outnumber those of the 1990s. Greenville (Mercer County) produced the first report on June 13, 2001. An unnamed witness watched the bird for twenty minutes, first believing it to be a small airplane or ultralight aircraft before he recognized it as a living thing. During the time that it was visible, the bird also perched in a tree, permitting the witness to estimate its body length at five feet, with a fifteen-foot wingspan. A neighbor also saw the thunderbird on June 14, calling it "the biggest bird I ever saw."[44]

Three weeks later, on July 6, another anonymous witness logged a sighting from Erie County, once again outside the range described by Robert Lyman Sr. in 1973. Aside from its massive wingspan, estimated between fifteen and seventeen feet, the bird was described as "dark gray with little or no neck, and a circle of black under its head. Its beak was very thin and long—about a foot in length."[45]

Another errant thunderbird appeared over Westmoreland County on September 25, 2001. Teenage witness Mike Felice was first attracted by the sound it made, like "flags flapping in a thunderstorm," and looked up to see a huge bird passing fifty to sixty feet over his head. "I wouldn't say it was flapping its wings gracefully," Felice later told researcher Dennis Smeltzer, "but almost horrifically flapping its wings very slowly, then gliding above the passing big rig trucks" on Route 119 in South Greensburg. Observing the bird for some ninety seconds, Felice estimated that its head was three feet long, and its wingspan ten to fifteen feet.[46]

A pair of thunderbirds turned up over Tunkhannock (Wyoming County) at 9:30 P.M. on June 26, 2002. One anonymous witness first thought they were herons, then realized "they were huge, much larger than any bird I have ever seen." They landed together atop a tall coniferous tree, flexing "bat-like" wings that were wider than the tree's longest branches. The observer called to a relative inside his house, and the second witness emerged in time to see the birds pass overhead, then vanish into nearby woods. After measuring the tree's branches, both witnesses said the birds measured six feet from beak to tail, with wingspans of twelve feet or more.[47]

While most reported thunderbirds range from brown to gray or black in color, the next on record was snowy-white. An anonymous witness logged the sighting on May 18, 2005, from an undisclosed site in Washington County. Professing great familiarity with local wildlife, he or she described the bird as "huge," with "an extremely large wingspan."[48]

Our most recent sighting to date comes from South Greensburg. Four witnesses assembled for a backyard barbecue on August 26, 2010, were suddenly distracted by a "swooshing" sound and saw a large bird passing overhead. They watched it fly a quarter-mile within twenty seconds, later describing the creature as dark brown or black, with a wingspan of ten feet or more. Its head was oval, with a beak eight to ten inches long, and its body was "very bulky and husky," twenty-five to thirty inches in diameter. The observers said its tail was two feet long and "came out wide to a point." If standing, they guessed, the bird would be four to five feet tall.[49]

Loose Ends

Thus ends our list of more-or-less traceable sightings, but five more cases remain, lacking various details required for substantiation. The first comes from Robert Lyman Sr., who described a couple frightened when a thunderbird swooped toward their car on some unidentified highway, date undisclosed. Supposedly, the woman "said the claw was at least four times as big as her hand, and its legs as large as her arm."[50]

The remaining cases all come from Gerald Musinsky, whom I was unable to contact for clarification or additional details. The vaguest of his tales refers to truck drivers on Boot Jack Hill, in Elk County's Ridgway Township, who were "harassed by large dark birds resembling 'big buzzards' over the last few years."[51]

We have more details for the case of Tammy Golder and her two-year-old son, who allegedly met a thunderbird "early one April evening," year unknown. While driving up Frantz Hill, near Hughesville (Lycoming County), Golder saw a large bird framed in her headlights. "It jumped and circled over the hood," she said, "then hit the truck above the windshield on the passenger side and flew off. It wasn't a turkey or a vulture." The bird left an apple-sized dent in the roof of Golder's pickup truck.[52]

Musinsky's next event occurred in June of some unknown year, reported by witnesses Erin Goundie and Todd Hackenberg. While en route to hunt crayfish on Young Woman's Creek, near North Bend (Clinton County), they were startled by a peculiar sight. "Down from the spillway stood an awfully big, whitish bird," Goundie said. As she recalled it later, the bird was "about five feet tall, had a long beak, thick legs as long as the stocky body. The neck was long, not skinny, not thick. It didn't look like a bird that belonged around here, it was so big and strange." According to Hackenberg, "The wings were as wide as the creek. Two and half times longer than the body...held straight like an airplane when it flew off."[53]

"Later that summer," Musinsky informs us, still omitting the year, witness Allison Stearn went hiking near Shingletown (Centre County). Along her chosen trail she saw a bird "like a small plane, dark brown or black, and maybe some yellow. I guess it could've been a golden eagle. Do they get that big? I mean, it was like an airplane."[54]

Musinsky's last case is the most detailed—although devoid of any dates—and also the most suspicious. He starts by telling us that witnesses Denny Eckley and Russ Powers Jr. were driving "through the Algerines" near Bear Run, thus sowing the seeds of confusion. Twenty Pennsylvania counties boast twenty-seven streams called "Bear Run," while five other features—a camp, church, ridge, trail, and junction share the same name. Lycoming County has two Bear Runs, while Tioga County has three. Those counties also claim four geographical features including the name "Algerine." None are mountains, as implied by Musinsky's turn of phrase. They include Lycoming County's Algerine Swamp Bog, Algerine Trail and Algerine Wild Area, plus Tioga's Algerine Swamp Natural Area.[55]

In short, we have no way of knowing when or where Musinky's final incident allegedly occurred.

Leaving pesky details aside, the tale is simply told. Eckley and Powers were driving *somewhere*, when they stopped for a group of deer crossing the highway. Simultaneously, they beheld a bird whose wings "spanned the forest road," fourteen to sixteen feet across. The deer bolted, except for one yearling that was instantly eviscerated by the raptor. As it dined, the bird turned once to peer at the human intruders, standing tall enough to face them at eye-level in their car.[56]

Eckley and Powers observed that its head was flat, covered with "feathers like on a chick." The bird had "a longer and less hooked beak than an eagle, dark grayish brown plumage, thick legs, talons larger than a man's hand, and grayish legs." Powers subsequently perused *The Guinness Book of World Records* (a title shortened after 1999, our only clue to date), and allegedly matched the bird he had seen to one depicted in a photo captioned "Thunderbird," which showed a large bird nailed to a barn wall.[57]

In fact, no such photo appeared in *Guinness*—or anywhere else, as far as diligent research by multiple authors has thus far revealed. The legendary "thunderbird photo" is usually said to depict a monster shot in Arizona, sometime in 1886 or 1890 (reports vary). Pulp author Jack Pearl first mentioned the photo in the May 1963 issue of *Saga* magazine, apparently inspired by correspondence with Pennsylvania's own Hiram Cranmer—who embellished the story further in a March 1966 letter to *Fate*. Muskinsky does not help his case by citing pages 65-66 of Mark Hall's *Thunderbirds* as his source for the Bear Run event. In truth, Hall never mentions the case.[58]

What Goes There?

How, finally, may we explain the many incidents allegedly involving Pennsylvania thunderbirds? One option is dismissal of reports across the board as tall tales spun by early settlers and modern pranks or hoaxes. It seems unlikely that so many "normal" citizens—including an elected county sheriff with two sightings on record—would fabricate monster encounters, but in these days of abject public spectacles like television's *Jersey Shore, The Jerry Springer Show* and *Pretty Wild,* anything is possible.

A more charitable explanation involves simple mistakes. Estimating size and distance may be difficult, especially for airborne objects, and even experienced naturalists may confuse birds seen on the wing against backgrounds of sun, sky, and clouds. That problem is compounded where a witness has imperfect knowledge of the species found within a given area.

North America's largest known bird is the endangered California condor (*Gymnogyps californianus*), with a record standing height of 55 inches and a wingspan of 9.8 feet. The 188 specimens known to exist in the wild, as of August 2010, all live in the American Southwest or along the West Coast. A condor found in Pennsylvania would qualify for cryptid status in its own right, and would not approach the size of thunderbirds described by witnesses.[59]

More likely candidates for mistaken identity within the Keystone State include four native species. In descending order of size they include:

Golden eagles, with a record length of forty-four inches and a wingspan of nine feet two inches.[60]

Bald eagles, reaching forty inches long, with an eight-foot wing-span.[61]

Great blue herons, with a record length of 4.5 feet and a top wingspan of six feet seven inches.[62]

Turkey vultures (*Cathartes aura*), with a top recorded length of thirty-two inches and a record six-foot wingspan.[63]

A frequent candidate for West Coast thunderbird sightings, the wandering albatross (*Diomedea exulans*), may boast a wingspan exceeding eleven feet, but its official range is limited to the Pacific and Indian Oceans. Indeed, no albatross of any species should be found on the Atlantic coast of North America.[64]

Large exotic species include the Andean condor (*Vultur gryphus*), with a record wingspan of 10.5 feet, officially confined to the Andes Mountains of South America; the African fish eagle (*Haliaeetus vocifer*), with an eight-foot wingspan; Steller's sea eagle, at 7.9 feet; South America's black-chested buzzard-eagle (*Geranoaetus melanoleucus*), 6.6 feet; the Philippine eagle (*Pithecophaga jefferyi*), 6.6 feet; the Madagascar fish eagle (*H. vociferoides*), 6.6 feet; and so on.[65] The bottom line: none should be found in Pennsylvania, and even if some negligent owner has released an exotic raptor somewhere, at some time, it is absurd to use that explanation for all thunderbird sightings statewide, spanning a period of some 170 years.

Our closest models for the thunderbirds described by Pennsylvania witnesses are teratorns, members of the Family *Teratornithidae*, presumed to be extinct since the end of the Pleistocene epoch, 10,000 years ago.[66] All occupied the Western Hemisphere. Four species are known from fossil remains, so far. In descending order of size, they include:

Argentavis magnificens, identified from remains found in Argentina, with a length of 11½ feet, a twenty-six-foot wingspan, and an estimated weight of 240 pounds.[67] Clearly this creature meets thunderbird criteria in all respects.

Aiolornis incredibilis (formerly *Teratornis incredibilis*), known from fossil wing bones and a partial beak unearthed in California and Nevada. Archaeologists project a wingspan of seventeen to eighteen feet, with a total mass of fifty pounds.[68]

Teratornis merriami, best known of the teratorns, with partial remains of more than 100 individuals recovered. Most hail from California's La Brea Tar Pits, but others have been found in Arizona, Nevada, and Florida. They depict a bird close to thirty inches tall, with a top wingspan of 12½ feet and a projected weight of thirty-three pounds.[69]

Cathartornis gracilis, known only from a couple of fossilized leg bones found at La Brea, hypothesized to be slightly shorter and clearly more slender than *Teratornis merriami.*[70]

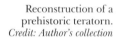

Reconstruction of a
prehistoric teratorn.
Credit: Author's collection

The obvious drawback with proposing any teratorn as a prospective thunderbird is the presumed extinction of all known species. Add to that the fact that no remains of the most likely candidate, *Argentavis magnificens,* have been found outside of Argentina, and mainstream scientists predictably scoff at the notion of living teratorns at large in Pennsylvania—or anywhere on Earth, for that matter.

But are they right?

Three out of four known teratorns were clearly North American birds. The discovery of *Argentavis* fossils at three sites in north-central Argentina does not prove that the birds were confined to that region, or to South America. Archaeologists estimate that individual *Argentavis* specimens roamed over a hunting range of 500 square kilometers (193 square miles) and may have lived for fifty to 100 years. It is no great stretch of imagination to suppose that some reached North America during the Miocene or Pleistocene epochs, which spanned some twenty-six million years.[71]

Imagination, however, does not prove the case. The most that we can say, with any certainty, is that sightings of large birds unknown to science continue from Pennsylvania. As with giant snakes and other cryptids seen statewide, hard scientific evidence remains elusive.

Chapter 7
Apes Among Us?

Mention of the ape-like creature known as Bigfoot or Sasquatch normally evokes images of misty forests in the Pacific Northwest. Some readers of this book may also know that similar monsters are frequently seen in southern swamps and bayous from Florida's Everglades to Louisiana and eastern Texas. But how would Bigfoot find its way to Pennsylvania?

How, indeed?

East Coast researcher Rick Berry, writing in 1993, listed 296 Pennsylvania Sasquatch reports between the 1830s and 1989. The Bigfoot Field Researchers Organization (BFRO) reports ninety-three Keystone sightings logged between 1921 and 2009. The Pennsylvania Bigfoot Society (PBS) claims "over 200" sightings on its Internet website, but the actual total listed in September 2010 included 362 incidents reported between 1956 and 2009. The Pennsylvania Research Organization (PRO) lists 376 alleged encounters between 1931 and 2007. All published lists include overlapping cases, and some contain duplicate entries.[1]

Using those sources and others listed in the bibliography, I have compiled 490 specific Bigfoot sightings from Pennsylvania spanning some 175 years. Also examined were seventeen reports of multiple sightings claimed by individual witnesses, plus 167 cases of footprints, sounds, smells, or other evidence attributed to Bigfoot without visual contact. Based on those figures, Bigfoot is the state's second most common cryptid, after phantom cougars. Its appearances outnumber those of giant snakes and thunderbirds combined.

Nineteenth-Century Bipeds

Aboriginal tribesmen met Pennsylvania's earliest white settlers with tales of the cannibal giant *Mesingw,* but no actual sightings by Anglo-European witnesses were logged until the 1830s.[2] Ten sightings were recorded by the end of the nineteenth century.

The first two incidents, from Susquehanna County, have confused modern authors, prompting mistaken dates and inaccurate reportage of duplicate sightings. According to contemporary newspaper reports, a berry-picker from Bridgewater claimed the first sighting in summer 1837, describing a timid, whistling biped "having the appearance of a child seven or eight years old although somewhat slimmer and covered entirely with hair." In early August 1838, a teenage hunter in Silver Lake Township saw "the same or a similar looking animal," failing to drop it with a hasty shot.[3]

Two decades passed before the next report, from Lancaster in December 1858, where multiple witnesses saw "a thing like a man, but hairy as a bear." One farmer found the "wild man" in his corral, "sucking the cows," before it "turned and fled, bounding like a deer."[4]

Welsh Mountain (Lancaster County) produced the next reports of a "hairy man" in August 1871. Vague reports of the creature "afflicting" children and livestock remain unexplained, while a newspaper's charge that it was "high time that this formidable monster was brought to terms and put under durance" produced no results.[5]

Three years later, in September 1874, Williamsport's *Sun Gazette* reported "a wild man of immense stature and aspect" prowling around Morgantown—the same Berks County village plagued by a thirty-foot snake and "a wild beast of unknown species, which strikes terror into the hearts of the inhabitants." That triple threat apparently resolved itself, as none of the monsters was killed or captured.[6]

Another bipedal "what-is-it" disturbed Berks County residents in October 1879, plaguing Muhlenberg and Ruscombmanor Townships. According to the Indiana (Pennsylvania) *Progress*, this unusual beast was hairless and yellowish-brown, with "small eyes and face, arms about fourteen inches long, legs somewhat longer, the hands and feet resembling those of a human being, and has two horns on the top of its head."[7]

A rival newspaper ridiculed sightings of a hairy monster that left sixteen-inch footprints around Nicktown (Cambria County) in July 1888. The *Weekly Messenger*'s Republican editor blamed liquor for those sightings, opining that the witnesses were "in training for campaign liars for Democratic newspapers."[8]

Three years later, in July 1891, a monster "half man and half beast" troubled farmers in Erie and environs, reportedly killing 500 to 600 chickens by early August. In each case, allegedly, the birds were drained of blood but otherwise untouched.[9]

On August 14, 1894, several residents of Galeton (Potter County) were frightened by "a wild man of immense stature all covered with hair." Ten days later, the *McKean County Monitor* dismissed that story, claiming that the creature was "a large bear walking on its hind feet as they frequently do." While true, with strict limitations on bipedal speed and distance of travel, the *Monitor* failed to explain how the bear was identified after the fact.[10]

The century's last Bigfoot report is also the least detailed: a passing mention in Warren's *Ledger* of November 15, 1895, that a "wild man in the woods is terrorizing the natives of Bolivar and vicinity" (Westmoreland County).[11]

Close Encounters
(1901-12)

The first dozen years of the twentieth century produced eight reports of Bigfoot-type creatures in Pennsylvania. The first tale, if in fact it describes a Sasquatch, came from Pennsbury Township (Chester County) in July 1901. Nocturnal hunters Tom Lukens, Milton Brint, and Taylor Brint were stalking raccoons in the midst of a rainstorm, when a creature with a man's head and neck atop a "wild beast's body and legs," leapt from a tree and frightened their dogs. A short time later, near the same location, Lewis Brooks and Jack Murphy saw "the same beast" walking on all fours. It was impervious to bullets and escaped by "passing through" a fence.[12]

The "wild man" seen in Allegheny County during July 1906 was more conventional, described as "a man with long hair all over his body and who had the appearance of a full grown gorilla." Four residents of Ben Avon—Charles and Robert Crawford, J.S. Wagoner and John Trust—allegedly captured the beast, binding its wrists with a handkerchief, but the prisoner escaped, leaving his captors scarred by painful bites and scratches. An Ohio newspaper suggested, without any evidence, that the "lunatic" was an unnamed escapee from nearby Dixmont State Hospital.[13]

Four months later, a distant California newspaper reported that black residents of Delaware County had armed themselves against nocturnal visits from "a wild and uncanny thing, resembling a gorilla." Tagging the creature a "ghost," the Oakland *Tribune* claimed that it "manifests itself only to persons of African descent." One man who tried to shoot the beast reported that his bullet was deflected, as if by armor plating.[14]

Later in November 1906, the action shifted to Luzerne County, where a "strange beast" showed itself around Georgetown, Laurel Run and outside of Wilkes-Barre. Some witnesses believed it was a bear, while others described it as "an enormous ape."[15]

December 1906 closed with fresh reports of a "gorilla" at large in Delaware County. This time the witnesses were white, and thus *presumably* more credible to journalists. From Utah came a "rumor" that unnamed staffers from Philadelphia's zoo were tracking "a lost simian" in the neighborhood, but zoo spokesmen quickly denied it. Trappers failed to catch the beast and wound up blaming a still-unidentified "practical joker."[16]

In June 1909, a resident of Westfield (Tioga County) penned a letter to the Wellsboro *Agitator,* describing a "wild man" seen near Broughton Hollow and Mill Creek. While occasionally walking on all fours, and thus prompting suspicion of a bear at large, the creature also "raise[d] itself upon its hind legs to travel and gets itself along at a very good pace." In that manner, it chased one man but failed to catch him, and retreated from a youth armed with a shotgun.[17]

Warren County played host to an "unknown monster" resembling a tall man with "fiery eyes" in July 1909. The apparition shrieked and howled around Russell and Putnamville, while eluding all pursuers.[18]

Gorilla My Dreams

Pennsylvania's "gorilla" returned with a vengeance in December 1920, a hundred miles northwest of its original stomping ground in Delaware County. On December 14, Charles Bolig of Snyder County reported that his son had been attacked and injured by "a huge ape" on the family's farm, between Kreamer and Middleburg. Lewiston's *Daily Sentinel* proclaimed that the creature was "supposedly an escaped gorilla from a carnival company, that has been roaming about the woods near Meiser for at least several weeks." The escape allegedly occurred at Williamsport (Lycoming County), sometime during the summer. As usual, the carnival was not identified.[19]

Pennsylvania witnesses reported many gorilla sightings in 1920-21.
Credit: U.S. Fish & Wildlife Service

The incident made Bolig a local celebrity, but he never saw the ape himself, despite two more reported visits to his farm. Son Samuel allegedly wounded the creature with a .22-caliber rifle on its second appearance; on the third he used a pistol, which misfired. Young Bolig described the prowler as seven feet tall, "having a color between black and brown, a human-like face and large lips." It normally walked upright, but fled on all fours when wounded.[20]

A $1,000 reward for the gorilla's capture—or $500 for its corpse—brought hunters no closer to their prey, but public uproar sent it roaming farther afield. By December 17, it had traveled to Blair County, startling Canoe Creek residents and looting a local smokehouse. On December 19, back at Middleburg, it leaped from the darkness to frighten motorist Bruce Yeager, then fled when he blazed away with a pistol.[21]

January 1921 brought the prowling ape—now described as a fugitive from "a New York City zoo"—to Wallaceton (Clearfield County). It killed and partially devoured an unnamed farmer's calf on January 13, knocked one Jim Barron unconscious with a club, then escaped toward Morriston with fifty hunters on its heels.[22]

Still traveling swiftly, the ape next surfaced near Pen Mar (Franklin County, on the Maryland border) on January 29. Witness John Simmons was unarmed and in no mood to tackle a gorilla when they met in broad daylight.[23]

A six-month hiatus ensued, during which the vanished ape became a comic figure. Gettysburg's *Star and Sentinel* described its return on August 20, with tongue firmly planted in cheek.

> Miles are nothing in the life of this animal whose fame has spread throughout southern Pennsylvania and northern Maryland. One night he is seen cavorting over the hillsides between York Springs and Gardners in northern Adams county. The next night he looms up in Biglerville, then Gettysburg and ere a week flits by he is seen in the hills of Franklin county or Maryland. What an asset to a football coach planning for a successful season would be this never weary animal who flits from mountain top to mountain.[24]

The laughter faded on August 13, when multiple witnesses saw the gorilla shambling along York Street, in downtown Gettysburg. A shotgun blast dropped it, but the ape recovered as its would-be slayer approached, and chased the man back to his home before fleeing the scene. Searchers found "footprints of a strange beast" in a nearby vacant lot.[25]

The creature made its last known appearance near Fairfield, on August 22, 1921. It crossed a country road in front of horseman Ray

Weikert, walking on its hind legs before it scaled a roadside fence and disappeared into the woods. Weikert described the hairy beast as roughly five feet tall.[26]

Apemen at Large
(1926-46)

Whatever the gorilla's destination on that summer evening, it vanished for the next five years. In early August 1926, a "big ape" frightened several Indiana County children "near Lucerne"—presumably referring to the company town of Lucerne Mines. Two men intrigued by that report went looking for the beast on August 16, reporting that they met "a real, live ape and it was a pretty big one." Hunters found "plenty of tracks," but no ape. Predictably, the local *Evening Gazette* claimed that the beast was "thought to be" a fugitive from an unnamed circus, which escaped in Johnstown "some time ago."[27]

Two months later, Fayette County residents blamed "an escaped gorilla" for wholesale slaughter of livestock on farms between Brier Hill and Masontown. Aside from a cow and horse disemboweled on October 19, the night-prowler killed "hundreds of chickens and pigs." While no one caught "giant creature" red-handed, and hunters followed blood trails in vain, the Charleroi *Mail* dubbed the outbreak "an alarming gorilla scare."[28]

So end the Roaring Twenties, with terror by night. The 1930s offer four more incidents, beginning once again in Fayette County, where an unnamed woman saw a "tall, hairy, man-like creature" near Indian Head, sometime in 1931. The witness claimed multiple sightings but offered no further details.[28]

On January 21, 1932, while hiking five miles north of Downingtown (Chester County), witness John McCandless saw "a hideous form, half-man, half-beast, on all fours and covered with dirt or hair." He returned with armed friends, scouring the local woods for seven straight days, but never met the thing again.[29]

Our last case of the Depression decade dates from September 1938, when a "furry thing resembling an ape" made two appearances in Erie County. Three young members of the Clabbatz family met the creature first, on September 18, in the woods south of Corry. Four days later, farmers Frank Ross and Fred Lindstrom saw a hairy creature four feet tall stroll past their property, while hunters searched the nearby woods in vain. Unnamed pundits speculated that the beast was "probably a bear cub walking on its hind legs."[30]

The 1940s yield two Bigfoot sightings, both from 1946, and neither dated any more precisely. One incident involves a Lebanon farmer who heard nocturnal noises from his pasture and surprised a "tall, hairy, man-like creature" feeding on the body of a fallen cow. The farmer fired a shot but failed to drop the prowler, which fled into darkness.[31]

In the other case, young Caroline McAdoo was playing in the woods near Dicksonburg (Crawford County), when she placed her hand on what she mistook for a tree stump. At once, the "stump" rose to reveal itself as "a large, black hairy bi-pedal creature with dark eyes, wide mouth, and large square teeth." McAdoo—who claimed repeat sightings in 1959 and 1960, recalled that the creature's hair felt like pine needles.[32]

Cold War Creatures
The 1950s

This decade produced five Bigfoot sightings, the first of which has no specific date. Rick Berry tells us that a group of unnamed Crawford County residents heard "banging" on an old farm house and lay in wait with guns, confronting a hairy biped eight to ten feet tall around midnight. Their shots apparently missed, since the prowler escaped.[33]

In July 1954, an anonymous witness saw Bigfoot walking through a cornfield near Latrobe. It was roughly seven feet tall and left corn stalks smashed by large footprints.[34]

In autumn 1956, Sasquatch invaded Pittsburgh proper, prowling through Chatham Village in the Mount Washington district. The witness, a young boy, described it as a large creature covered in dark orange or reddish hair.[35]

Late one night in 1957, a Mrs. Weaver parked her car in the woods south of Hanover, for reasons undisclosed. While there, she was reportedly accosted by a tall Sasquatch with outstretched arms, which "appeared to be very old." Rick Berry, reporting the case, failed to explain *which* Hanover he had in mind: Pennsylvania has three towns of that name, in Luzerne, Northampton, and York Counties.[36]

Caroline McAdoo, now a young woman, logged her second Crawford County sighting in 1959, while walking near Conneautville. This time, the creature had a "huge body and small head," smelled rank, and touched McAdoo's shoulder while uttering a riot of "whistling, laughing, and screaming sounds."[37]

Swinging Sixties

Pennsylvania Bigfoot sightings increased 320 percent in the 1960s, with sixteen incidents reported. Repeat witness Caroline McAdoo was first on the books, with a sighting from Springboro (Crawford County) in summer 1960. Once again, the creature's head seemed undersized for its large torso, but its deep-set eyes "glowed white like a light bulb even in daylight."[38]

On July 1, 1961, a teenager playing hide-and-seek with friends at Greenmount, south of Gettysburg, met a musky-smelling biped roughly five feet tall, "covered with hair not like a bear but long like hair on the hooves of Clydesdale horses." The unnamed witness met with disbelief when he informed his friends of the event.[39]

Nine months later, in April 1962, a fisherman at Beaver County's Brady Run Park saw a six-foot-tall biped "too massive for a bear." It watched him briefly, then "raised its arms and slipped back into the forest."[40]

A larger, more aggressive creature reportedly chased two youths along Church Street (now South Center Street) in Bradford (McKean County) on October 1, 1963. Forty years after the fact, one unnamed witness recalled the beast as being eight to ten feet tall.[41]

Sometime in 1963 or '64, an anonymous Sullivan County hunter heard sounds of large rocks being tossed about in the woods and went to investigate. He glimpsed "a very large dark hair covered animal running away on two legs," then recalled a prior discovery of huge footprints resembling bear tracks.[42]

The year 1964 produced two more sightings. At Garrison (Greene County), a "giant" ape-like creature peered through a woman's window, then fled, leaping over a five-foot-tall fence. In September, at Lignoier (Westmoreland County), a slump-shouldered "ape" with orange eyes reportedly killed a calf in front of a 12-year-old witness.[43]

On July 31, 1966, five witnesses at Erie County's Presque Isle Bay watched a shaggy "man/ape-like creature" walk past their car, leaving footprints on the beach. On August 17, the creature showed itself to seven Erie County witnesses at Edinboro Lake. Gunshots chased it off, with no apparent ill effects.[44]

In August 1967, *Real* magazine published a letter from one Mario Pinardi, claiming that he and another witness had trailed a nine-foot-tall bipedal creature across a field near Allison (Fayette County). No other details are available.[45]

A month later, in Westmoreland County, an 8-year-old boy at Camp Fairfield saw "a big gorilla looking thing" peer through the open doorway of his cabin, its conical head brushing the eight-foot doorway's upper frame. Before departing, it took time to rummage through some nearby garbage cans.[46]

In August 1968, a Bigfoot visited Tohickon Valley County Park, near Point Pleasant (Bucks County). Years later, a solitary witness described it as "the most frightening and butt ugly creature I have ever seen," with "a wild eyed look upon its face with the body language being restless." The witness claimed another sighting near the same site, in 1979.[47]

Tohickon Valley County Park, scene of a 1968 Bigfoot sighting.
Credit: U.S. National Oceanic and Atmospheric Administration

In September 1968, a group of hikers in the woods outside Ford City (Armstrong County) met a long-armed "gorilla man" seven feet tall, covered with long hair. Unlike the creatures seen by Caroline McAdoo, this one had "a large head which was proportioned to the rest of the body."[48]

We have three incidents on file from 1969. The first involves a group of teenage skinny-dippers in Greensboro, who patronized the Monview Park swimming pool after hours. Surprised by an approaching car, they fled into the nearby woods, where one of them collided an eight-foot, foul-smelling creature "manlike in form" and "covered in a long hair like element from the head to the feet."[49]

Sometime in autumn 1969, four residents of Northumberland County got an unpleasant surprise while spotlighting deer. Instead of a trophy buck, their lights revealed a black-haired, ape-like creature sitting on the ground, in a flattened circle of grass some twenty feet wide. The hunters did not fire or wait around to watch the beast.[50]

The young, unnamed witnesses from our last 1960s case had been fishing near West Newton (Westmoreland County) sometime during 1969. While walking home along some railroad tracks, they reported being followed by "a dark figure" whose arms dangled below its knees. The creature frightened them, but made no effort to attack.[51]

Hectic Seventies

Nothing thus far had prepared Pennsylvania monster-watchers for a sudden explosion of Bigfoot cases in the 1970s. All told, the decade produced 149 individual sightings, four vague claims of multiple encounters, and twenty-seven incidents involving footprints, strange smells or noises—an astounding 934-percent jump in eyewitness reports.

January 1970 brought the decade's first sighting, by a Centre County motorist who saw an ape-like creature leaning on a fence post beside Route 45. Later, three-toed footprints measuring twenty-one inches long were found in snow nearby.[52]

On April 18, 1970, a Potter County fisherman saw "a dark colored figure" standing beside his favorite trout stream. The following month, a family of five returning from church saw a reddish-brown biped "walking slumped" at Footedale (Fayette County). On June 16, two children from Emsworth (Allegheny County) saw a beast resembling Chewbacca from the *Star Wars* films in nearby woods. One of the kids claimed a second sighting of the same creature during the late Seventies but offered no further details.[53]

Another case from 1970, undated, involved a driver and his passenger who saw a hairy "man" outside Costello (Potter County). Two witnesses from Crawford County knew it was November when they saw a light-brown biped "jogging slightly hunched" along a rural highway, forty miles southeast of Erie, but by 1997, when they publicized the incident, neither could say if it occurred in 1970 or 1971.[54]

Witness Daniel Burkhart waited three decades to report his childhood encounter with Bigfoot at Steam Valley (Lycoming County) during spring 1971. The "massive" beast was covered with hair, except for its "bald-like face." Around the same time—April 20—a group of teenage campers saw a "very large hairy creature" at Hammonds Rocks, in Cumberland County.[55]

Summer 1971 produced two—and perhaps three—sightings. At Allison Park (Allegheny County), an unnamed hiker saw a tall, gray ape-like creature in an open field. Sometime later, two witnesses in Hampton Township saw a gray-and-white biped seven to nine feet tall, making sounds like a bird call. A third summer report, from a Westmoreland County equestrienne, placed Bigfoot on the outskirts of Keystone State Park. However, after thirty years' delay, the woman could not recall if the sighting occurred in 1971, 1972, or 1973.[56]

An autumn case completes our tally for 1971. Near Reynoldsville (Jefferson County), a hunter followed large "human" footprints and met their maker: "a tall man covered with hair." It had long arms, stood "swaying back and forth," then fled at his approach.[57]

Jan Klement's Kong

One of the more peculiar documents in Bigfoot literature was published in 1976 by Allegheny Press, based in Elgin (Erie County). Titled *The Creature: Personal Experiences with Bigfoot,* it claimed to relate a series of encounters between author "Jan Klement"—an admitted pseudonym—and a Sasquatch he dubbed "Kong." While most of the events are left undated, with locations deliberately obscured, certain events mentioned in the text—the death of baseball player Roberto Clemente (December 31, 1972); an independent Bigfoot sighting on Labor Day 1973—provide a broad a framework for the supposed events.

"Klement," a self-described scientist and college professor of unknown credentials, reportedly spotted Kong for the first time in August, near a cabin in the vicinity of Chestnut Ridge and Whymps Gap (Fayette County). Over time, he watched the creature kill a deer, two chipmunks, an opossum, a dog, and a robin—all of which it devoured. Klement also suspected the beast of killing a man on Chestnut Ridge, and suffered personal injury when Kong attacked his station wagon. Stranger still, on one occasion he observed Kong copulating with a cow![58]

Despite such incidents, Klement maintained that Kong accepted food from him and learned to obey a series of simple commands: "stay," "go," "lie [down]," etc. It came to visit Klement regularly, but despite near-daily contact spanning months, Kong fled at the sight of a camera, frustrating Klement's plan to photograph the beast.[59]

"Jan Klement" published his story of "Kong" in 1976.
Credit: Author's collection

So it went, for months on end, if we believe Klement's account. On once occasion he supposedly drove Kong to the Allegheny State Forest and left the beast whimpering, with orders to "Go!" but Kong quickly returned to the cabin, having "covered over two hundred miles in less than a day." After spoiling Klement's love life—his girlfriend suspects him of spending time with "some whore," instead of a Sasquatch—Kong died around New Year's Day 1972, from an unexplained illness. After dismembering Kong with an axe, Klement buried its remains near the West Virginia border.[60]

Fact or fiction? A thirtieth-anniversary edition of *The Creature*, released in 2006, reiterates the publisher's vow to preserve "Jan Klement's" anonymity, while stating that the author's cabin was destroyed by an arsonist in 1986, replaced by "several very expensive houses." Published speculation that "Klement" might be retired Professor Walter Skinner of Pittsburgh's Duquense University remains unconfirmed.[61] The tale remains entirely uncorroborated.

Bigfoot Bonanza

Before *The Creature* went to press, Pennsylvania experienced an unprecedented outbreak of Sasquatch sightings—a veritable deluge of encounters so numerous that only brief descriptions may be offered here. Cases from the remainder of the 1970s include:

1972

June: After flooding produced by Hurricane Agnes, during June 21-25, a woman in Salona (Clinton County) claimed that a Bigfoot raided her back porch for canned food.[62]

September: Multiple witnesses saw a large biped prowling their property near Glendale (Allegheny County).[63]

Autumn: A teenage hunter met a "big hairy animal" six to seven feet tall near Clarion (Clarion County).[64]

October: A family in Champion claimed multiple encounters with a beast they called "the Cookie Monster," which on one occasion killed their dog. Rick Berry misplaces the event in Somerset County, which has no such town. Others exist in Allegheny and Fayette Counties.[65]

October 31: While driving past Jumonville Rocks (Fayette County), several witnesses saw a gray-haired biped with "long arms, short legs, and self-illuminated eyes."[66]

November: Reckless children lobbed stones at a six-foot snarling biped, near Jumonville Rocks.[66]

1973

Undated: Two brothers saw a gray Sasquatch with "a white mane" on their farm, near Lancaster.[67]

Undated: A woman in Lancaster saw Bigfoot steal two of her geese. When she gave chase, the beast hurled one goose at her, knocking her down.[68]

Undated: Bigfoot charged another Lancaster farmer, tearing a scythe from his hands before the man fled.[69]

Undated: A Westmoreland County resident saw an 8.5-foot creature peering through his bathroom window.[70]

June: Several youths saw a "gorilla-like creature" walking near Greensburg's Greengate Mall.[71]

June: Stan Gordon's website subsequently claims 118 Bigfoot sightings in seven Pennsylvania counties, involving 245 witnesses, but published accounts describe only fifty-eight sightings during that period.[72]

July: Another window-peeping incident occurred, in New Sewickley Township (Beaver County), with large footprints discovered.[73]

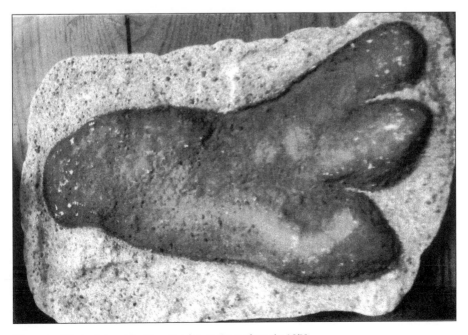

Three-toed footprint cast by Stan Gordon at Greensburg in 1973.
Credit: Stan Gordon Productions

July: A Greensburg physician fired shots at a creature attempting to enter his home. (Rick Berry dates this event from August 29.)[74]

July: Another Greensburg resident saw a nine-foot biped pass his upstairs bedroom window, then walk into the woods.[75]

July: Multiple witnesses saw a broad-shouldered creature at Jumonville Rocks.[76]

August 1: While shaving, a Greensburg man caught Bigfoot staring through his bathroom window. Six days later, huge footprints appeared at his home.[77]

Early August: Five witnesses on a Greensburg golf course saw three hairy bipeds, ranging from four to nine feet in height.[78]

August 7: Police in New Sewickley Township found eighteen-inch footprints after witnesses reported an ape-like creature with "glowing red eyes."[79]

August 8: Bigfoot looked through another bathroom window, in Westmoreland County.[80]

August 14: Two Greensburg men saw a foul-smelling Bigfoot emerge from the woods and cross a railroad track.[81]

August 16: A woman in Derry (Westmoreland County) saw a Sasquatch near her home.[82]

August 17: A resident of Bradenville (Westmoreland County) reported a Bigfoot sighting.[83]

August 17: A motorist told Kingston police that he had nearly struck a screaming, red-eyed biped on Route 30.[84]

August 19: An ape-like biped chased a housekeeper in Herminie (Westmoreland County).[85]

August 20: Bigfoot strolled along Donahue Road in Latrobe, "approaching drivers in a docile manner."[86]

August 21: A Derry resident saw Bigfoot looking through her bedroom window, nine feet above ground.[87]

August 21: State police received multiple reports of a hairy biped walking through Latrobe.[88]

August 23: A resident of Luxor (Westmoreland County) saw Bigfoot walking in daylight.[89]

August 24: A seven-foot, foul-smelling creature left eighteen-inch tracks at a trailer court in Herminie.[90]

August 25: Bigfoot returned to the Herminie trailer park, damaging one mobile home and leaving three-toed footprints.[91]

August 26: Two witnesses saw Bigfoot walking through Luxor.[92]

August 27: Two Beaver County girls saw an eight-foot creature "carrying a luminescent sphere in its hand."[93]

August 27: A Beech Hills (Westmoreland County) woman saw a UFO hovering near her home. Her husband later fired point-blank at an ape-like creature, without apparent effect.[94]

August 27: Multiple residents of Bradenville claimed a daylight Bigfoot sighting.[95]

August 28: A Sasquatch with "protruding fangs" was seen near Beech Hills.[96]

September 1: Bigfoot accosted a woman and child at Youngstown's St. James Church (Westmoreland County). Later, two other witnesses saw the creature near the first woman's home, five miles away.[97]

September 2: A resident of Indiana, Pennsylvania, saw an eight-foot hairy biped walking with "a stride three times that of a human."[98]

September 2 or 3: Chester Yothers and his wife saw an eight-foot creature outside their home at Whitney (Westmoreland County). Police found tracks at the scene.[99]

September 3: A female resident of Indiana, Pennsylvania, reported a "slumped over" Sasquatch walking with long strides.[100]

Early September: Three women driving near Penn (Westmoreland County) allegedly saw a seven-foot ape-like creature emerge from "a large metallic rectangular-shaped object" beside the highway.[101]

September 9: A resident of Westmoreland County reported an ape-like beast with "red glowing eyes" staring through the upstairs bedroom window of her rural home.[102]

September 11: A Westmoreland County fisherman told state police that he saw two Sasquatches swimming submerged in Keystone Lake.[103]

September 13: Residents of Indiana, Pennsylvania, found a Bigfoot sitting on an apple barrel outside their home. It fled when one witness fired gunshots.[104]

September 21: Several Greensburg boys reported a Bigfoot sighting to state police. Officers found footprints and collected hair samples.[105]

September 21: Bigfoot fought a dog at a home outside Latrobe, then fled "with tremendous leaps."[106]

September 24: Two Greensburg boys found Bigfoot asleep on a pile of grass clippings. It left before they returned with adults.[107]

September 24: A boy delivering newspapers in Greensburg saw a stooped Sasquatch walking "like it was drunk."[108]

September 27: Two Beaver County girls reported an eight-foot, red-eyed white creature carrying "a luminous sphere."[109]

October 2: A hunter met a gray eight-foot biped near Beaver Run Dam (Westmoreland County).[110]

October 25: Three witnesses approached the scene of a UFO sighting outside Uniontown and observed two large hairy bipeds. Some accounts claim that shots were fired at the creatures.[111]

Autumn: Several women reported a "strange animal" with glowing green eyes, seen near Midland. Towns of that name exist in Beaver and Washington Counties.[112]

November 3: Witnesses in Industry (Westmoreland County) reported a Bigfoot sighting to police.[113]

November 24: Four young motorcyclists claimed a nocturnal Sasquatch sighting near Latrobe.[114]

November: A Uniontown man claimed two Bigfoot sightings. He fired at the creature both times.[115]

1974

Undated: A Fayette County motorist saw Bigfoot cross the road in front of his car.[116]

Undated: Several young men saw a bipedal creature running near railroad tracks, outside West Newton.[117]

Undated: Thirteen witnesses in cars pursued a Bigfoot near Jumonville Rocks. It "seemed to move almost instantaneously from one side of them to the other."[118]

February 6: During a UFO sighting at Uniontown, a witness saw Bigfoot outside her home. When she fired a shotgun at it, the beast "disappeared in a flash of light." Her son-in-law responded to the gunshot and fired a pistol at several creatures gathered nearby, without apparent effect.[119]

August: Two boys reported sighting a brown-haired Bigfoot outside Dawson (Fayette County).[120]

December 29: Children saw a seven-foot biped outside their Allegheny County home, admiring a lighted Christmas tree. Investigators found four-toed footprints sixteen inches long and twelve inches wide.[121]

Mid-1970s

Young boys in Beaver County reported a brownish-black Sasquatch eating blueberries, sometime between 1972 and 1975.[122]

An unnamed York County witness claimed multiple sightings of a "large man-like creature" near the Peach Bottom Power Plant, during summer and November through December, 1973-76.[123]

A West Newton resident fired shots at a creature on his back porch in 1974 or '75. Fleeing, it ran through a barbed-wire fence built to confine a 1,500-pound bull.[124]

Sometime in the mid-Seventies, a deer hunter lost his kill to a snarling monster in "Mercer Swamp." Mercer County has three swamps, none named for the county.[125]

Two farmhands at Worthington (Armstrong County) caught an eight-foot biped watching them in summer 1976 or 1977.[126]

1975

Undated: A motorist saw a tall hairy biped near Jeannette.[127]

Undated: Rick Berry reports a sighting at North Hills, in Allegheny County—which has two schools, but no towns of that name. Towns called North Hills are found in Montgomery, Northumberland, and York Counties.[128]

Undated: Several witnesses watched a Sasquatch "float rather than walk" on a foggy night near Jumonville Rocks.[129]

February: An Allegheny County girl saw Bigfoot pass her family's farmhouse, "ostensibly teasing horses."[130]

March 28: Two women driving past North Park (Allegheny County) saw a seven-foot biped with orange reflective eyes "walk into" a steep roadside embankment. Two investigators from the Pennsylvania Center for UFO Research arrived the same day and found a three-toed footprint twenty-three inches long. Near midnight, they claimed a sighting of two "tall figures with red eyes."[131]

April: Children walking to Bradford Woods Elementary School (Allegheny County) reported a Bigfoot sighting.[132]

May: Five persons at a used-car lot in Etna (Allegheny County) observed three hairy bipeds from a distance, surmising that they comprised a "family."[133]

May: Two North Hills schoolteachers saw a twelve-foot hairy biped cross Harts Road at 1 a.m. Investigators later found twenty-one-inch, three-toed footprints separated by a five-foot stride.[134]

May 19: Another ape-like biped was seen near Jeannette, one day after a UFO sighting.[135]

Summer: Several Fayette County witnesses saw a "huge hairy creature" cross Route 981.[136]

July 2: An "overgrown gorilla," nine feet tall and the width of a refrigerator, left three-toed footprints outside Youngwood (Westmoreland County).[137]

July 10: A Washington County police officer saw a "stooped over," seven-foot biped cross a rural road at 4 a.m.[138]

July 14: A father and son saw Bigfoot run across Interstate 70 in Washington County.[139]

July 17: A off-road motorcyclist saw a brown-and-white Sasquatch in Washington County's Fallowfield Township.[140]

July: Investigating "large" sounds outside his home near Uniontown, an unnamed man saw "very large red eyes...up too high to be a deer."[141]

July: An eight-foot, green-eyed creature peered through the windows of a mobile home in Gibsonia (Allegheny County). It left claw marks on a door and three-toed, fourteen-inch tracks in the yard.[142]

August: A bicyclist watched Bigfoot climb a highway embankment on Route 410, near Luthersburg (Clearfield County).[143]

October 9: A hunter saw Bigfoot eating apples in an orchard near Monongahela (Washington County). Returning with two friends, he found a pair of creatures in the same spot. All three men fired rifles at the bipeds with no visible effect.[144]

1976

Undated: A "huge figure" frightened a hunter near Claysville (Washington County).[145]

Undated: Children playing near Ebensburg's Cambria County Fairgrounds saw an "orange/brown colored creature" and tried to shoot it with a pellet gun from 100 yards.[146]

Undated: A hunter glimpsed a hairy biped four to five feet tall near West Newton's elementary school.[147]

Undated: Several hikers met Bigfoot in a Crawford County forest. It was eight feet tall, smelled rank, and walked with "the deepest slouch [they] had ever seen."[148]

February 29: One night after a UFO sighting, two Oakdale residents saw an eight-foot Sasquatch at Settlers Cabin County Regional Park.[149]

May: A family driving past a lake at Suscon (Luzerne County) saw four bipeds eight to ten feet tall, all "waddling from side to side as if they were stiff-legged."[150]

A fabricated tabloid view of Bigfoot.
Credit: Author's collection

May: Two teenagers saw a seven-foot biped with "a cross between a gorilla face and a human" on Woodbourne Road in Levittown (Bucks County).[151]

Summer: Two youths working at a "mushroom mine" near Worthington (Armstrong County) saw a bipedal creature seven to eight feet tall.[152]

August: Bigfoot ran past a hiker in the woods near Mercer, allowing a glimpse of one hairy arm and leg.[153]

September 18: Witness Angelo Bufalino saw an eight-foot, dark-haired creature four miles from Cambridge Springs (Crawford County).[154]

Autumn: A hunter collided with Sasquatch in a thicket outside Cadogan (Armstrong County). Both parties fled in opposite directions.[155]

1977

Undated: A Coaltown resident saw Bigfoot standing outside her home, next to an upright ladder.[156]

Undated: A shrieking, long-haired biped tried to enter a cabin occupied by several men, near Clinton County's Kettle Creek State Park.[157]

Undated: Sasquatch rapped on the door of a home in Derry (Westmoreland County), then fled when the occupant answered.[158]

Undated: Bigfoot approached and scratched a car parked near Latrobe, with multiple witnesses inside.[159]

Undated: A motorist reported a midnight sighting near Prospect (Butler County).[160]

April: A Cadogan resident saw a tall, hairy biped in the woods behind his home.[161]

May: Three children saw a reddish-brown creature walking "slumped over" in Fayette County's German Township.[162]

May 15: A Fayette County couple saw a seven-foot shaggy biped "glide" across a road near Footedale.[163]

Spring: A driver parked at a dump near Grays Landing (Fayette County) first smelled, then saw a nine-foot hairy biped with yellow-orange skin and a "curly beard."[164]

June 14-15: A college student claimed two Bigfoot sightings near his Uniontown home.[165]

June 15: John Tiskus saw a hairy biped drinking from his swimming pool, in the Allison Park neighborhood of Glenshaw (Allegheny County). Conflicting reports place this incident in mid-July.[166]

July: A Cadogan resident viewed Bigfoot from a distance.[167]

July 10: A teenage camper saw a beige Sasquatch in the woods near Quakertown (Bucks County).[168]

August: The same Cadogan witness from July's sighting claimed another long-distance glimpse of Bigfoot.[169]

Labor Day weekend: Three campers saw Bigfoot outside their cabin, near Sinnemahoning (Cameron County). In a separate report, one of the witnesses claimed the sighting occurred on "September 31," during Memorial Day weekend (legally observed in May).[170]

September 5: Cadogan's lucky, anonymous witness claimed his third Bigfoot sighting, this one from thirty feet.[171]

September 10: The same unnamed witness claimed his fourth sighting since July.[172]

September 17: A relative of Cadogan's repeat witness allegedly saw Bigfoot in the same vicinity.[173]

Autumn: An Erie County boy saw a black, seven-foot creature "tearing off tree limbs and pushing over rotted trees" near West Springfield.[174]

October: A Latrobe resident found his dog "hung by its neck," then saw an eight-foot, red-eyed biped nearby. His bullets "bounced off [the creature] with no effect."[175]

October 11: Several witnesses saw an 8.5-foot creature with knee-length arms on Dutch Hollow Road, in Cadogan.[176]

November 16: A Washington County farmer saw Bigfoot on his property. The PBS adds UFOs to the report.[177]

December 23: Two boys saw a Bigfoot with "glowing white eyes" outside Trent (Somerset County). Again, the PBS reports a UFO nearby.[178]

1978

Undated: A motorist fired shots at Bigfoot, south of Uniontown. Police followed a blood trail to an abandoned mine in neighboring West Virginia, but did not explore it.[179]

Undated: Near the same location, two boys watched a hairy biped limp across a field.[180]

January: Rick Berry reports a Bigfoot sighting from "Laurel State Park." No such park exists, although Somerset County has Laurel Hill State Park and Laurel Summit State Park, while Laurel Mountain State Park is found in Westmoreland County.[181]

January 10: A resident of Fawn Grove (York County) reported a ten-foot-tall biped with "shining white" eyes near a local school.[182]

March 2: Motorist Norval Thomas saw a seven-foot creature near York County's Peach Bottom Power Plant. Security guards heard "bone-chilling screams" and found footprints equivalent to a size-10.5 boot.[183]

Early March: A York County driver saw Bigfoot near Spring Grove. Police found its tracks in snow.[184]

April: A resident of Hooversville (Somerset County) fired shots at "an apparent Bigfoot creature."[185]

May: In Apollo (Armstrong County), Sasquatch pounded on a homeowner's air-conditioner, then fled into the woods.[186]

Late August: A boy saw Bigfoot chasing horses on his family's farm, near Clearfield.[187]

September: Sasquatch woke tourists at Gifford Pinchot State Park by screaming and pounding on their camper.[188]

November: On the first day of deer season, a hunter met Bigfoot near Airville (York County).[189]

1979

Undated: An Apollo resident saw Sasquatch in his driveway.[190]

January: A rank-smelling Sasquatch visited the Semelsburger farm, neat Patton (Cambria County).[191]

April 19: Witnesses reported an eight-foot, "humped over" biped "racing back and forth" across a Dauphin County bridge, between Dauphin and Harrisburg.[192]

May: Bigfoot approached a mobile home in Apollo, then fled in the face of gunfire.[193]

July: A Derry resident followed Sasquatch into the woods, where it eluded him.[194]

July 4: An unnamed witness saw Bigfoot at New Florence (Westmoreland County).[195]

August 15: Residents of White Oak (Allegheny County) watched a shrieking bipedal creature circle their home.[196]

August 18: After another White Oak sighting, searchers found three-toed, sixteen-inch tracks at a nearby mine.[197]

September: Three witnesses observed Bigfoot in the woods near Lagonda (Washington County).[198]

October 20: A young Derry witness saw Sasquatch near his home and reported frequent nocturnal vocalizations from "three to five" creatures.[199]

November: Two witnesses riding snowmobiles near Kingwood (Somerset County) saw Bigfoot crossing a distant field.[200]

Late Seventies

Undated: A West Newton resident reported Bigfoot staring through his window, late at night.[201]

Undated: A young girl saw a hairy biped near a farm outside Scottdale (Westmoreland County).[202]

Apes of the Eighties

Sightings declined slightly in this decade, but still remained fairly frequent, with 133 specific individual reports, four vague claims of multiple sightings, and fifty-four cases of footprints, strange odors or noises, and so forth. Again, the frequency of sightings permits only brief descriptions.

Hollywood often portrays Big-foot as a vicious man-eater. *Credit: Author's collection*

1980

Undated: A resident of Markleton (Somerset County) saw Bigfoot lurking in his driveway.[203]

January 6: Near Trafford (Westmoreland County), a woman heard growling and saw "the shadow of a large biped."[204]

January 10: Several Trafford boys saw a red-eyed Bigfoot that smelled like sulfur breaking branches in the woods. The PBS adds "a strange white light" to the report.[205]

June 26: Two citizens of Guffey (Westmoreland County) saw a large, "very coordinated" biped cross their backyard.[206]

June 30: Another Guffey resident followed Sasquatch but lost it in woods near his home.[207]

July: Witnesses in Guffey saw a tall hairy biped walking near a "strange blue light."[208]

July 18: Rick Knovich saw a black-haired creature cross railroad tracks at Scotch Run, outside Mainville (Columbia County).[209]

July 20: Witnesses in Guffey glimpsed another Sasquatch.[210]

August: A dune buggy driver saw a nine-foot monster holding a log above its head, near Latrobe.[211]

August 18: Near Jonestown (Columbia County), Bill and Tom Talanca saw Bigfoot walking with "a stride three times that of a human."[212]

August 25: A seven-foot creature smelling of sulfur was seen near abandoned coal mines outside South Fork (Cambria County).[213]

September: A woman saw Bigfoot in a cornfield near Boile Run. Sixteen-inch footprints later appeared in the same vicinity.[214]

September 22: Two boys from Trafford saw a hairy biped that "appeared to float or glide, rather than walk" through nearby woods.[215]

October: A man walking his dog outside Kingwood saw a ten-foot hairy biped near the entrance to an abandoned mine.[216]

October 22: Two brothers from Kingwood claimed a Bigfoot sighting from a distance of 250 yards. The PBS dates this case from November 22.[217]

1981

April 18: Sam Frew, a resident of Westmoreland County's Bell Township, fired shots at a four-foot-tall ape-like creature, to no effect. He described it as weighing 550 pounds, though the PBS claims 1,500.[218]

July 7: Sam Frew and wife Ruth heard "the typical sound of the creature" and saw "a black mass with yellow colored eyes" near their home.[219]

August: A young bicyclist saw Bigfoot crossing a pasture beside Route 189, in Westmoreland County's Bell Township.[220]

August 12: Another Bell Township witness saw a twelve-foot-tall biped cross a gas line road.[221]

Autumn: Sam Frew saw a fifteen-foot Sasquatch in the woods near Apollo.[222]

Autumn: Witness J.D. Frew glimpsed a "bulky" ten-foot biped in a forest clearing near Apollo.[223]

October 31: A resident of Vandergrift (Westmoreland County) saw a hairy creature seven to eight feet tall crossing her neighbor's lawn.[224]

November 30: Two Fayette County trappers met Bigfoot near Keisterville, repelling it with a shower of stones.[225]

December: While hunting with his father in Columbia County, a boy observed a seven-foot Sasquatch "with its legs bowed out in front," which ran with "a strange jerking motion to its arms."[226]

1982

Undated: Two Westmoreland County witnesses saw Bigfoot "slumped over" in a Bell Township thicket.[227]

March 20: Rick Berry reports that Bigfoot visited a farm near Grantville (Dauphin County) "on several occasions."[228]

June 12: Berry says that camper Robert France saw a biped seven to eight feet tall "near Hillside" and photographed its footprints. Towns of that name exist in Luzerne and Westmoreland Counties.[229]

July 30: Two witnesses saw Bigfoot at a baseball field in New Stanton (Westmoreland County).[230]

September 1: ATV riders saw a four-foot apelike creature picking berries near West Newton, then observed an eight-foot beast nearby.[231]

September 10: While driving through Cambria County's Conemaugh Township, David Gustdey saw a seven-foot creature cross Truman Boulevard with four strides.[232]

October: Three Fayette County children saw two bipedal creatures walking in the woods: One was seven feet tall, the other about three feet.[233]

October 6: While doing laundry in her basement, a Bell Township woman saw a red-eyed monster peering through the window.[234]

October 28: A Bell Township resident fired three rifle shots at a red-eyed Bigfoot, with no visible effect.[235]

November: Two witnesses from the October Fayette County incident saw a lone Sasquatch on the same forest trail.[236]

November: Two Bell Township residents saw a biped with reddish-orange eyes outside their home.[237]

November: On the first day of deer season, three hunters met a 6.5-foot Sasquatch near Sigel (Jefferson County).[238]

Late Autumn: A couple driving from York to their rural home saw a beige, ten-foot creature walking past a garbage dump.[239]

December 31: A wildlife photographer met Bigfoot near North Park (Bucks County) but "forgot" to snap its photo.[240]

1983

Undated: A couple hiking in the woods near Luxor saw a "partially hair covered" bipedal creature with "oily and wrinkled skin."[241]

Undated: A Kingstown resident saw a Bigfoot with "a very tall head" on Chestnut Ridge Road.[242]

Undated: Two West Newton boys heard branches breaking and saw "a white left arm sticking out of the thicket."[243]

Undated: While hunting in a Port Vue cemetery (Allegheny County), a young man saw "two huge hair covered legs up to the waist."[244]

January 2: Two men watched a pair of twelve-foot bipeds cross a field near Greensburg. One creature carried "a large object" over its shoulder.[245]

February 15: Rick Berry writes that an unnamed witness fired shots at Bigfoot with no result, location unknown.[246]

March 19: Berry reports that several Girl Scouts met an ape-like creature walking erect, outside Freeport. Towns of that name exist in Armstrong and Erie Counties.[247]

July 6: Berry relates another shooting incident at an unknown location, apparently wounding a creature described as "a huge mass of blondish-brown hair."[248]

Summer: An ATV rider saw Bigfoot near a strip mine outside Mahaffey (Clearfield County). She also saw several partially-devoured turkeys, surrounded by large humanoid footprints.[249]

Summer: A camper reported seeing Bigfoot at a remote location west of Clarendon (Warren County).[250]

September or October: Children playing in the woods near Jefferson (Greene County) saw Bigfoot running on two legs.[251]

1984

Undated: A Bedford boy saw Bigfoot while delivering newspapers.[252]

Undated: Two witnesses saw Sasquatch in the woods near Ligonier (Westmoreland County). It left footprints seventeen inches long and nine inches wide.[253]

March 23: A Bell Township motorist saw a black, four-foot-tall biped cross Rubright Road.[254]

Late September or early October: A resident of Catawissa Township (Columbia County) watched a Bigfoot "sway back and forth" in tall grass. It smelled "like an open sewer."[255]

Autumn: Two Boy Scouts claimed a Bigfoot sighting at Hell's Hollow, near Greenville (Mercer County).[256]

October 27: A woman riding with her husband near Harveyville (Luzerne County) saw a Sasquatch standing near an old barn.[257]

November 3: A Somerset County resident smelled, then saw Bigfoot near Laurel Hill Tunnel.[258]

1985

Undated: A hunter saw "a tall, hairy, erect walking creature" near Jo Jo (McKean County).[259]

Undated: A mother and son watched two red-eyed bipeds cross Dime Road near North Vandergrift (Armstrong County).[260]

Undated: Two young couples saw "a large hairy creature" near DuBois Reservoir (Susquehanna County).[261]

June: "Two or three" bipedal creatures eight to nine feet tall watched a man and boy work on a barn in Washington County's Borough of Long Branch.[262]

July: A Schuylkill County witness saw Bigfoot standing 500 feet behind his uncle's rural home.[263]

July 3: Two residents of Redstone Township (Fayette County) saw a "black human-like form" that emitted a "rotten" odor.[264]

July 7: Different Redstone Township witnesses saw and smelled the same creature.[265]

Late July: Robert Carnathan and Dan Meyers saw a four-foot-tall biped with chestnut-colored hair walking beside a road in Lebanon County's North Londonderry Township.[266]

August: Rick Berry reports that a Sasquatch with large teeth frightened a child in a cornfield, location undisclosed.[267]

Poster for the Pennsylvania Bigfoot Society's conference, 2008.
Credit: Author's collection

September 6 or 7: Edward Kreamer and his girlfriend reported an ape-like creature prowling around the home of Kreamer's parents, in Annville Township (Lebanon County).[268]

End of September: Tom Leach and a friend reported a Sasquatch with two-inch fangs at large in Cumberland County's East Pennsboro Township. Police Chief James Corbett called it a "Halloween prank," but his investigating officers disagreed.[269]

Late Autumn: A witness on horseback saw a five-foot-tall biped near Brady's Run Lake (Beaver County).[270]

1986

June: Rick Berry reports a farmer's Bigfoot sighting in Hickory Township. Townships of that name exist in Forest, Lawrence and Mercer Counties.[271]

June: Witness "Joey" saw Bigfoot while hunting in Westmoreland County. His father smelled a "sulfur odor" but saw nothing.[272]

Autumn: An anonymous report filed on the BFRO's website in 2002 claims a Bigfoot sighting by two teenagers at Hell's Hollow.[273]

December 13: Rick Berry describes an eight-foot biped throwing a stick at a hunter near "Greystation." No such town exists in Pennsylvania—or in the United States—but there is a town called Grays in Westmoreland County, and a Gray Station Road in Blairsville (Indiana County).[274]

December 14: Berry reports another sighting at "Greystation," by two witnesses.[275]

1987

January: A witness reported two hairy bipeds—one eight feet tall, the other half that size—walking through woods near Clarksburg (Indiana County).[276]

February 1: Rick Berry describes a 2 a.m. Bigfoot sighting at "Greystation, Derry Township." Four counties have townships of that name: Dauphin, Mifflin, Montour, and Westmoreland.[277]

February 1: Berry says another "Greystation" witness saw Bigfoot peering through her window, eight feet off the ground.[278]

February 8: Berry reports an unnamed man saw Sasquatch walking through the woods near "Greystation."[279]

March: A motorist glimpsed Bigfoot running through a field outside Donegal (Westmoreland County).[280]

March 5: Berry claims a Bigfoot sighting by several children at "Bressier," another untraceable location.[281]

March 6: Berry cites an "unconfirmed report of a police search" for Bigfoot, following sightings at "Coketown." No such town exists, although there is a Coketown Road in Coraopolis (Allegheny County).[282]

April 8: Berry claims two more sighting of a seven-foot, red-eyed creature at "Greystation," forty-five minutes apart.[283]

April 13: Berry says two more "Greystation" witnesses claimed separate sightings of Bigfoot.[284]

May 5: Berry notes a Sasquatch sighting at Hillside, without specifying a county.[285]

May 16: Two men saw Bigfoot cross a road near New Alexandria (Westmoreland County). One fired a shot over the creature's head.[286]

June: Multiple sightings emerged from Harrisburg, including several reports of slaughtered animals.[287]

July 3: Several witnesses saw Bigfoot standing by a creek outside Latrobe.[288]

Summer, possibly August: An orange-eyed biped appeared in response to a hunter's rabbit distress call in Greene County's Jackson Township.[289]

August: Berry reports a motorist's Bigfoot sighting near Hillside, county unspecified.[290]

November 22: A hunter reported being followed by "a monkey" in Westmoreland County's North Huntingdon Township. Area zoos had no escapees.[291]

November 26: A mother and son saw a "long-haired gold-colored" biped in woods near Pittsburgh.[292]

1988

Undated: A camper saw a seven-foot "shadowy creature" following two of his friends in Elk State Forest (Elk County).[293]

February 14: A Cub Scout saw a seven-foot biped that smelled "like a wet dog," near Ligonier.[294]

February 20: Multiple witnesses saw Bigfoot prowling around a rural home at Point Marion (Fayette County).[295]

March 19: Rick Berry reports a sighting on Chestnut Ridge, in Derry Township. Pennsylvania has sixteen ridges of that name in twelve counties, and four Derry Townships in four counties. The only match is in Mifflin County, with two Chestnut Ridges.[296]

April: Berry reports another Bigfoot sighting by multiple witnesses at "Greystation."[297]

May 9 or 10: Bigfoot approached a man walking his dog near Rector (Westmoreland County).[298]

May 17: A 6.5-foot biped with glowing eyes the size of golf balls touched fisherman Samuel Sherry's shoulder at Loyalhanna Creek.[299]

May 22: A strolling couple saw Bigfoot outside Ligonier.[300]

June: Berry reports a lone-witness sighting from Laurel Ridge. Pennsylvania has five Laurel Ridges in as many counties.[301]

June 29: A Derry resident (Westmoreland County) sees Bigfoot in her backyard.[302]

July 3: Rick Berry claims a sighting at a trailer park in untraceable "Carey Station."[303]

July 12: Another dog-walker met Sasquatch, three miles east of Laughlintown (Westmoreland County).[304]

July 17: Witnesses observed a shrieking hairy biped in Westmoreland County's Keystone State Park.[305]

Week of July 19th: Berry reports another Bigfoot sighting from "Bressier."[306]

August: Various South Fork residents reported Bigfoot at large and blamed it for killing several dogs.[307]

August 7: A South Fork woman saw a gorilla-like creature watching her outside her home.[308]

August 13: Berry says that Sasquatch caused an auto accident in South Fork, by standing in the road.[309]

August 21: A resident of Germany (Indiana County) saw Bigfoot in the woods nearby.[310]

September: A Derry motorist saw "something hairy and around eight foot tall" standing near a house.[311]

September: A father and daughter fishing near Jo Jo heard "high-pitched screeching sounds." The girl saw "red eyes" in the woods, 7.5 feet above the ground.[312]

September 10: Berry reports a near-collision with Bigfoot on a road near "Bressier."[313]

Autumn: An Erie County resident saw a red-eyed biped eight to nine feet tall passing his rural home, between Erie and Wesleyville.[314]

Autumn: The Hell's Hollow witness from autumn 1986 claimed a second Sasquatch sighting near the same location.[315]

October: Three witnesses driving near Knox Dale (Jefferson County) saw a reddish-brown Sasquatch in a roadside field.[316]

October: Several witnesses saw Bigfoot while walking past a dump near Alfarata (Mifflin County).[317]

October: A family spotting deer near Punxsutawney saw a reddish-brown biped seven to eight feet tall.[318]

November: A Greensburg resident reported Bigfoot walking near a local cemetery.[319]

December 12: Two residents of Torrance saw a Sasquatch that "appeared to be female."[320]

1989

Early January: Berry reports another Bigfoot sighting from "Bressier."[321]

January 31: A hunter met Sasquatch in the woods near Blairsville.[322]

February 25: Two witnesses driving near Bentleyville (Washington County) glimpsed a hairy biped standing beside the highway.[323]

March: A Ligonier Township motorist saw an eight-foot hairy creature near the site of another encounter from July 12, 1988.[324]

April 16: Bigfoot ran through the woods and leapt over a fence outside Connellsville (Fayette County).[325]

April 20: Berry reports a fisherman's Bigfoot sighting near Donegal. Towns of that name exist in Clearfield and Westmoreland Counties.[326]

May: The PBS reports a nocturnal sighting near Logansport, an abandoned ghost town in Armstrong County.[327]

May 20: A fisherman saw Bigfoot "in profile," three miles east of Jennerstown (Somerset County).[328]

Week of June 4th: Berry cites "several" reports of Bigfoot roaming around Grove City (Mercer County).[329]

Week of June 11th: Berry reports Bigfoot attacking a trailer in Greenville. Pennsylvania has four towns of that name, in as many counties.[330]

Week of June 25th: Berry reports a Bigfoot sighting near Wheatland. Two towns of that name exist, in Lancaster and Mercer Counties.[331]

Early August: Four witnesses riding ATVs in Stonycreek Township (Somerset County) saw a large biped with "straggly" hair and a "bent over" posture.[332]

September: While driving near Rillton (Westmoreland County), a witness saw a small hairy creature running through a roadside field.[333]
October 7: Four witnesses saw Bigfoot cross a road near Homer City (Indiana County).[334]

Uncertain Dates

1980s: A Cambria County girl saw Bigfoot from her bedroom window, location unknown.[335]
Autumn 1980-81: Two boys say a red-eyed creature in the woods near East Stroudsburg (Monroe County). It left one large footprint in mud.[336]
Mid 80s: Two teenagers saw a 7.5-foot biped in the woods near Dravosburg (Allegheny County).[337]
1984 or '85: Eight or nine youths saw Bigfoot peering through a window of their house in Lykens (Dauphin County).[338]
November 1986-87: A seven-foot Sasquatch shrieked outside a home in Sweden Valley (Potter County).[339]
1986-1994: The PBS reports that a couple living near Jamestown had "several unusual encounters with an unforeseen creature," but offers no details. Oddly, the report places Jamestown in Crawford County, where no such town exists. Pennsylvania's three Jamestowns are found in Cambria, Carbon and Mercer Counties.[340]

Nineties' Nightmares

Bigfoot sightings declined by forty-one percent in the twentieth century's last decade. The 1990s produced fifty-five individual reports and twenty-nine accounts of other evidence with no creatures seen. The sighting cases include:

1990

March: A shrieking hairy biped, four feet tall with "blazing red eyes," frightened a Ligonier resident.[341]
June 22: Two motorists and their passengers saw Bigfoot jump over a highway guardrail in Clinton County's Bald Eagle Township.[342]
October or November: The PBS website describes a teenager's sighting of Bigfoot in Indiana County's "Ruffington Township." The report presumably refers to *Buff*ington Township.[343]

1991

February 3: Another screaming, red-eyed creature, this one five feet tall, frightened residents and horses at a home near Darlington (Westmoreland County).[344]

Early February: A hunter saw Bigfoot on State Game Lands No. 110, west of Hamburg in Berks County.[345]

April 2 or 3: A night watchman saw a red-eyed, seven-foot biped at a steel mill on the Juniata River, near Harrisburg.[346]

June: Two men saw a biped seven to 8.5 feet tall, covered with "stringy" dark hair, in Centre County's Bald Eagle State Park.[347]

June 7: Two campers in Union County's White Deer Township saw a "tall jogger," subsequently recognized as Bigfoot. It left one sixteen-inch footprint.[348]

July: A woman driving on Route 192 near Livonia (Centre County) saw a creature 3.5 to 4 feet tall, "covered in reddish brown hair like a fox."[349]

Summer: A resident of Tarentum saw a brownish-gray creature eight to nine feet tall in the woods a half-mile from his home.[350]

December: A Clearfield County hunter saw "a shadowy dark figure" near Penfield and smelled its "foul odor like decaying flesh."[351]

1992

Undated: A Cambria County motorist saw a five-foot apelike creature hop a guardrail on Route 22, between Altoona and Galitzin.[352]

February 3: Eric Hess and two friends saw a red-eyed Sasquatch while camping near Evans City (Butler County).[353]

July: On a Sunday afternoon, two bicyclists and a jogger met Bigfoot on a trail two miles north of Sigel.[354]

July or August: A lone witness saw four shaggy bipeds cross a road near Wylandville Elementary School (Washington County). Two were seven or eight feet tall, the others a foot or two shorter.[355]

August 5: Three campers in Elk County heard high-pitched vocalizations, then saw "the legs of a hairy, bi-pedal creature" in their flashlight beams. The PBS reports an identical case from Erie County on the same date, suggesting a duplicate listing.[356]

November 29: Three friends followed humanoid tracks through the snow in Somerset County, until one saw a nine-foot "shadow" and collapsed when the "hairy thing" touched his cheek.[357]

December 1: A hunter fired at Bigfoot near an abandoned mining town in Brush Valley (Indiana County), but missed the eight-foot target.[358]

1993

April: A driver and his passenger saw Sasquatch rise from a crouch beside Route 286 near Aultman (Indiana County).[359]

Late April: A hairy biped 5.5 feet tall chased two campers through an apple orchard outside Catawissa.[360]

August: A midnight fisherman saw Bigfoot running in the water near a bridge at Davidsville, misplacing the town in Cambria County (rather than Somerset) when he reported it to the GCBRO.[361]

October 18: A hiker saw Bigfoot standing near a mutilated deer carcass, somewhere in Butler County.[362]

December: A Wayne County hunter watched Sasquatch through his rifle's scope, on State Game Lands No. 299.[363]

1994

January or early February: Seven snowmobilers saw two hairy bipeds near the Black Forest Trail (Potter County). One creature was eight feet tall, while the other—an apparent female—was six inches shorter.[364]

February 5: Two residents of Washington County's North Strabane Township saw Bigfoot from their kitchen window. Eighteen-inch footprints, separated by a fifty-inch stride, were found nearby on February 6.[365]

April: A hiker at Raystown Lake found a dead pig, then saw a dark-colored bipedal creature walking nearby.[366]

April: Five teenagers roaming in the woods near Girard (Erie County) met a Sasquatch with "very large green glowing eyes."[367]

Summer: A resident of Export (Westmoreland County) saw a tall hairy biped cross the road near his home.[368]

October 2: Two tourists from Ohio saw an apelike creature eight to nine feet tall at a picnic area in Westmoreland County, along the Pennsylvania Turnpike.[369]

October 15: A teenager saw Bigfoot in the woods near Connellsville. Returning with his parents the next day, he found footprints and broken saplings.[370]

December: Several hunters observed two bipeds—the larger one brown, its companion "dirty white"—along Big Run Creek (Jefferson County).[371]

1995

January 5: A Washington County motorist reported a predawn Bigfoot sighting near Canonsburg.[372]

June 25: A driver and his passenger saw Bigfoot on Route 422, west of Revloc (Cambria County).[373]

Autumn: A hunter glimpsed a "large dark creature" from eighty yards, near Westline (McKean County).[374]

October 14: Three boys heard screams and saw an eight-foot biped near Shamokin (Northumberland County).[375]

1996

Undated: While walking his dog three miles south of West Newton, a man saw a creature seven to eight feet tall, noting its "long nose that was not very wide" and the fact that its "lip line ran to the sides of its face, not on the front of its face like a human."[376]

January 22: A state trooper saw Bigfoot walking along State Road 1004 in Armstrong County's Madison Township. The officer found six eighteen-inch footprints.[377]

October 12: A motorist saw a "huge manlike form" walking beside Route 780 near Milligantown (Westmoreland County).[378]

1997

July: Two youths driving ATVs saw Bigfoot cross Breakneck Road near Connellsville.[379]

August 3: Two hikers saw a seven-foot, long-armed biped near Big Run, outside Nisbet (Lycoming County).[380]

September: "Robert M." saw a "white human form" eight to nine feet tall cross his yard near Sewickley (Allegheny County).[381]

Late October: A hunter got "a fairly good look" at three ape-like creatures, one of them "dragging a baby," in Adams County's Michaux State Forest.[382]

1998

January: A couple driving on Route 116, between Fairfield and Gettysburg, saw Bigfoot step over a fence and cross the road in two or three steps.[383]

February 25: A South Fork witness saw a creature eight to nine feet tall near the old Liberty Park swimming pool. Its face was "a cross between an ape and a man." The witness photographed its footprints.[384]

June 28: Two Erie County witnesses saw Bigfoot at a camp one mile south of Lake Erie.[385]

November: Two hunters saw a nine-foot biped standing on a bridge in Union County's Raymond B. Winter State Park. It charged and punched their truck after the driver blew his horn.[386]

1999

February: A fisherman claimed he saw Bigfoot eating a rabbit near the Clarion River.[387]

February: A camper reported seeing a nine-foot-tall creature in Centre County's Moshannon State Forest.[388]

April 24: While fishing near Laurelville (Westmoreland County), a lone witness saw Bigfoot leap twenty feet or more across a creek.[389]

May: A woman met Sasquatch while walking her dog near the wildlife preserve at Dead Man's Hollow (Allegheny County).[390]

July: While driving near Brisbin (Clearfield County) a motorist saw a seven-foot biped cross Route 153 in three strides.[391]

August: A hiker glimpsed a black creature seven to eight feet tall outside Weatherly (Carbon County).[392]

September: A Fayette County motorist driving from McClellandtown to Masontown saw Bigfoot rise from all fours to stand upright beside the highway. When he blew his horn, it screamed and ran into the woods.[393]

October: A resident of Penfield (Clarion County) saw a black seven-foot biped in the woods outside town.[394]

October 28: Three witnesses driving on a country road in Unity Township (Westmoreland County) watched a six-foot-tall reddish-brown biped cross in front of their car.[395]

1990s: Year Unknown

June 1992 or '93: A child residing near Gettysburg heard footsteps outside his bedroom window and saw a hairy creature 5.5 to six feet tall, with "a fairly large head and very broad shoulders."[396]

Monsters of a New Millennium

As this book went to press, the first decade of the twenty-first century had nearly doubled the 1990s' tally of Bigfoot encounters, producing 108 individual sightings in Pennsylvania, plus three claims of "ongoing" Sasquatch activity and fifty-seven cases of other evidence without visual contact. Eyewitness sightings include:

2000

March 19-24: Four hikers heard a "scream/moan" in the woods near Ebensburg, then saw Bigfoot peering from behind a tree. The witness who submitted their report to the BFRO claims "ongoing encounters with Bigfoot type creatures."[397]

May: A motorist saw Sasquatch with "the face of a Neanderthal" cross a rural road in Armstrong County.[398]

June 9: A woman driving to work in Jeannette saw a black biped cross Route 30 in three steps.[399]

July: A couple hiking near Reynoldsville saw a black biped 6½ to seven feet tall.[400]

July: A farmhand mowing a field near Wyalusing (Bradford County) noticed a hairy creature watching him from the nearby woods.[401]

July 15: While fishing at Cambria County's Bakerton Reservoir, a woman saw a "very hairy" creature six to seven feet tall.[402]

August: A motorist driving past Rockton Mountain, north of Clearfield, saw Bigfoot leaning against a highway guardrail.[403]

August 5: Three hikers photographed "a reddish brown object standing upright" in the woods near Rockton Mountain, but the blurry photo proved useless.[404]

August 6: A motorist driving on Route 322E near Knox Dale saw a shaggy biped with a face "puffy and wrinkled." It greeted her car with "a very piercing scream."[405]

August 12: An anonymous resident of Chester (Delaware County) claimed a frightening encounter with "a very ugly ape." Locals call it the "Josh Ape," after "a very dorky, lonely boy with no friends."[406]

August 27-29: Vague reports of Bigfoot activity prompted a PBS investigation at Wyalusing. Society members heard various odd sounds, but saw nothing.[407]

September: A school bus driver saw Bigfoot cross a road outside Curwensville (Clearfield County).[408]

November: A hunter reported being followed by "something large and brown in color" near Canton (Bradford County).[409]

2001

January 15: A screaming seven-foot creature with "almond colored" hair and "a skunk like odor" frightened a camper in Montgomery County's Wissahickon Valley Park.[410]

February: Rick Fisher saw an ape-like biped cross Route 23 near Lancaster. He described it as five feet tall and "skinny, perhaps 80 pounds."[411]

March: A motorist driving on Route 153 near Clearfield saw a seven-foot biped cross the highway.[412]

March 3: Three nocturnal walkers from West Salisbury (Somerset County) heard growling near Mount Davis, then saw a 7.5-foot creature with gray-white hair and "a hunch in its back."[413]

May 13: PBS researcher Scott Hangartner claimed a personal Bigfoot sighting near Rockton Mountain.[414]

June 2: A boy saw Bigfoot pass his family's cabin near Ickesburg (Perry County).[415]

June 6: The same Allegheny County witness from May 1999 reported her second encounter with Bigfoot, describing a shadowy figure with "a set of black legs."[416]

July: A bicyclist and his dog surprised a gray-and-brown Sasquatch resting against a tree in Clarion County, location undisclosed.[417]

July 20: An eight-foot biped with "glistening long black hair" woke a camper near Grove Run (Cameron County).[418]

Summer: An unnamed witness claimed a Bigfoot sighting near Avis (Clinton County).[419]

September 22: Two hunters heard "baby crying vocalizations" and saw a pair of hairy creatures walking on Rockton Mountain.[420]

October 20: A driver and his passenger saw Bigfoot cross Route 56E near Homer City.[421]

November 18: Three Mercer County witnesses, driving on Lamor Road between Hermitage and Mercer saw a "humanlike figure" covered with light-brown hair cross in front of their car.[422]

December: A witness at Monaca (Beaver County) reported seeing "a big, ugly, hairy, tall, dark colored creature" that "smelled real bad and walked in a long stride."[423]

2002

January 29: Monster-hunter Mike Morrow claimed that he had inadvertently photographed Bigfoot at Bald Eagle State Park. His photos have been removed from the GCBRO website as of November 2010.[424]

April 25: A couple driving near Towanda (Bradford County) saw a large biped cross Route 220.[425]

May 19: An unnamed witness glimpsed Bigfoot in Clinton County's Mount Logan Natural Area.[426]

June 28: A resident of Cross Fork (Potter County) saw two bipeds cross a pipeline outside town. One was seven to eight feet tall, the other around three feet.[427]

July 7: Roused by screams "like someone was being murdered," a camper saw Bigfoot running through woods near Route 68, in Clarion County's Brady Township.[428]

August: A "very tall" ape-like creature crossed a Snyder County road and ducked into a cornfield.[429]

September: Westmoreland County's Chestnut Ridge produced two Bigfoot sightings. First, a bicyclist encountered the creature. Then, two weeks later, the cyclist's mother saw it step over a four-foot roadside fence in the same area.[430]

September: Two Indiana County hunters smelled a "dead skunk" odor, then saw a "large and stealthy" figure in the woods.[431]

October 1: A resident of Archbald (Lackawanna County) saw a large hairy biped in a swamp near Salem Hill.[432]

October 6: After a month of nocturnal screaming, a Tarentum witness saw Bigfoot near his home.[433]

October 9: The GCBRO reports that two campers in Beaver County's Raccoon Creek State Park saw an eight-foot creature with "red eyes outlined with green." The PBS dates the incident from 2004.[434]

October 23: More Beaver County witnesses reported a "possible Bigfoot" from Hopewell Township.[435]

October: A couple hiking in Cowan's Gap State Park (Fulton County) watched deer fleeing "loud ape-like sounds," before the woman saw an unknown creature's "dark, muscular hindquarters."[436]

November: A hunter somewhere in Allegheny County saw a muscular biped roughly 7½ feet tall.[437]

2003

February: Bigfoot ran beside a car with two occupants on Route 274, near Elliottsburg (Perry County).[438]

April 13: Three Westmoreland County witnesses reported a beige-colored Sasquatch crossing a cornfield in Derry Township.[439]

Late April or early May: Two motorcyclists saw a large "hairy man" in Derry Township, near the Fayette County line.[440]

May 16: A motorist saw Bigfoot cross Route 60 north of New Castle (Lawrence County).[441]

July 18: Alerted by a foul smell and sounds of snapping wood, a witness glimpsed a black biped 8.5 feet tall in rural Pike County.[442]

August 15: A large hairy biped left footprints in a woman's garden, in Westmoreland County's Derry Township.[443]

August: A driver passing near Monroeville (Allegheny County) observed Bigfoot sitting on a pile of rocks.[444]

October 22: Two campers found a Sasquatch resting in the woods near Dickson City (Lackawanna County).[445]

November: A witness claimed that he saw Bigfoot swimming in Lake Erie, near Presque Isle.[446]

November 17-18: A group of boys from New Castle reported two Bigfoot sightings near town on successive days. PBS researchers considered the incidents possible hoaxes.[447]

November 28: Two hunters watched Bigfoot pass below their tree stands in Forbes State Forest (Westmoreland County).[448]

December: Two hikers reported a meeting with Sasquatch at an undisclosed site in Pike County.[449]

2004

January 20: A motorist driving near Ogletown (Somerset County) saw Bigfoot cross the road in three strides.[450]

February: Another Somerset County driver claimed a collision with Sasquatch on Route 56 near Windber. When she turned around and came back, the creature was gone.[451]

March: Two sightings emerged from the Murrysville area (Westmoreland County). First, a man saw Bigfoot cross his yard and an adjacent road. Days later, a motorist "almost hit" a creature in the same vicinity.[452]

March 8: A driver saw Sasquatch cross a road near Freeport (Armstrong County) and step over a three-foot-high guardrail without breaking stride. He found a four-toed footprint at the scene.[453]

April 9: A woman saw Bigfoot walking along a creek near her home in Brookhaven (Delaware County).[454]

May 7 or 9: A trucker saw Bigfoot standing beside U.S. Route 6 near Denton Hill, east of Coudersport.[455]

June 20: Four boys walking through woods near Chalfont (Bucks County) met a seven-foot red-eyed creature covered with white hair, which left a fifteen-inch footprint.[456]

June 26: Two residents of Clearville (Bedford County) saw a nine-foot creature run into a cornfield, leaving footprints and reddish-brown hair on a barbed-wire fence.[457]

July 3: A bicyclist met a white-haired biped, three feet tall, at a housing project in Fairview (Erie County).[458]

July 12: Two hunters watched a "huge" creature with a "big misshapen head" cross a country road somewhere in Luzerne County.[459]

August: A dog-walker glimpsed a "monkey like face" watching her from the woods at Brady's Run Park, in Beaver Falls.[460]

August 15: Four residents of Allegheny County's McCandless Township saw a reddish-brown biped four to five feet tall.[461]

September: A man living near Brady's Run Park glimpsed Bigfoot running past his home.[462]

September 26: Somewhere in Indiana County, two men heard screams and saw "a gorilla looking shape" near an abandoned house.[463]

September 29: Several witnesses saw an eight-foot biped and found its footprints outside Nemacolin (Greene County).[464]

October: While driving through Beaver County on Route 60, a woman saw three hairy creatures of different sizes walking across a roadside field.[465]

October 28: Several teens saw a "thing" cross Robinson Road near Blain (Perry County), noting legs that were "hairy and big."[466]

November: A hunter saw a 7.5-foot biped in Allegheny County's Moon Township, two miles from Pittsburgh International Airport.[467]

November 14: A Grove City motorist claimed a collision with Sasquatch, reporting that he preserved hair samples, but the witness declined a PBS interview and produced no evidence.[468]

November 23: Two bikers smelled "something horrible" and saw "a large creature" at an undisclosed site in Crawford County.[469]

November 26: A driver saw Bigfoot cross Route 48 near White Oak Run (Westmoreland County).[470]

2005

July 1: A delivery driver saw two hairy bipeds at a campsite near Route 87 and Loyalsock Creek (Lycoming County).[471]

2006

January 30: An employee of a business located near Allison Park saw Bigfoot run across an open field.[472]

March: Two men spotlighting deer near Allegheny County's Settler's Cabin Park saw a hairy biped running down a hillside.[473]

July 23: A resident of Plum (Allegheny County) saw a creature eight to nine feet tall outside her home. It had a face "part human, part... something else."[474]

2007

January 19: A motorist in Allison Park glimpsed a "black hairy creature" that was "grayish in color."[475]

February 27: Two Beaver County men observed a groaning Sasquatch near a mushroom "mine" outside Wampum.[476]

March 13: A lone witness saw an eight-foot biped emitting "weird screechy deep pitched howls" at Clarksville (Greene County).[477]

March 19: Two observers saw Bigfoot cross a field at Kempton (Berks County).[478]

March 31: A Clinton County motorist saw a six-foot creature with "long tangled hair" standing behind a guardrail on Route 120.[479]

April 24: Three Butler County girls off-roading near an unnamed cemetery, surprised a creature eight to nine feet tall. It left sixteen-inch footprints with a seven-foot stride.[480]

September 16: A stationary camera placed in the Allegheny National Forest snapped photos of a peculiar quadruped. While some observers dubbed it a juvenile Sasquatch, forest rangers dismissed it as a "skinny, mangy bear."[481]

September 27: A hiker met a creature seven to eight feet tall near Mount Lebanon (Allegheny County). PBS Assistant Director Dave Dragosin deemed the witness credible.[482]

October 24: A hunter observed Bigfoot from 180 yards, outside Argus (Bucks County).[483]

December: Bigfoot visited a mobile home on Route 706 west of Montrose (Susquehanna County), peering through a window fourteen feet above ground.[484]

2008

July 18: A camper at Allegheny County's North Park claimed that Bigfoot raided his food cache.[485]

August 25: Late-night screeching roused a resident of Shaler Township (Allegheny County), who saw a creature eight to nine feet tall "with ape-like arms swinging back and forth."[486]

September 13: A motorist saw Bigfoot standing beside Interstate 80, fifteen miles west of Clearfield.[487]

2009

February 3: Two hikers observed a chestnut-colored Sasquatch, somewhere in Lackawana County.[488]

February 9: A Tioga County hiker claimed a Bigfoot sighting. PBS researchers could not locate the witness.[489]

May 4: A motorist saw a biped covered in long reddish hair standing atop a roadside hill north of Media.[490]

May 8: Bigfoot surprised a Pike County driver, crossing a road at some undisclosed location.[491]

May 9: A hunter in Blair County sighted "an approximately human like creature," location unknown.[492]

May 17: A motorist saw Bigfoot standing beside a highway sign on Route 30, near Raccoon Creek State Park.[493]

Early July 10: A motorist swerved to avoid striking Sasquatch on a highway near Uniontown.[494]

August: A driver narrowly avoided hitting Bigfoot outside Jumonville.[495]

Late August: Another Jumonville motorist saw "a reddish brown orangutan-like animal" cross the road on all fours.[496]

August 31: Three witnesses saw a gray-haired Sasquatch standing behind a roadside tree, somewhere in southern Beaver County.[497]

September 23: A mother and daughter sightseeing near Dunbar (Fayette County) watched a hairy biped run across a gas well line into the woods.[498]

2010

January 31: Heath Landman and his son saw a Sasquatch more than six feet tall cross Ferguson Road in Dunbar (Fayette County). They found footprints in the snow and collected hair samples. PBS director Eric Altman announced that he "may send the hair to a lab for testing." No results had been announced when this book went to press.[499]

March 17: Unionville's *Herald Standard* reported that the PBS has logged eight Bigfoot sightings from Fayette County since August 2009, including four around Dunbar, two at Jumonville (see above), one at Confluence and one at Connellsville.[500]

2011

March 1, 2011: A Fayette County resident saw "something" running from his yard after his dogs "went ballistic" overnight, followed by "screeching"sounds persisting for fifteen minutes.

Summing Up

So, if Bigfoot exists, what is it? Based on eyewitness descriptions, the creatures most closely resemble great apes, but discovery of three- and four-toed footprints contradicts that notion, since all know primates have five digits on their hands and feet. Aside from individual cases of birth defects or accidental mutilation, the sole exceptions to that rule are members of the Vadoma tribe in western Zimbabwe, most of whom display two-toed "ostrich" feet caused by inherited ectrodactyly.[501]

Levittown: Another troubling aspect of the Pennsylvania Bigfoot phenomenon—at least, for "flesh-and-blood" cryptozoologists who reject paranormal explanations—is the repeated mention of bipedal creatures seen in conjunction with UFO sightings. Those cases comprise only two percent of Keystone reports—ten incidents claiming airborne craft or lights and two claims of creatures carrying luminous spheres, out of 490 eyewitness sightings—but they are often selected by critics to discredit the entire Bigfoot phenomena.

Reports of "glowing" eyes, likewise, suggest some paranormal force, but most can be explained with reference to eyes reflecting artificial light from houses, vehicles, or flashlights.

Among cryptozoologists, the hands-down favorite Bigfoot candidate is *Gigantopithecus,* a prehistoric ape known from fossil teeth and mandibles found in Asia since 1935. While no complete skeletons have been recovered, paleontologists using modern apes as models estimate that "Giganto" stood approximately ten feet tall and weighed up to 1,200 pounds.[502] In theory, it may have crossed the Beringian land bridge with early human migrants, from the area of present-day Siberia to Alaska and beyond, spreading throughout the Americas over time.

Gigantopithecus, a popular Sasquatch candidate among cryptozoologists.
Credit: Author's collection

If Giganto made that crossing—and survived its own presumed extinction some 10,000 years ago—it might still require evolutionary changes to match modern Sasquatch descriptions. Although still waiting for the skeletal remains to prove it, mainstream scientists believe Giganto had feet like modern apes, with opposable great toes, and that it moved primarily by knuckle-walking, like modern great apes. Its teeth also suggest an herbivorous diet, which contradicts claims of Bigfoot devouring wildlife and domestic animals.[503]

More imaginative authors—Ivan Sanderson, Mark Hall, Loren Coleman, and Patrick Huyghe among others—have proposed multiple species of unclassified primates to explain sightings of creatures in different places and sizes, but one fact remains: Until the day we have a specimen in hand, the mystery shall remain unsolved.

Chapter 8
Something Else

As always, when the major "families" of unknown creatures have been catalogued, there still remains a gibbering menagerie of other entities who fit none of the groups described. A few are known only from bones unearthed in bygone days, then lost, while others lurch, hop, creep and soar across the Keystone landscape to the present day. Examining the misfits chronologically, as best we can, the list offers a startling—and sometimes frightening—diversity.

Giants in the Earth

Our first notice of human giants in Penn's Woods dates from 1608, when English explorer John Smith met members of the Susquehannock tribe whom he described as "gyant-like." Such terms are relative, but excavations conducted three centuries later, in neighboring New York, revealed a Susquehannock skeleton that measured eight feet tall.[1]

Meanwhile, in 1822, workmen digging a cellar in Bradford County's Burlington Township uncovered a nine-foot sarcophagus containing a human skeleton eight feet two inches long from head to foot.[2]

Next up, in 1852, came the discovery of a "very large" femur, said to be human, on Charles Hooker's farm in Bradford County. Interviewed by the *Towanda Daily Review* nearly half a century later, Dr. Theodore Wilder opined that the bone's original owner must have been seven feet tall.[3]

Construction of the Erie & Pittsburgh Railroad began in April 1858 and concluded in March 1860. Sometime between those dates, laborers unearthed a "great mass of bones" in Erie County, including the remains of "a giant, side by side with a smaller one, probably that of his wife. The arm and leg bones of this native American Goliath were about one-half longer than those of the tallest man among the laborers; the skull was immensely large, the lower jawbone easily slipped over the face and whiskers of a full-faced man, and the teeth were in a perfect state of preservation."[4]

Nor was that the only local find. When the *History of Erie County, Pennsylvania* was published in 1884, it noted that "Another skeleton was dug up in Conneaut Township some years ago which was quite remarkable in its dimensions. As in the other instance, a comparison was made with the largest man in the neighborhood, and the jawbone readily covered his face, while the lower bone of the leg was nearly a foot longer than the one with which it was measured, indicating that the man must have been eight to ten feet in height."[5]

In 1885, the journal *American Antiquarian* reported a discovery of more oversized remains, retrieved from an Indian mound near Gastonville (Washington County; misspelled "Gasterville" in the original text). According to that article, the find included "the skeleton of a giant measuring seven feet two inches. His hair was coarse and jet black, and hung to the waist, the brow being ornamented with a copper crown. The skeleton was remarkably well preserved."[6]

Folklorist Robert Lyman Sr. reports yet another discovery of giant remains in the 1880s, at Tioga Point, near Sayre (Bradford County). His information presumably came from Louise Murray's *History of Old Tioga Point and Early Athens*, published in 1908, which stated that "[a] number of huge skeletons found in the various Indian burial grounds of Tioga have suggested, by the size, that they are Andastes" (a French name for the Susquehannocks).[7]

Fresh excavation accompanied the opening of a new historical museum in Athens (Bradford County), on June 27, 1895. The dig revealed "two large flat stones, full of [D]evonian fossils," concealing "a skeleton of six feet or more in height." Also found was a clay pot, eighteen inches in diameter, which clearly did not belong to the Devonian period (416–359.2 million years ago).[8]

A more lively giant appeared in Buffalo Mills on August 19, 1973. He passed along Main Street, where witnesses noted his nine-foot stature, "dark penetrating gaze," and "strange clothing" sewn from "shimmering material." Sadly, Pennsylvania has two towns called Buffalo Mills, in Armstrong and Bedford Counties, and no published report tells us which community enjoyed the stranger's visit.[9]

An even larger humanoid, described as ten feet tall, with "large white glowing eyes," appeared to Alston Blankenship and Richard Tincher outside Fawn Grove (York County) on January 10, 1977. Shocked as they were, the witnesses supplied no further details.[10]

A Mammoth Mystery

In spring of 1872, farmer Barnard Hassell's plow turned up a peculiar stone on his land east of Doylesville (Bucks County). It was a piece of slate, later described as part of an ornamental necklace. Both sides of the fragment bore etchings of various animals and human figures, presumably carved by some artist of the Lenape people, also known as the Delaware Indians. Hassell sold the slate to researcher Henry Paxon in 1881, then "coincidentally" found its missing half before year's end, near the same site where he dug up the original piece.[11]

The Lenape stone—a hoax or depiction of a mammoth hunt in Pennsylvania?
Credit: Author's collection

Reunited at last, the complete "Lenape stone" revealed carvings of turtles, fish, birds, and snakes on one side, while the other depicted a group of hunters battling a beast that resembled an elephant. Members of the Bucks County Historical Society questioned Hassell's account of his discoveries, but archaeologist/historian Henry Mercer deemed the stone a portrayal of aboriginal tribesmen hunting a wooly mammoth (*Mammuthus primigeniusi*), deemed extinct since 3750 B.C.E. The earliest confirmed Lenape carvings, meanwhile, date from roughly 1000 B.C.E., suggesting that no native artist could have seen a living mammoth.[12]

Did Pennsylvania Aborigines hunt woolly mammoths?
Credit: U.S. National Oceanic and Atmospheric Administration

Chapman defended the artifact's authenticity in a book, *The Lenape Stone or the Indian and the Mammoth,* published in 1885. He concluded that the stone proved the existence of "a race of savages as old or older than the now famous river-drift and cave-men of Europe," depicted in the act of hunting a mammoth or its contemporary relative, the American mastodon (*Mammut americanumi*). Most modern researchers dismiss the stone as a nineteenth-century hoax.[13]

Horns of a Dilemma

In 1879, according to Irish author Ronan Coghlan, a curious creature appeared somewhere in Pennsylvania. Dubbed a "what-is-it," after a phrase coined by showman P.T. Barnum, the beast was "almost four feet tall, long armed and toeless, lacking hair. Its colour was yellowish brown and it had horns." Regrettably, Coghlan supplies no more precise location, and no source for his report.[14] We might dismiss the claim out of hand, except...

On July 12, 1916, a newspaper in Bradford County reported that members of a scientific expedition led by state historian Dr. G.P. Donehoo, Professor A.B. Skinner of the American Investigating Museum, and Professor W.K. Morehead of Phillips Andover Academy had unearthed sixty-eight remarkable human skeletons buried around 1200 C.E. As summarized by Robert Lyman Sr. in 1971, "The average height of these men was 7 feet, while many were much taller. On some of the skulls, 2 inches above the perfectly formed forehead, were protuberances of bone, evidently horns that had been there since birth." The remains were packed off to Philadelphia's American Investigating Museum, from which they vanished forever.[15]

Or, did they?

In fact, a letter penned by Professor Skinner on July 14, 1916, declared that diggers had found only fifty-seven skeletons, all "perfectly normal individuals," though one was "covered by a deposit of deer antlers." As for the museum in Philly, it never existed.[16]

Haunted Skies

Huge thunderbirds are not the only cryptids found aloft in Pennsylvania. In September 1897, the *Pittsburgh Chronicle* claimed that factory workers in nearby Etna had seen a "monster air snake" twenty-five feet long, flying overhead at an altitude of 500 feet. According to the article:

It was jet black and in thickness looked like an ordinary keg. The ponderous jaws of the reptile were frequently seen to open, from which emerged a large tongue. It sailed in a regular course, but when the jaws opened it then took a downward course and seemed as though it would fall to the ground below. On the descent the mouth remained open, and after a fall of about 100 feet the jaws would close and the snake would raise its head and slowly wend its way up to its former height.[16]

The startling air show continued for an hour, until the flying reptile vanished in a northeastern direction.[17]

Another airborne snake appeared on August 1, 1906, startling young campers Harold Boynton and Jackson Miller at Titusville (Crawford County). The boys suffered ridicule until October, when multiple witnesses saw a snake with eyes the size of saucers and "two enormous fin-like wings" swimming in the Allegheny River near Grunderville (Warren County). Ferryman Hank Jackson opened fire with a rifle, first prompting the serpent to flight, then disabling its wings. As described in press reports, "It emitted a piercing shriek, then hit the water with a great splash and swam rapidly down the river," soon vanishing from sight.[18]

Pennsylvania's next winged visitor, reported from Harrisburg in June 2003, was none other than Mothman. Best known for its appearances in West Virginia during 1966-67, and its starring role in two Hollywood horror films, the flying omen of disaster allegedly buzzed an unnamed motorist on a country road outside town. Four months later, PBS director Eric Altman said:

> I talked to a state trooper out of the Somerset barracks and he said they get a lot of calls on stuff like this, but don't have the staff to investigate. They dismiss it, rather than following up.[19]

Mothman, depicted in this West Virginia statue, has also appeared in Pennsylvania.
Credit: Author's collection

Such was also the case with a larger bat-like creature, seen in Washington County on May 20, 2008. Witness "Jim" was driving on Route 43, near Brownsville, when the beast swooped overhead at 2 p.m. He "could see no feathers, only short dark gray or black hair on the body. The wings appeared to be a membrane stretched over bone." Another motorist stopped nearby, brandishing a camera, but if he secured any photos they remain a closely-guarded secret. Before the creature vanished over nearby trees, Jim pegged its wingspan at twenty feet, minimum.[20]

Seal of Approval?

On April 18, 1889, the Philadelphia *Record* announced that fishermen Charles Adams and Charles Wooden had pulled a strange creature from the Delaware River at Burlington (Bradford County). It was "about six feet long, with a large head shaped like a bulldog's and an immense mouth furnished with two rows of sharp teeth. The head is attached to the body by a long, sinuous neck and the small and deep sunken eyes are protected by long lashes. The body, which gradually tapers to a tail, is covered by a short fine fur, and two short imperfectly formed legs, with webbed feet like those of a duck, are attached just below the neck. The tail is peculiarly formed, having four blades exactly like the screws of a propeller."[21]

Researcher Chad Arment believes the beast was some kind of pinniped. And, in fact, a 300-pound seal was found in marshy suburban Philadelphia, fifty miles up the Delaware River from the Atlantic, in June 2007.[22]

Hideous Herps

The giant snakes covered in Chapter 5 have no monopoly on spooking Pennsylvania witnesses. One morning in November 1892, three Montgomery County youths set out to pick chestnuts near Old Oaks Cemetery. There, they met a sort of dragon covered in heart-shaped scales, which nonetheless also sported a "bristle-like mane" resembling a mule's on its head and neck. Its primary color was "a beautiful bronze green," with purple stripes on each side. Before the beast disappeared into a railroad culvert, the boys saw enough to judge its length (equivalent to a fence rail) and its twelve-inch girth. They also heard the animal, whose scales "gave out a metallic ring that sounded like a small sleigh bell, though more silvery." Its tail was "like that of a fish."[23]

Our next report, vaguely dated from "the late 1800s," involves alleged witness William Johnson of Somerset County. According to Johnson, a huge scaly creature once lived beneath a local schoolhouse, showing itself only on moonless nights. That said, he also claimed that people entering the school had to step over the monster's foot-thick body, sheathed in "sharp scales that apparently were electrically charged," capable of stunning anyone who touched it. Speculation on the beast's status as "a multi-dimensional reptile" lends no credibility to Johnson's tale.[24]

Equally strange was the "baby dinosaur" supposedly seen by four New Kensington boys in 1981. They pulled the creature from a sewer drain, but it quickly escaped. New Kensington's police chief told reporters, "The creature was described as about three feet tall, [with] two arms and a tail, and hunched over on two legs." Fourteen years later, author Rosemary Guilley muddied the waters by placing the incident in nearby Arnold, adding a fifth boy to the mix, and stating that the creature "had no fur or hair, [but] had 'nipples' and a short tail." Chad Arment suggests that the boys may have seen a fugitive exotic pet, perhaps a plumed basilisk (*Basiliscus plumifrons*) from Latin America, which may run on its hind legs for short distances.[25] Neither the basilisk nor any other reptile has nipples.

On the afternoon of September 19, 2009, while driving near Youngwood, an anonymous married couple saw "a black snake about four feet long," with a "shiny wet" texture, crossing the road in front of them. Instead of slithering, the reptile was "gliding real slow"—until it suddenly broke into eight equal parts, each sprouting four feet and scrambling for safety. According to the witnesses, each mini-monster moved "individually, erratically, and extremely fast in the road." The experience "was surreal, like watching computer generated graphics or animation."[26]

A Water-Hog

On July 18, 1903, the Elizabeth *Herald* warned Allegheny County readers of a strange amphibious creature at large. Witnesses described the beast as "a quadruped about four feet long, with a head like that of a hog." It emerged from the Allegheny River on occasion, chasing boys through cornfields and leaving cattle "in a state of terror." The thing "left tracks of two web feet and two like those made by the hoofs of an ordinary hog." Chad Arment opines that the beast was a South American capybara (*Hydrochoerus hydrochaeris*), Earth's largest living rodent, presumably imported and released in Pennsylvania by persons unknown.[27]

Was a capybara at large in Allegheny County during 1903?
Credit: U.S. Fish & Wildlife Service

Up Jumps the Devil

The Jersey Devil is one of America's oldest reported cryptids—and the most flexible, in terms of appearance. Initially, it was supposed to be the cursed thirteenth child of a New Jersey colonist, born with wings and other odd appendages forty years before the American Revolution. Today, the "Jersey Devil" name is equally applied to cryptids ranging from Bigfoot to black panthers and incomprehensible hybrid monstrosities. Nor, we should note, are its ramblings confined to New Jersey.

The Devil's first Pennsylvania outing occurred on the night of January 16-17, 1909, when a policeman in Bristol met a huge winged creature screeching on a city street. Nearby, another local watched it fly across the Delaware River, describing a beast with "a ram-like head with curled horns, a long neck, thin wings and four legs, the front pair shorter than the back." The thing left weird hoof-prints in Bristol, and another trail in Burlington.[28]

On January 21 the Devil returned, allegedly touching off an explosion in Clayton (Berks County), then perching atop a telegraph pole in Pleasantville, where a lineman shot it through one wing. Wounded, it still escaped, and surfaced in a barn at Morrisville on January 27, eluding pursuers once more.[29]

Twenty years later, in December 1929, Philadelphia resident Norman Jefferies "confessed" to donning a kangaroo suit and impersonating the Jersey Devil during its Keystone rampage. His credibility was damaged when he claimed the incidents occurred in 1906—nor could he explain his invincibility to gunfire.[30]

An early artist's concept of
the Jersey Devil.
Credit: Author's collection

And the Devil kept appearing, without help from Jefferies. In January 1932, it terrorized Linden (misspelled "Lindell" in some reports). July 1937 brought sightings of a kangaroo-like beast from Dorlan and Milford Mills (Chester County). Posses scoured North Coventry Township for an elusive Devil in November 1945. Locals also blamed the Jersey Devil in March 1973, when a "huge cat-like creature" killed chickens and rabbits in Upper Pottsgrove Township. Two Philadelphia police officers reported a sighting on August 8, 1996. Multiple witnesses saw the Devil in a park, on January 10, 2000, but published accounts provide no location. Through it all, the beast(s) remained elusive and invulnerable, always one leap ahead of the hunters.[31]

Mystery Maulers

Transient Jersey Devils are not alone in preying on Pennsylvania livestock and domestic animals. In November 1912, A.R. McKain returned from "a gunning trip" to his home in Marietta (Lancaster County) and found that some unknown wild beast had devoured two of his beagles. The dogs were chained in a kennel, but when McKain's wife went to feed them one morning, she found "the collars empty with chains attached and bones lying around." Newspapers blamed a bear, but noted that a "wildman" had been seen at nearby Kinderhook "some time ago," while a recent "hole and automobile mystery" had caused excitement in Maytown. Armed men stood watch for the beast, all in vain.[32]

On January 27, 1919, farmers at Shamburg (Clarion County) turned out in force to stalk a nocturnal predator resembling a wolf or an oversized fox. William Roth killed the beast on January 29, near Rattlesnake School, but it remained unidentified. As described in the Titusville *Herald*, it "resemble[d] a grey hound, excepting in color, it being a reddish dark brown, has [a] long pointed nose, short ears, short hair and a long bushy tail. The pelt measured a little over six feet in length from the tip of the nose to the end of its tail."[33]

Pottstown claimed its own monster in 1945, accused of raiding chicken coops and "snarling at children coming home from school." Press reports claimed that it "screams like a panther, barks like a dog, wails like a banshee, and laughs like a hyena. Those who claim to have seen him describe him in odd shapes, various colors and a hodgepodge of features. It was agreed, however, that he possesses a most magnificent tail."[34]

Another case from 1945 involved two hunters at West Newton. The men first heard a "strange cry," followed by yelping and howling as some unseen creature mauled their hunting dogs. Details are sparse, and while the PBS lists the incident as a Bigfoot encounter, no reported evidence supports that claim.[35]

After a lapse of nearly three decades, in March 1973, the Pottstown *Mercury* noted a new rash of cryptid sightings, including a report of a nocturnal raid against a rabbit hutch in Hilltown Township. Once again, the beast escaped while leaving no clues to its true identity.[36]

In September 1977, an unnamed resident of Cadogan reported that "a strange animal" was "bothering and mutilating" his livestock, including cattle, geese, and turkeys. Some published reports blame the attacks on Bigfoot, though no one saw the predator.[37]

Another quarter-century passed before "a mysterious huge cat-like creature" began killing livestock by night, in Washington County. Once again, farmers suffered without recourse and the attacks ceased as suddenly as they began.[38]

Hybrid Horrors

Mythology is filled with tales of strange composite beasts that violate accepted rules for interbreeding between disparate species. Such things are not restricted to the realm of ancient lore, however. They continue to appear in modern times, astounding frightened witnesses.

On February 11, 1939, while spreading fertilizer on his fields near Westwood (Natrona County), farmer Sylvester Scott caught his first glimpse of a peculiar creature. It was "two or three feet high and was colored like a deer in front, with white on the flanks...It had paws rather than hooves. It had a foot long neck, a small head, and no tail." As Scott watched, it leaped two feet into the air, then ran across his field and vanished in the woods. He later saw the thing on three occasions, and sometimes heard it screaming after nightfall.[39]

In 1945, three months after Pottsdown's mauler slaughtered chickens and terrorized children, Coatesville residents claimed sightings of a "monster described as a cross between a giraffe, a dog, and a deer," complaining that it "wails like a woman."[40]

Twenty-eight years later, in August 1973, Amish residents of Lancaster County lived in fear of a beast "the size of a good heifer, gray in color with a white mane. It had tiger-like fangs and curved horns like a billy goat. It ran upright on two legs, and had long grizzly claws."[41]

In 1979, four Lancaster County farmhands saw a strange figure crossing the field where they were at work. Initially mistaken for a naked man, it was in fact a monstrosity with "with semi-human features...covered with coarse, sandy hair, and bounding along with this strange hopping motion" reminiscent of a kangaroo. At a range of 100 feet, one witness felt "a stabbing sensation, like an electric jolt," then the monster shouted at him in "a foreign language" and raced into some nearby woods at "superhuman speed."[42]

Ronan Coghlan reports another strange tale from Columbia (Lancaster County), where creatures described as half-cat and half-fox allegedly startled drivers on local roadways. Unfortunately, Coghlan lists no dates or other details, and his reputed source—the Gulf Coast Bigfoot Research Organization's website—carried no such stories when I checked it in November 2010.[43]

Bucks County suffered an outbreak of monster-fever in October 2003. On October 27, *Bucks County Courier Times* reporter Alison Hawkes received seventeen calls from from locals who had glimpsed the creature, described as having "the ears of the Pennsylvania red fox, the body of the Colorado cougar, the snout of the African jackal and the tail of a hideous New Hope house poodle." Asked for his opinion of an eyewitness sketch, PBS member Rick Fisher said, "I don't have a clue. But it's Halloween. We always get more reports around this time." PBS director Eric Altman quickly stepped in to quash talk of a hoax. "People are seeing something," he declared. "There is something out there."[44]

Yet another freakish hybrid surfaced in August 2006, this one frolicking in a wooded section of Philadelphia. According to unnamed witnesses, "It had a face like a fisher or weasel, sort of bear-like, with small ears, and had a short stubby hairy tail. It was gray, moderately heavy, [and] was perched vertically in the tree. It appeared clumsy like a sloth or koala bear."[45]

Almost Human

Cryptids—like Mothman—are sometimes linked in the public mind to disasters. One such Pennsylvania case supposedly involved a 1944 cave-in at the Dixonville Mine, located at Clymer (Indiana County). As reported on various Internet websites, the collapse claimed fifteen lives. Three decades later—on July 14, 1974—one Stoney Brakefield published an article in a Keystone newspaper called the *News Extra*, reporting that mine inspector Glenn Berger had blamed the cave-in on malicious subterranean humanoids. Several miners' corpses allegedly bore "large claw marks," while a survivor described monstrous beings "not of this world."[46]

All very dramatic ... if any of it were true.

In fact, Clymer's only mining disaster was an explosion that killed forty-four men on August 26, 1926. The nearest incidents to that described online were an explosion at Minersville's Primrose Colliery that killed fourteen on September 24, 1943, and another blast that killed fifteen at Plymouth's Nottingham Mine on January 15, 1947. The only mine disaster of 1944 was a fire that claimed six lives at Clarksville's

Emerald Mine on June 7. Add to that the fact that neither "Stoney Brakefield" nor the *News Extra* apparently existed, and the case collapses like its fictional mine shaft.[47]

A more whimsical tale from the 1990s, specific date and place unknown, is a two-witness sighting of a "leaf man." One observer described the figure as "a gingerbread man with leaves," and while a friend who blogged about the incident online described her as "TOTALLY serious," no supporting evidence exists.[48]

On August 16, 2005, four members of an unnamed family were fishing at Wilmore Reservoir, near Portage in Cambria County, when they saw a frightening figure. Although "hunched over," the man-thing was seven to eight feet tall, with arms "almost as long as its body." It was, they later said, "bright white but not shiny like an albino and it moved as if its knees were in backwards." The thing's face, briefly glimpsed, "was definitely not human."[49]

Two years later, in June 2007, an anonymous teenager claimed several sightings of "a thin white creature" in the backyard of his Blair County home. Sparking memories of the Portage humanoid, it was a "tall, thin figure with an odd gait and unusual bends in its limbs." The youth's father also claimed multiple encounters with "white blob-like creatures" on his property.[50]

Another Blair County beastie, seen sporadically along Ridge Road, is known only from undated Internet postings. As described online, the thing is "roughly human-like, but with hairless, gray skin, a skull-like face, and red, reflective eyes. It is also taller than a human." One anonymous blogger declares: "It may be a primate, but it is unusual for any form of life. It is either a Type #1 or Type #3 cryptid"—whatever that means.[51]

Hopping Mad

Phantom kangaroos, or some other entities resembling those marsupials from Down Under, have been sighted across North America for generations. Pennsylvania's experience with such cryptids is more recent, beginning in 1969.

In September of that year, residents of Delaware County pestered police with reports of a curious creature at large. Witnesses described "a black animal standing no more than three feet high with a two-foot long tail. The tail was tapered and curled. The strange thing about the animal was that it leaped and hopped, like a kangaroo or wallaby, and it left tracks measuring four inches long."[52]

Phantom kangaroos appear throughout North America.
Credit: U.S. Fish & Wildlife Service

Six years later, two residents of Bensalem (Bucks County) were wakened by strange sounds from their laundry room, "as if something were clawing its way up the drainpipe." Fearing to investigate in darkness, they found "small tracks in the virgin snow resembling small hoof prints." Subsequently, the male witness took his dog for a walk and met a beast resembling "a miniature kangaroo," which hopped a few yards, then "suddenly disappeared in plain sight." If all that were not strange enough, in 1976 a "terrific explosion" of unknown origin rocked the property, shattering neighbors' windows.[53]

Bad Moon Rising

Every civilization on Earth has produced tales of shape-shifting humans, either empowered or cursed with the ability to take on various animal forms. Most famous of the lot, thanks to Hollywood, are the lycanthropes or werewolves. Today, we all know that such manimals are simply products of imagination—and yet, creatures resembling classic wolfmen keep appearing and terrifying witnesses.

During 1951-52, Henry Shoemaker regaled readers of *New York Folk Lore Quarterly* with a series of articles on "The Werwolf [sic] in Pennsylvania." Author Linda Godfrey names Shoemaker's primary source as aforementioned "Indian fighter" Peter Pentz, spinning yarns for Shoemaker in 1900, but that can hardly be the case, since Pentz lived in the eighteenth century. He was a grown man when he staged his legendary panther hunt in 1797 (see Chapter 3), and would thus have been pushing 140 years old, at a minimum, in 1900.[54]

In any case, the tale related by Shoemaker, courtesy of whomever, involved Pentz's aunt, Clinton County resident Divert Mary DePo. One night in the 1850s, while returning from her duties as a midwife, DePo met a "werewolf in the shape of an enormous black dog," which rose on its hind legs and attacked her with her forepaws. She escaped and ran home, where her husband shot the beast with pewter bullets dipped in "sacramental wax" and watched it turn into a well-known neighbor as it died.[55]

Whether Shoemaker placed any credence in that tale or not, if Pentz advanced it as the truth, perhaps his first-person accounts of panther-slaying exploits should be reconsidered as "tall tales."

More recently, a quasi-lycanthrope terrorized northwestern Pennsylvania's Shenango River Valley with repeat appearances, from 1972 to 1998. According to artist-researcher Jason Van Hoose, the beast was "four to five feet tall, covered with patches of long, black hair, [with] a piglike nose, large round 'fisheyes,' a disturbing mouthful of snaggle teeth, and perhaps the strongest feature of all, its elbow and knee joints bend opposite of a human['s], somewhat like a dog but not really...It can run on all fours and is also bipedal...Its hands are similar to humans', with digits, but when running the fingers are clenched, giving the appearance of paws. There is no tail."[56]

Coming Up Short

Legends of "little people" rival those of shape-shifters worldwide, from Old World gnomes and leprechauns to the *kowi anukasha, Yehasuri, and Yunwitsandsdi* described by Native American tribes. Penn's Woods, predictably, are not devoid of pint-sized denizens.

In early October 1973, teenager Paul Flurosek claimed a sighting of a "little man" near his Hanlin Station home (Washington County). The wrinkled figure made a buzzing noise, then "just disappeared into the clouds." Researcher Alberto Rosales links the incident to local UFO sightings, though Flurosek mentioned no airborne craft.[57]

Lancaster County reportedly harbors a race of half-human pygmies known as albawitches—"apple snitchers"—who steal fruit from picnickers, then pelt their unwilling donors. Typically thin to the point of being called stick-figures, albawitches are covered with dark hair or fur, and rarely reach four feet in height. Chickies Rock County Park, located on the Susquehanna River between Columbia and Marietta, is the epicenter of modern albawitch sightings.[58]

In February 2002, Rick Fisher saw an albawitch while driving on Route 23 between Marietta and Lancaster. The sighting was both fortuitous and suspicious, since Fisher served as director of the Paranormal Society of Pennsylvania. "I'm a Bigfoot researcher," he told author Linda Godfrey. "My first thought was that this must be a skinny one. It walked like a human, not ape-like although its arms were longer, and it was swinging its arms."[59]

While derided by skeptics, Fisher uncovered another albawitch witness, known only as "Dwight," who, with two unnamed friends, saw an identical creature near the same location sometime in 1999. Online postings claim another albawitch encounter during May 2005, but provide no details.[60]

46. Chickies Rock County Park, scene of modern *albawitch* sightings.
Credit: U.S. National Oceanic and Atmospheric Administration

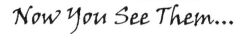

Now You See Them...

Reports of see-through humanoids at large transport us to a new level of high strangeness. The first supposed event occurred in July 1999, in Huntingdon, as a group of anonymous friends were driving home at 2:30 a.m. The hour may suggest a party's aftermath, though none such was admitted. According to the witnesses, a humanoid figure "encased in a pale green aura" suddenly appeared before their vehicle, then vanished as the pickup truck passed through it.[61]

Ten years later, in August 2009, an unnamed resident of Mechanicsburg (Cumberland County) reported an equally curious sighting. While standing on the front porch of his home, the man heard rustling noises from a nearby tree, then saw a strange figure rushing toward a brick wall at the edge of his property. Though less than four feet tall, the intruder "sounded heavy, like an adult human." According to the witness, "It didn't have fur or feathers. I saw two skinny bone like legs, but didn't look as though it had feet like a human, similar to that of a bird...The body seemed transparent-like. I didn't notice if it had wings/arms, as my vision was concentrated on the body. It moved so quickly that I didn't have time to get a better look, so as far as the head goes, I cannot say." Six photographs attached to the report online, purporting to show footprints on smashed grass, are indistinct at best.[62]

Badger Games

In Chapter 2 we examined the controversy surrounding existence of badgers in Pennsylvania. Whether or not those mustelids survive today within the state, none match the size of the creature reported by a U.S. Marine and his wife from Minersville (Schuylkill County) in May 2003. The driver struck it with his vehicle, then watched the creature flee, unharmed. No huge surprise, perhaps, since both observers claimed the badger was as long as their car![63]

The Yardley Yeti

Whimsical nicknames are often applied to cryptids, but few are less appropriate than that of the "Yardley Yeti," a beast reported roaming through Bucks County, around Yardley and Lower Makefield Township, in autumn 2006. Students of cryptozoology will recognize the Yeti as a Bigfoot-type creature said to inhabit Asia's Himalaya Range, also known since 1921 as the "Abominable Snowman." The Yardley Yeti, however, was something else entirely.

News of the creature first broke in the *Bucks County Courier Times*, on September 19, 2006. That article described a long-tailed quadruped, gray or tan in color, compared by various witnesses to a fox, wolf, jackal, hyena, or cougar. Some remarked on its "oddly shaped snout," while one saw "long fangs." Observers disagreed as to whether its tail was covered in sleek fur, or hairless like a rat's.[64]

Photos of the beast soon surfaced, snapped by Jonathan Maberry and Sara Jo West. One showed the creature in relation to a compact car, and thereby solved the mystery. As with a rash of "chupacabras" trapped and killed in Texas during recent years, the Yardley Yeti was a simple victim of disease—specifically, a red fox (*Vulpes vulpes*) plagued with mange.[65]

Don't Bug Me!

The latest entrant to our Keystone Cryptid Sweepstakes appears to be a giant caterpillar of unknown species, seen by four witnesses driving near Mount Pleasant (Westmoreland County) on June 27, 2009. Although the sun had set, their headlights clearly framed "something strange" on the pavement, slowly crossing the road. It was roughly seven inches long, "appeared to be segmented, and moved like a grub. It was primarily a very iridescent white color with a bluish tint." It had no legs, and no apparent head or tail. Its body was "skinnier at the tip ends, and fatter in the center."[66]

The driver waited for the giant "grub" to clear his path, and then proceeded. Seconds later, he saw a second, similar thing cross the highway, moving in the opposite direction from the first. Before they cleared a quarter-mile, the witnesses counted seven oversized caterpillar-creatures inching their way over blacktop, into the surrounding woods.[67]

"Giant" invertebrates are well known to science, including tarantulas with ten-inch legs, moths with twelve-inch wingspans, and earthworms nearly ten feet long. With rare exceptions, though, such behemoths thrive only in tropical climates, and nothing like the "caterpillars" seen near Mount Pleasant are recognized by science.

They belong, like the rest of our cryptids, to a world of mystery.

Conclusion

Where should prospective monster-hunters seek their prey in Pennsylvania?

Those seeking Bigfoot should concentrate in the southwest, where seven counties claim thirty-eight percent of the state's reported sightings, and Westmoreland County alone boasts 107.

Thunderbird enthusiasts, by contrast, should look to the state's northern border, among the remnants of the once-great Black Forest, where huge raptors reveal themselves most frequently.

Searchers who crave encounters with a giant snake have more ground to cover, ranging statewide from Black Forest glades to Bedford County's Broad Top and Gettysburg at the southern extreme.

As for black panthers, phantom cougars, and the random, incomprehensible beasts that appear any time, anywhere, no given range improves the odds for a prospective sighting. They are everywhere and nowhere, surfacing at will and vanishing as suddenly as they appear.

Some researchers suggest that we exist in close proximity to other realms—parallel times, dimensions, universes, take your pick—that may be breached from time to time, allowing denizens from haunted netherworlds to drop in on our own. Most "flesh-and-blood" cryptozoologists reject such theories of a Goblin Universe—a name coined by Colin Wilson and Ted Holiday in 1986—but who can say with any certainty?

This much is certain: We are tenants of a world where mysteries abound and multiply. Each time another "expert" takes the stage, proclaiming that we know it all, he proves himself a fool.

The mysteries endure. We are merely tourists, with our noses pressed against the glass.

Endnotes

Note: Abbreviated citations refer to sources listed in the bibliography. Sources not listed there are cited with full details on their first appearance below.

Introduction

1. "History of Pennsylvania," http://en.wikipedia.org/wiki/History_of_Pennsylvania; "Early Exploration of Pennsylvania," Pennsylvania Roots Online, http://www.pennsylvaniaroots.com/history-2.html.
2. "History of Pennsylvania"; "Philadelphia," http://en.wikipedia.org/wiki/Philadelphia.
3. "History of Pennsylvania."
4. Ibid.; "State Nicknames," 50States.com, http://www.50states.com/bio/nickname4.htm.
5. "History of Pennsylvania."
6. Ibid.
7. "Pennsylvania," http://en.wikipedia.org/wiki/Pennsylvania.
8. Coleman, *Mysterious America*, pp. 144-9; Arment, *Boss Snakes*, p. 283; Arment, *Historical Bigfoot*, pp. 271-2; The Conneaut Giants, http://solomonspalding.com/SRP/saga2/sagawt0a.htm; Clark, pp. 280, 284, 286; Hall, p. 99.
9. "List of cities in Pennsylvania," http://en.wikipedia.org/wiki/List_of_cities_in_Pennsylvania.
10. "Allegheny National Forest," U.S. Forest Service, http://www.fs.fed.us/r9/forests/allegheny; "State Forest Index," Pennsylvania Dept. of Conservation and Natural Resources,http://www.dcnr.state.pa.us/forestry/stateforests/index.aspx; "List of Pennsylvania state forest wild areas," 209 named swamps: "Pennsylvania," USA Place Names, http://www.placenames.com/us/42.
11. Arment, *Cryptozoology: Science and Speculation*, p. 16.

Chapter 1

1. Pennsylvania Biological Survey (hereafter PABS), http://www.altoona.psu.edu/pabs/index.html.
2. PABS, http://www.altoona.psu.edu/pabs/pdfs/Fishes_tech_Comm2008.pdf; "Aquatic Invasive Species," Pennsylvania Fish & Boat Commission (hereafter PFBC), http://www.fish.state.pa.us/ais.htm.

3. PABS, http://www.altoona.psu.edu/pabs/pdfs/Fishes_tech_Comm2008.pdf; "Aquatic Invasive Species," PFBC; "*Petromyzon marinus* Linnaeus 1758," U.S. Geological Survey, http://nas.er.usgs. gov/queries/GreatLakes/SpeciesInfo.asp?NoCache=6%2F10%2F2010+4%3A32%3A40+PM &SpeciesID=836&State=&HUCNumber=DgreatLakes.

4. PABS, http://www.altoona.psu.edu/pabs/pdfs/Fishes_tech_Comm2008.pdf.

5. "Northern Snakehead," PFBC, http://fishandboat.com/water/fish/snakehead/snakehead.htm; "Northern Snakehead 'Frankenfish' Information," Scinet, http://www.scinet.cc/articles/northern-snakehead/frankenfish.html.

6. "Another exotic species confirmed in Pa. waters," PFBC (July 23, 2004), http://www.fish.state. pa.us/water/fish/snakehead/2004press_snakehead.htm; Bresswein.

7. "Northern Snakehead," Pennsylvania Fish & Boat Commission, http://fishandboat.com/water/ fish/snakehead/snakehead.htm.

8. Montgomery; Milford and Byrd.

9. "Pacu," http://en.wikipedia.org/wiki/Pacu_(fish); "Piranha," http://en.wikipedia.org/wiki/Piranha.

10. "Pacu, Not Piranha," PFBC, http://www.fish.state.pa.us/images/pages/qa/fish/pacu.htm.

11. "Nonindigenous Aquatic Species," U.S. Geological Survey, http://nas.er.usgs.gov/queries/factsheet.aspx?SpeciesID=419; Dyer; "4-Year-Old Pulls Piranha From Lancaster County River;" Weisberg, "Local fisherman reels in a piranha."

12. PABS, http://www.altoona.psu.edu/pabs/amphibians_and_reptiles.htm.

13. Ibid.

14. Ibid.; Distribution of the Invasive Red-Eared Slider Turtle in the Lower Delaware River Basin, http://www.pserie.psu.edu/seagrant/research/Urban%20Final%20Report.pdf; "Nonindigenous Aquatic Species," U.S. Geological Survey, http://nas.er.usgs.gov/queries/FactSheet. aspx?speciesID=1261.

15. PABS, http://www.altoona.psu.edu/pabs/amphibians_and_reptiles.htm.

16. "Nonindigenous Aquatic Species," US Geological Survey, http://nas.er.usgs.gov/queries/FactSheet.aspx?speciesID=222.

17. Weisberg, "Alligator found near dam."

18. "Cayman Found in DelCo."

19. "Alligator found in downtown Pittsburgh fountain;" "Alligator found in Homewood."

20. "Alligator on the lam in Philadelphia pond;" "Crocodile found in Pennsylvania."

21. "Alligator found in Pennsylvania hasn't been claimed yet."

22. "Lake City firefighters capture alligator in Elk Creek."

23. Melissa Barclay, "Giant Toad," Cryptozoology.com, http://www.cryptozoology.com/sightings/ sightings_show.php?id=1651.

24. "Cane toad," http://en.wikipedia.org/wiki/Cane_toad.

25. PABS, http://www.altoona.psu.edu/pabs/bird.html.

26. Ibid.; "Rock Pigeon," http://en.wikipedia.org/wiki/Rock_Pigeon; "House Sparrow," http:// en.wikipedia.org/wiki/House_Sparrow; "European Starling," http://en.wikipedia.org/wiki/ European_Starling.

27. PABS, http://www.altoona.psu.edu/pabs/bird.html; "Mute Swan," http://en.wikipedia.org/wiki/ Mute_Swan; "Common Pheasant," http://en.wikipedia.org/wiki/Common_Pheasant.

28. McKee.

29. Patton, "Traffic-tying emu tasered"; "State Police tase loose emu on Pa. Turnpike."

30. PABS, http://www.altoona.psu.edu/pabs/mammals.htm.

31. Ibid.; "Hogs Wild In Pennsylvania," The Pig Site, http://www.thepigsite.cn/swinenews/13926/ hogs-wild-in-pennsylvania.

32. Crable; "Officials say wild boar problems continue."

33. Frye, "Wild hogs join exotic species in Pa.;" Gorden.

34. Frye, "Five counties in Pennsylvania are home to wild hogs."

35. Ibid.; Schneck.

36. "Feral Rhesus Macaque," http://en.wikipedia.org/wiki/Feral_Rhesus_Macaque; Ed Baker, "The legendary snow monkeys of Texas," *Austin Chronicle*, August 5, 2005.

37. Bord, *Unexplained Mysteries*, p. 242; Arment, "A Pennsylvania Primate," pp. 67-8.

38. Bord, *Unexplained Mysteries*, p. 242; Guilley, p. 148; Arment, "A Pennsylvania Primate," p. 69.

Chapter 2

1. PABS, http://www.altoona.psu.edu/pabs.

2. PABS, http://www.altoona.psu.edu/pabs/pdfs/Fishes_tech_Comm2008.pdf.

3. PABS, http://www.altoona.psu.edu/pabs/amphibians_and_reptiles.htm; "Pennsylvania Native Reptile & Amphibian Species," PFBC, http://www.fishandboat.com/water/amprep/native.htm.

4. PABS, http://www.altoona.psu.edu/pabs/amphibians_and_reptiles.htm.

5. Roger Conant and Joseph Collins, *A Field Guide to Reptiles and Amphibians: Eastern and Central North America* 3rd edition (Boston: Houghton Mifflin, 1998), pp. 528-9; (PABS, http://www.altoona.psu.edu/pabs/amphibians_and_reptiles.htm.

6. "Pennsylvania Native Reptile & Amphibian Species," PFBC.

7. PABS, http://www.altoona.psu.edu/pabs/bird.html.

8. Ibid.; "Passenger Pigeon," http://en.wikipedia.org/wiki/Passenger_Pigeon.

9. PABS, http://www.altoona.psu.edu/pabs/bird.html; Eberhart, pp. 87-8.

10. PABS, http://www.altoona.psu.edu/pabs/mammals.htm.

11. Ibid.; Shoemaker, *Stories of Pennsylvania Animals*; "Mammals of Pennsylvania," Carnegie Museum of Natural History, http://www.carnegiemnh.org/mammals/collections/PAmamm/PAmamD/elk.html.

12. Shoemaker, *Stories of Pennsylvania Animals*; "Mammals of Pennsylvania," http://www.carnegiemnh.org/mammals/collections/PAmamm/PAmamD/castor.html.

13. Shoemaker, *Stories of Pennsylvania Animals*; "Mammals of Pennsylvania," http://www.carnegiemnh.org/mammals/collections/PAmamm/PAmamD/otter.html.

14. Pennsylvania Department of Conservation and Natural Resources, http://www.dcnr.state.pa.us/polycomm/jan/fisherjan98.htm; Weisberg, "Fishers are making a comeback."

15. Shoemaker, *Stories of Pennsylvania Animals*; "Mammals of Pennsylvania," Carnegie Museum of Natural History, http://www.carnegiemnh.org/mammals/collections/PAmamm/PAmamD/lynx.html; Van Wagner and Karl Shellenberger, "What Once Was," http://www.vanwagnermusic.com/once.html.

16. PABS, http://www.altoona.psu.edu/pabs/mammals.htm; "Mammals of Pennsylvania," Carnegie Museum of Natural History, http://www.carnegiemnh.org/mammals/collections/PAmamm/PAmamD/ratrat.html.

17. PABS, http://www.altoona.psu.edu/pabs/mammals.htm; Joseph Merritt, Guide to the Mammals of Pennsylvania. (Pittsburgh: University of Pittsburgh Press, 1987), p. 176.

18. PABS, http://www.altoona.psu.edu/pabs/mammals.htm; "Mammals of Pennsylvania," Carnegie Museum of Natural History, http://www.carnegiemnh.org/mammals/collections/PAmamm/PAmamD/marten.html.

19. PABS, http://www.altoona.psu.edu/pabs/mammals.htm; "Mammals of Pennsylvania," American Society of Mammalogists, http://www.mammalsociety.org/statelists/pamammals.html; "List of mammals of Pennsylvania," http://en.wikipedia.org/wiki/List_of_mammals_of_Pennsylvania; "Mammals of Pennsylvania," Carnegie Museum of Natural History, http://www.carnegiemnh.org/mammals/collections/PAmamm/PAmamD/badger.html.

20. "Mammals of Pennsylvania," Carnegie Museum of Natural History, http://www.carnegiemnh.org/mammals/collections/PAmamm/PAmamD/wolf.html; Shoemaker, *Stories of Pennsylvania Animals*; Zagofsky.

21. The Wolf Sanctuary of Pennsylvania, http://www.wolfsancpa.com/home.html.

22. "Pennsylvania Game Commission Seeks Information About Illegal Release of Wolves in Adams County" (February 23, 2006), http://www.timberwolfinformation.org/info/archieve/newspapers/viewnews.cfm?ID=2934; Moyer, "Don't believe rumors."

23. Alan Locken, personal communication with the author, April 3, 2004; Schneck, "Pennsylvania coyotes have a bit of the wolf in their background;" Zagofsky.

24. "North American Cougar," http://en.wikipedia.org/wiki/North_American_Cougar.

25. "Mammals of Pennsylvania," Carnegie Museum of Natural History, http://www.carnegiemnh.org/mammals/collections/PAmamm/PAmamD/mtnlion.html; Schneck, "Pennsylvania protects wild hogs in five counties"; "America's Mountain Lion Bounty and Sport Hunting History," Mountain Lion Foundation, http://mountainlion.org/Cougar_Timeline.asp.

26. Quoted in Bolgiano and Roberts, p. 8.

27. "America's Mountain Lion Bounty and Sport Hunting History"; Bolgiano and Roberts, pp. 22-3; Shoemaker, *Stories of Pennsylvania Animals*.

28. Shoemaker, *Extinct Pennsylvania Animals*; "Was the last wild panther in Pennsylvania shot in Berks County?" *Reading Eagle*, March 4, 2010; "America's Mountain Lion Bounty and Sport Hunting History."

29. Shoemaker, "The Panther in Pennsylvania;" USA Place Names; Bolgiano and Roberts, p. 25; Downing, p. 37.

30. Shoemaker, *Stories of Pennsylvania Animals*; Shoemaker, "The Panther in Pennsylvania;" Shoemaker, *Extinct Pennsylvania Animals*; Downing, p. 37.

31. Arment, *Varmints,* pp. 539-40.

32. Downing, p. 37.

33. Herbert Sass, "The panther prowls the East again!" *Saturday Evening Post* (March 13, 1954), pp. 33-6; Arment, *Varmints*, pp. 582-3.

34. Bolgiano and Roberts, pp. 26-7; Butz, p. 106; Downing, p. 37; "Mammals of Pennsylvania," Carnegie Museum of Natural History.

35. Eberhart, pp. 156-7, 159; Shuker, p. 155; Downing, p. 37.

36. Eberhart, p. 159; Lutz, p. 31.

37. Are There Mountain Lions In PA?, http://zormsk.tripod.com/mtlions.html; USA Place Names.

38. Are There Mountain Lions In PA?; USA Place Names.

39. Are There Mountain Lions In PA?

40. Ibid.

41. Ibid.

42. Peyre-Ferry; Shalaway.

43. Are There Mountain Lions In PA?; "Story, Rumor, or Fact?" Pennsylvania: Hunt. Fish. Shoot., http://pahuntfishshoot.com/?p=242.

44. Frye, "Mountain lions coming home."

45. Berg, "In search of the elusive Pennsylvania mountain lions"; McKeever; "Lions, tigers and bears, oh boy!"

46. "USFWS Begins Review of Mountain Lion Status in East," http://www.prnewswire.com/news-releases/usfws-begins-review-of-mountain-lion-status-in-east-51592522.html; "Eastern Cougar," U.S. Fish & Wildlife Service Northeast Region (December 3, 2008), http://www.fws.gov/northeast/Ecougar.

47. Young.

48. "Lions Confirmed," Pennsylvania: Hunt. Fish. Shoot., http://pahuntfishshoot.com/?p=242.; Patton, "Large animal attacks Lancaster County man;" Hayes; Mueller.

49. Mueller.

50. Serrao; "Lions Confirmed;" "Deer management and thoughts on predator control," Buck Manager, http://www.buckmanager.com/2009/04/17/deer-management-and-some-thoughts-on-predator-control.

51. Kuhns, "Does the mountain lion roam Pa?"

52. Ibid.; "Infrared Aerial Deer Survey 2005 Final Report," Pennsylvania Department of Conservation and Natural Resources, http://www.dcnr.state.pa.us/forestry/deer/report.aspx.

53. Kuhns, "Pocono readers 'swear' they've seen elusive mountain lion."

54. Schneck, "Bigfoot in Pennsylvania."

55. Ibid.

56. Ibid.

Chapter 3

1. "Big cat," http://en.wikipedia.org/wiki/Big_cat.

2. Shoemaker, *Juniata Memories*, p. 204.

3. Shoemaker, "The Courage of Peter Pentz," pp. 23-4.

4. Ibid., p. 24.

5. Ibid., p. 25.

6. Ibid., p. 26.

7. Quoted in Bolgiano and Roberts, p. 21.

8. "Ocelot," http://en.wikipedia.org/wiki/Ocelot; "Jaguar," http://en.wikipedia.org/wiki/Jaguar.

9. Warco.

10. Ibid.

11. Shoemaker, *Felis Catus in Pennsylvania?*, p. 27; USA Place Names.

12. Shoemaker, *Felis Catus in Pennsylvania?*, p. 27.

13. Ibid., pp. 27-8.

14. Ibid., p. 28.

15. Arment, *Varmints*, p. 540.

16. Ibid.; USA Place Names; Nockamixon Township, http://www.nockamixontownship.org; Eberhart, p. 551.

17. Arment, *Varmints*, pp. 541, 544.

18. Ibid., p. 544.

19. Ibid., pp. 541, 544; "European Wildcat," http://en.wikipedia.org/wiki/European_Wildcat; Shoemaker, *Felis Catus in Pennsylvania?*, p. 28; Eberhart, p. 552; "Jaguarundi," http://en.wikipedia.org/wiki/Jaguarundi.

20. Arment, *Varmints*, p. 548.

21. Ibid., pp. 549-50.

22. Ibid., pp. 581-2.

23. Ibid., p. 536

24. Ibid.

25. Ibid., p. 538

26. Ibid., p. 548.

27. Ibid., p. 590; Coleman, *Mysterious America*, p. 142.

28. Arment, *Varmints*, pp. 537-8.

29. "Canada Lynx," http://en.wikipedia.org/wiki/Canadian_lynx.

30. "Black panther," http://en.wikipedia.org/wiki/Black_panther.

31. Arment, *Varmints*, pp. 550-1.

32. Ibid., p. 552.

33. Ibid., pp. 552-3.

34. Ibid., pp. 554-5.

35. Ibid., pp. 555-6.

36. Ibid., p. 556.

37. Ibid., p. 557.

38. Ibid., pp. 557-61.

39. Ibid., pp. 561-5.

40. Ibid., pp. 565-6.

41. Ibid., pp. 566-7.

42. Ibid., pp. 568-9.

43. Ibid., pp. 567-8.

44. Ibid., pp. 570-2.

45. Ibid., pp. 572-3.

46. Ibid., pp. 574-5.

47. Ibid., pp. 575-8.

48. Ibid., pp. 578-80.

49. Ibid., pp. 580-1.

50. Ibid., pp. 582-3.

51. Ibid., p. 583.

52. Bord, *Unsolved Mysteries*; USA Place Names.

53. Arming, *Varmints*, p. 584.

54. Ibid., p. 585.

55. Ibid., pp. 586-7.

56. Ibid., pp. 587-8

57. Ibid., p. 589.

58. Ibid., p. 590.

59. Ibid.

60. Lutz, p. 31.

61. Are There Mountain Lions in PA?, http://zormsk.tripod.com/mtlions.html.

62. Ibid.

63. Miller, "House cat or cougar?" Arment, *Varmints*, p. 590.

64. Becker, "Mystery cat's eyes glowed in the night;" Becker, "Mystery cat passes up BBQ after man yells out."

65. McCloy and Miller, p. 146.

66. Ibid., p. 147; Coghlan, *Further Cryptozoology*, p. 48.

67. Georges Leclerc, *Natural History, General and Particular* (London: A. Strahan and T. Caldwell, 1791), Vol. 5, pp. 210-4.

68. Thomas Pennant, *Synopsis of Quadrupeds* (Chester, England: J. Monk, 1771), p. 180.

69. Shuker, p. 162; Arment, "Black Panthers in North America," p. 42.

70. Richard Lydekker, Harmsworth Natural History (London: Carmelite House, 1910), p. 392.

71. Shoemaker, *Extinct Pennsylvania Animals*.

72. "American Lion," http://en.wikipedia.org/wiki/American_Lion.

73. Coleman, *Mysterious America*, pp. 128-32, 153.

74. Mike Grayson, *Fortean Times* No. 36 (winter 1982): 58-9; Shuker, pp. 170-2.

75. Coleman, *Mysterious America*, pp. 153-4.

Chapter 4

1. Eberhart, pp. 655-90.

2. USA Place Names.

3. "Pennsylvania Lakes," PFBC, http://www.fish.state.pa.us/lakes.htm.

4. Charles Skinner, *Myths and Legends of Our Own Land* (Philadelphia: Lippincott, 1896), vol. 2, p. 304.

5. "*Esox*," http://en.wikipedia.org/wiki/Esox; "Pennsylvania Fishes," PFBC, http://fishandboat.com/fishes.htm.

6. Raystown Lake Online, http://www.lakeraystown.com; "Raystown Lake," http://en.wikipedia.org/wiki/Raystown_Lake.

7. Raystown Lake Online.

8. Raystown Ray, http://www.raystownray.com/index.asp?section=Home.
9. Ibid.
10. Ibid.; "Pennsylvania State Record Fish," BFBC, http://fishandboat.com/strecord.htm.
11. Raystown Ray, http://www.raystownray.com/index.asp?section=Sightings.
12. Ibid.
13. Ibid.
14. Ibid.
15. Ibid.
16. Ibid.
17. Ibid.
18. Ibid., http://www.raystownray.com/index.asp?section=What's New.
19. Ibid., http://www.raystownray.com/index.asp?section=Sightings.
20. Ibid.
21. Ibid., http://www.raystownray.com/index.asp?section=Home.

Chapter 5

1. PABS, http://www.altoona.psu.edu/pabs/amphibians_and_reptiles.htm; "Snakes of Pennsylvania Species Checklist," PFBC, http://www.fish.state.pa.us/snakespaspecies.htm.
2. "New tenants find python in Lancaster home," WGAL-TV, Channel 8 (Lancaster, PA), February 19, 2010; "Dead python found in rental car," http://www.autorentalnews.com/Channel/Rental-Operations/News/Story/2010/05/Dead-Python-Found-in-Rental-Car.aspx; Joe Elias, "Python found in Annville Township," *Patriot-News* (Harrisburg, PA), July 10, 2009.
3. Arment, *Boss Snakes*, p. 295.
4. Ibid., p. 283.
5. Eberhart, p. 202; Arment, "Giant Snakes in Pennsylvania," pp. 37-8.
6. Arment, "Giant Snakes in Pennsylvania," pp. 37-8.
7. "More Beastly Legends!" Philadelphia Weirdness, http://phillyist.com/2008/07/30/philadelphia_weirdness_6.php; "Tumbling Run Monster," Pennsylvania Dutch Haunts & History, http://sites.google.com/site/hauntsandhistory/pennsylvaniadutchhaunts&history3.
8. Arment, *Boss Snakes*, pp. 310-11.
9. Ibid., pp. 283-4.
10. Ibid., pp. 284-5.
11. "Battle of Gettysburg," http://en.wikipedia.org/wiki/Battle_of_Gettysburg.
12. Arment, "Giant Snakes in Pennsylvania," p. 37.
13. Arment, *Boss Snakes*, pp. 285-6.
14. Ibid., p. 298.
15. Ibid., p. 286.
16. Hall, "More giant snakes alive," p. 81.
17. Arment, *Boss Snakes*, p. 312.
18. Ibid., pp. 287-8.
19. Ibid., p. 288.
20. Ibid., p. 312.

21. Ibid., p. 288.

22. Ibid., p. 289.

23. Ibid., p. 290.

24. Ibid.

25. Ibid., pp. 290-1.

26. Ibid., p. 291.

27. Ibid., p. 292.

28. Ibid., pp. 292-4.

29. Ibid.

30. Ibid., p. 295.

31. Ibid., p. 296.

32. Ibid., pp. 296-7.

33. Ibid., p. 297.

34. Ibid.

35. Ibid., p. 313.

36. Ibid., p. 298.

37. Ibid., pp. 298-9.

38. Ibid., p. 299.

39. Ibid., pp. 299-300, 313.

40. Ibid., p. 301.

41. Ibid.

42. Ibid., pp. 301-2.

43. Ibid., pp. 302-3.

44. Ibid., p. 303.

45. Ibid.

46. Ibid., p. 304.

47. Ibid., pp. 304-5.

48. Ibid., p. 305.

49. Ibid., p. 306.

50. Ibid., pp. 306-7.

51. Ibid., p. 313; Arment, "Giant Snakes in Pennsylvania," p. 39.

52. Arment, *Boss Snakes*, pp. 307-8.

53. Ibid., p. 308.

54. Ibid., p. 309.

55. "King Cobra," http://en.wikipedia.org/wiki/King_Cobra.

56. Arment, *Boss Snakes*, p. 309.

57. Ibid., p. 313; Arment, "Giant Snakes in Pennsylvania," p. 39; USA Place Names.

58. Arment, *Boss Snakes*, pp. 313-14.

59. Ibid., pp. 309-10.

60. Arment, "Giant Snakes in Pennsylvania," p. 39.

61. Arment, *Boss Snakes*, p. 314.

62. Ibid.

63. Arment, "Giant Snakes in Pennsylvania," p. 39.

64. Ibid.

65. Arment, *Boss Snakes*, p. 315; Arment, "Giant Snakes in Pennsylvania," pp. 39-40.

66. Arment, "Giant Snakes in Pennsylvania," p. 39; Arment, *Boss Snakes*, p. 315.

67. Arment, "Giant Snakes in Pennsylvania," p. 40.

68. Arment, *Boss Snakes*, p. 316.

69. David Barker and Tracy Barker, *On Burmese Pythons in the Everglades*. Boerne, TX: VPI Library, 2009.

Chapter 6

1. Hall, *Thunderbirds*, pp. 47-69.

2. Ibid., p. 96.

3. "Allegheny National Forest," http://en.wikipedia.org/wiki/Allegheny_National_Forest; "List of Pennsylvania state forests," http://en.wikipedia.org/wiki/List_of_Pennsylvania_state_forests.

4. "Cowboys & Dragons," *Strange Magazine*, http://www.strangemag.com/strangemag/strange21/thunderbird21/thunderbird6_21.html; Lyman; Hall, *Thunderbirds*.

5. Lyman, pp. 94, 97; Hall, *Thunderbirds*, pp. 99, 103.

6. Hall, *Thunderbirds*, pp. 101, 191.

7. Ibid., p. 103.

8. Ibid., pp. 103-4.

9. Ibid., pp. 101, 191.

10. Lyman, p. 97; Bord, *Alien Animals*, p. 120.

11. Hall, *Thunderbirds*, pp. 101, 191.

12. Gerald Musinsky, "Return Of The Thunderbird: Avian Mystery of the Black Forest," Reflections on Cryptozoology, http://www.cryptozoology.net/english/reflections/return.html.

13. Ibid.

14. Lyman, p. 94; Hall, *Thunderbirds*, pp. 104, 191.

15. Hall, *Thunderbirds*, pp. 104, 191.

16. "The Giant Claw," http://en.wikipedia.org/wiki/The_Giant_Claw.

17. Hall, *Thunderbirds*, pp. 104, 191.

18. Musinsky.

19. Hall, *Thunderbirds*, p. 104; Clark, *Unexplained!*, p. 511; Musinsky; 1969 Humanoid Reports, http://www.ufoinfo.com/humanoid/humanoid1969.shtml.

20. Hall, *Thunderbirds*, p. 105; Clark, *Unexplained!*, p. 511; Musinsky.

21. Clark, *Unexplained!*, p. 512; Hall, *Thunderbirds*, p. 105; "Piper J-3," http://en.wikipedia.org/wiki/Piper_J-3; "Cessna 140," http://en.wikipedia.org/wiki/Cessna_120.

22. Hall, *Thunderbirds*, p. 105.

23. Ibid., p. 100.

24. Ibid., p. 105; Lyman, p. 97.

25. Hall, *Thunderbirds*, pp. 105-6.

26. Musinksy; "Hurricane Agnes," http://en.wikipedia.org/wiki/Hurricane_Agnes.

27. Hall, *Thunderbirds*, p. 106.

28. Ibid.

29. Ibid., pp. 98-9.

30. Ibid., pp. 106-7.

31. Musinksy.

32. Hall, *Thunderbirds*, pp. 107-8; Musinsky.

33. Clark, *Unexplained!* p. 511.

34. Hall, *Thunderbirds*, p. 108; Musinsky.

35. Hall, *Thunderbirds*, p. 108; Musinsky.

36. Hall, *Thunderbirds*, p. 108.

37. Ibid.

38. Ibid., p. 109; Musinsky.

39. Musinsky; "Great Blue Heron," http://en.wikipedia.org/wiki/Great_Blue_Heron.

40. Hall, *Thunderbirds*, p. 109; Musinsky.

41. Musinsky.

42. Ibid.; Hall, *Thunderbirds*, p. 109.

43. Hall, *Thunderbirds*, p. 109; Musinsky.

44. "The Giant Thunderbird Returns," About.com, http://paranormal.about.com/library/weekly/aa100801a.htm.

45. Ibid.

46. Ibid.; The Humanoid Contact Database: Humanoid Reports—2001, http://iraap.org/rosales/2001.htm.

47. "Two giant 'black birds,'" Phantoms & Monsters, http://naturalplane.blogspot.com/2010/02/humanoid-cryptid-encounter-reports-8.html.

48. Albert Rosales, http://www.skyscan.org/humanoid05.htm.

49. Stan Gordon, "Was this another close range encounter with a thunderbird near South Greensburg, Pennsylvania?" Paranormal News, http://www.paranormalnews.com/article.asp?ArticleID=1432.

50. Lyman, p. 96.

51. Musinsky.

52. Ibid.

53. Ibid.

54. Ibid.

55. Ibid.; USA Place Names.

56. Musinsky.

57. Ibid.

58. Ibid.; "Cowboys & Dragons;" Hall, *Thunderbirds*, pp. 133-7.

59. "California Condor," http://en.wikipedia.org/wiki/California_Condor.

60. "Golden Eagle," http://en.wikipedia.org/wiki/Golden_Eagle.

61. "Bald Eagle," http://en.wikipedia.org/wiki/Bald_Eagle.

62. "Great Blue Heron."

63. "Turkey Vulture," http://en.wikipedia.org/wiki/Turkey_Vulture.

64. "Albatross," http://en.wikipedia.org/wiki/Albatross.

65. "Andean Condor," http://en.wikipedia.org/wiki/Andean_Condor; "Eagle," http://en.wikipedia.org/wiki/Eagle.

66. "Teratornithidae," http://en.wikipedia.org/wiki/Teratornithidae.

67. *"Argentavis,"* http://en.wikipedia.org/wiki/Argentavis.

68. "Teratornithidae."

69. *"Teratornis,"* http://en.wikipedia.org/wiki/Teratornis.

70. "Teratornithidae."

71. *"Argentavis."*

Chapter 7

1. Berry, pp. 94-126; BFRO, http://www.bfro.net/GDB/state_listing.asp?state=pa; PBS, http://www.pabigfootsociety.com/sightings.html; PRO, http://www.paresearchers.com/Bigfoot_Research/Bigfoot_Database/bigfoot_database.html.

2. Eberhart, p. 333.

3. Arment, *Historical Bigfoot,* pp. 271-2; Berry, p. 95; Bord, *Bigfoot Casebook,* pp. 6-7, 219.

4. Arment, *Historical Bigfoot,* p. 272.

5. Ibid.

6. Ibid., pp. 273-4.

7. Ibid., pp. 274-5.

8. Ibid., p. 275.

9. Ibid., pp. 275-6.

10. Ibid., p. 276.

11. Bord, *Bigfoot Casebook,* p. 223.

12. Arment, *Historical Bigfoot,* pp. 276-7.

13. Ibid., p. 277.

14. Ibid., p. 278.

15. Ibid., pp. 278-80.

16. Ibid., p. 280.

17. Ibid.

18. Ibid., p. 281.

19. Ibid., pp. 282-3.

20. Ibid., pp. 284-5.

21. Ibid., pp. 286-8.

22. Ibid., pp. 288-9.

23. Ibid., p. 289.

24. Ibid., p. 291.

25. Ibid., p. 290.

26. Ibid., p. 292.

27. Ibid., p. 293.

28. Berry, p. 95.

29. Clark and Coleman, *Creatures of the Outer Edge,* p. 65.

30. Arment, *Historical Bigfoot,* p. 294.

31. Berry, p. 95.

32. Ibid.; Pennsylvania Bigfoot Society (PBS).

33. Berry, p. 95.

34. Ibid., p. 96.

35. PBS.

36. Berry, p. 96.

37. Ibid.; PBS.

38. Berry, p. 96; PBS.

39. BFRO #12951.

40. PBS.

41. BFRO #9546.

42. PBS.

43. Berry, p. 96.

44. Ibid.; Green, pp. 257-8; Keel, pp. 126-7.

45. Keel, p. 126.

46. BFRO #23956.

47. BFRO #19170.

48. PBS.

49. Ibid.; BFRO #3566.

50. Berry, p. 96.

51. PBS.

52. Ibid.; Berry, p. 97.

53. PBS; Bord, *Bigfoot Casebook*, p. 258; BFRO #856.

54. PRO; BFRO #3559.

55. BFRO #5563; GCBRO.

56. PBS; PRO; BFRO #1089, 14707.

57. PBS.

58. Klement, pp. 6, 16-17, 66-7, 69.

59. Ibid., pp. 11, 34-7.

60. Ibid., pp. 54-8, 70-3, 81-5.

61. Ibid., p. 90; Craig Woolheater, "Is This Jan Klement?" Cryptomundo, http://www.cryptomundo.
com/bigfoot-report/klement-2.

62. PBS.

63. Ibid.

64. BFRO #3554.

65. Berry, p. 97; USA Place Names.

66. Berry, p. 97; PBS.

67. Ibid.

68. Berry, p. 97.

69. Ibid.

70. Ibid.

71. Ibid., p. 98.

72. Green, pp. 260-1, 263.

73. Bord, *Bigfoot Casebook,* p. 271.

74. Ibid.; Berry, p. 100.

75. Bord, *Bigfoot Casebook*, p. 271.
76. PBS.
77. Berry, pp. 97-8.
78. Ibid., p. 98; PBS.
79. Ibid., p. 102; PBS.
80. Berry, p. 98.
81. Ibid.; PBS; Bord, *Bigfoot Casebook*, p. 272.
82. Berry, p. 98; PBS.
83. Ibid.
84. Berry, p. 98; PBS; 1973 Humanoid Reports, http://www.ufoinfo.com/humanoid/humanoid1973.
    shtml.
85. Berry, p. 98.
86. Ibid.; PBS.
87. Berry, p. 99; PBS; 1973 Humanoid Reports; Bord, *Bigfoot Casebook*, p. 272.
88. Berry, p. 99; PBS.
89. Berry, p. 99; PBS.
90. PBS; Bord, *Bigfoot Casebook*, p. 272.
91. PBS.
92. Berry, p. 99; PBS; 1973 Humanoid Reports; Bord, *Bigfoot Casebook*, p. 272.
93. PBS.
94. Berry, p. 99; PBS; 1973 Humanoid Reports.
95. Berry, p. 99; PBS.
96. Berry, p. 100; Bord, *Bigfoot Casebook*, p. 272.
97. Berry, p. 100; Bord, *Bigfoot Casebook*, p. 273; PBS.
98. Berry, p. 100; PBS.
99. Berry, p. 100; Bord, *Bigfoot Casebook*, p. 273; PRO.
100. Berry, p. 100; PBS.
101. 1973 Humanoid Reports.
102. Berry, p. 100.
103. Ibid.
104. Berry, p. 101; PBS.
105. Berry, p. 101; Bord, *Bigfoot Casebook*, p. 273; PBS.
106. Berry, p. 101; Bord, *Bigfoot Casebook*, p. 273.
107. Berry, p. 101; Bord, *Bigfoot Casebook*, p. 273; PBS.
108. Berry, p. 101; Bord, *Bigfoot Casebook*, p. 273.
109. Berry, p. 101; Bord, *Bigfoot Casebook*, pp. 130-1; Green, p. 261; 1973 Humanoid Reports.
110. Berry, p. 101.
111. Ibid.; Bord, *Bigfoot Casebook*, pp. 133-5; Coleman and Clark, pp. 97-105; Green, pp. 261-2;
    PBS; 1973 Humanoid Reports.
112. Berry, p. 102; Bord, *Bigfoot Casebook*, p. 274; 1973 Humanoid Reports.
113. Berry, p. 102; PBS; 1973 Humanoid Reports.
114. Berry, p. 102; PBS.
115. Berry, p. 102; Bord, *Bigfoot Casebook*, p. 275; PBS; 1973 Humanoid Reports.

116. Berry, p. 102; PBS.

117. PBS.

118. Berry, p. 102; Bord, *Bigfoot Casebook*, p. 280; 1974 Humanoid Reports, http://www.ufoinfo. com/humanoid/humanoid1974.shtml.

119. Berry, p. 102; Bord, *Bigfoot Casebook*, p. 276; Green, pp. 262-3; PBS.

120. BFRO #2712L PBS.

121. Berry, p. 103; PBS.

122. PBS.

123. BFRO #3572.

124. PBS.

125. GCBRO; PBS; USA Place Names.

126. PBS.

127. Berry, p. 103.

128. Ibid., p. 105; PBS; USA Place Names.

129. Berry, p. 105; PBS; 1975 Humanoid Reports, http://www.ufoinfo.com/humanoid/humanoid1975.shtml.

130. Berry, p. 103.

131. Ibid., p. 103; PBS.

132. Berry, p. 104; PBS.

133. Ibid.

134. Ibid.

135. Ibid.; PRO.

136. Berry, p. 105; PBS.

137. Berry, p. 104.

138. Ibid.; PBS.

139. Berry, p. 105; PBS.

140. Berry, p. 105.

141. BFRO #3562; PRO.

142. Berry, p. 105; PBS.

143. BFRO #3556; PRO.

144. Berry, p. 105.

145. Bord, *Bigfoot Casebook*, p. 290.

146. PBS.

147. Ibid.

148. GCBRO.

149. Berry, p. 105; Bord, *Bigfoot Casebook*, p. 147; PBS.

150. Berry, p. 106; PBS.

151. BFRO #3122; PRO.

152. BFRO #3547.

153. PRO.

154. BFRO #3560; PRO.

155. Berry, p. 106; PBS.

156. Berry, p. 108; PRO.

157. PRO.
158. Ibid.
159. Berry, p. 108; PRO.
160. Berry, p. 106; PBS.
161. Bord, *Bigfoot Casebook,* p. 292.
162. Berry, p. 106; Green, p. 264; PBS.
163. Bord, *Bigfoot Casebook,* p. 292.
164. PRO.
165. Berry, p. 106; Bord, *Bigfoot Casebook,* p. 293.
166. Berry, p. 106; Bord, *Bigfoot Casebook,* p. 294; Green, p. 264; PBS.
167. Berry, p. 107; PBS.
168. BFRO #2932.
169. Berry, p. 107; PBS.
170. BFRO #3280; GCBRO.
171. Berry, p. 107; PBS.
172. Ibid.
173. Ibid.
174. BFRO #11506.
175. Berry, p. 108; PRO.
176. Berry, pp. 107-8; PBS.
177. Berry, p. 108; PBS.
178. Ibid.
179. Berry, p. 108.
180. Ibid., p. 109.
181. Ibid.; USA Place Names.
182. Berry, p. 109.
183. Ibid.; Bord, *Bigfoot Casebook,* p. 299.
184. Berry, p. 109; Bord, *Bigfoot Casebook,* p. 299.
185. Berry, p. 110; PRO.
186. Berry, p. 110; PBS.
187. BFRO #10632.
188. PBS.
189. Berry, p. 110.
190. Ibid., p. 112: PBS.
191. BFRO #2452; PRO.
192. PRO.
193. Berry, p. 110; PBS.
194. Berry, p. 111; PBS.
195. Ibid.
196. Ibid.
197. Ibid.
198. PBS.
199. GCBRO.

200. Berry, p. 110; PRO.
201. PBS.
202. Ibid.
203. Berry, p. 115; PBS.
204. Berry, p. 112; PBS.
205. Ibid.
206. Ibid.
207. Berry, p. 112; PBS.
208. PBS.
209. Berry, p. 113; PBS.
210. Berry, p. 113.
211. Ibid.
212. Ibid.; PBS.
213. Berry, p. 114; PBS.
214. Berry, p. 114.
215. Ibid.; PBS.
216. Ibid.
217. Ibid.
218. Berry, p. 115; PBS.
219. Berry, p. 116; PBS.
220. Ibid.
221. Ibid.
222. Berry, p. 116.
223. Ibid.
224. Ibid., pp. 116-17; PBS.
225. Berry, p. 117; PBS.
226. Ibid.
227. Berry, p. 118; PBS.
228. Berry, p. 117.
229. Ibid.
230. Ibid.
231. Ibid.
232. Ibid., p. 118; PBS.
233. PRO.
234. Berry, p. 118; PBS.
235. Ibid.
236. PRO.
237. Berry, p. 118; PBS.
238. BFRO #1134L PRO.
239. PBS.
240. Berry, p. 118.
241. PBS.
242. Ibid.

243. Ibid.
244. Ibid.
245. Berry, p. 118.
246. Ibid., p. 118.
247. Ibid., pp. 118-19; USA Place Names.
248. Berry, p. 119.
249. PBS.
250. Ibid.
251. Ibid.; BFRO #3567.
252. PBS.
253. Berry, p. 119.
254. Ibid.; PBS.
255. PBS.
256. BFRO #3584; PRO.
257. Berry, p. 120; PBS.
258. BFRO #3571; PBS.
259. PBS.
260. Ibid.
261. Ibid.
262. Ibid.
263. Ibid.
264. Berry, p. 120.
265. Ibid.
266. Ibid.
267. Ibid.
268. Bord, *Bigfoot Casebook*, pp. 179-80; PBS.
269. Bord, *Bigfoot Casebook*, p. 180.
270. PBS.
271. Berry, p. 121; USA Place Names.
272. GCBRO.
273. BFRO #3647.
274. Berry, p. 121; USA Place Names.
275. Berry, p. 121.
276. Ibid.
277. Ibid.; USA Place Names.
278. Berry, p. 121.
279. Ibid., p. 122.
280. PBS.
281. Berry, p. 122.
282. Ibid.; USA Place Names.
283. Berry, p. 122.
284. Ibid.
285. Ibid.

286. Ibid.

287. Ibid.

288. Ibid.

289. PBS.

290. Berry, p. 122.

291. BFRO Media Article #265.

292. PBS.

293. Ibid.

294. Berry, p. 123.

295. Ibid.

296. Ibid.; USA Place Names.

297. Berry, p. 123.

298. Ibid.; PBS.

299. Ibid.

300. Berry, p. 123.

301. Ibid., p. 124; USA Place Names.

302. Berry, p. 124.

303. Ibid.

304. Ibid.; PBS.

305. Berry, p. 124.

306. Ibid.

307. Ibid.

308. Ibid.

309. Ibid.

310. Ibid.

311. PRO.

312. PBS.

313. Berry, p. 125.

314. BFRO #3634; PBS; PRO.

315. BFRO #3647.

316. PRO.

317. PBS.

318. Ibid.

319. Berry, p. 125.

320. Ibid.

321. Ibid.

322. Ibid.

323. Ibid.

324. PBS.

325. Berry, p. 125.

326. Ibid.

327. PBS; Ghost Town USA's Guide to the Ghost Towns of Pennsylvania, http://freepages.history.
rootsweb.ancestry.com/~gtusa/usa/pa.htm,

328. Berry, p. 125.

329. Ibid.
330. Ibid.; USA Place Names.
331. Berry, p. 126; USA Place Names.
332. PBS.
333. Berry, p. 126.
334. Ibid.; PBS.
335. GCBRO.
336. PBS.
337. BFRO #11228.
338. GCBRO; PRO.
339. BFRO #24301.
340. PBS; USA Place Names.
341. Keel, p. 127.
342. PBS.
343. Ibid.; USA Place Names.
344. PBS.
345. Ibid.; BFRO #2758.
346. PBS.
347. Ibid.
348. Ibid.; Keel, pp. 127-8.
349. PBS.
350. Ibid.
351. Ibid.
352. Ibid.
353. Ibid; BFRO #3551.
354. BFRO #4478; PBS.
355. PBS.
356. Ibid.
357. Ibid.
358. Ibid.
359. BFRO #4117.
360. BFRO #3558.
361. GCBRO.
362. Ibid.
363. BFRO #1005.
364. PBS; PRO.
365. PBS.
366. Ibid.; PRO.
367. BFRO #3866.
368. PBS.
369. Ibid.
370. BFRO #9607.
371. PBS.

372. Ibid.
373. Ibid.
374. Ibid.
375. Ibid.
376. Ibid.
377. Ibid.
378. BFRO #14677.
379. BFRO #3563; PBS.
380. BFRO #3569; PBS; PRO.
381. BFRO #105; PBS.
382. BFRO #3542; PRO.
383. BFRO #3360; PRO.
384. BFRO #1214; PRO.
385. BFRO #3561; PBS; PRO.
386. PBS.
387. Ibid.
388. PRO.
389. GCBRO.
390. PBS.
391. PRO.
392. Ibid.; PBS.
393. BFRO #2898; PRO.
394. PBS; PRO.
395. PBS.
396. BFRO #571; PBS.
397. BFRO #208; PBS; PRO.
398. PBS.
399. Ibid.; Bord, *Bigfoot Casebook,* p, 200.
400. PBS.
401. Ibid.
402. BFRO #7137.
403. PBS.
404. Ibid.
405. PRO.
406. GCBRO.
407. PBS.
408. Ibid.
409. Ibid.
410. Ibid.
411. "Creepy Things in the Woods," Paranormal News, http://www.paranormalnews.com/article.
      asp?articleID=755.
412. PBS.
413. Ibid.; GCBRO.

414. PBS; PRO.
415. BFRO #2618.
416. PBS.
417. GCBRO.
418. PBS.
419. GCBRO.
420. PBS.
421. BFRO #3231.
422. BFRO #3401.
423. PBS.
424. GCBRO.
425. PBS.
426. GCBRO.
427. PBS.
428. Ibid.
429. Ibid.
430. Ibid; Jennings, "Bigfoot strikes in Derry Township."
431. GCBRO.
432. Ibid; PBS.
433. PBS.
434. PRO.
435. PBS.
436. Ibid.; GCBRO.
437. GCBRO.
438. PBS.
439. Jennings, "Bigfoot strikes Derry Township."
440. Ibid.; PBS.
441. Jennings, "Bigfoot strikes Derry Township."
442. GCBRO.
443. PBS.
444. Ibid.
445. Ibid.
446. Ibid.
447. Ibid.
448. Ibid.
449. Ibid.
450. Ibid.
451. Ibid.
452. Ibid.
453. Ibid.
454. Ibid.
455. BFRO #8633.
456. PBS.

457. Ibid.

458. Ibid.

459. GCBRO.

460. PBS.

461. Ibid.

462. Ibid.

463. GCBRO.

464. PBS.

465. Ibid.

466. BFRO #9694.

467. BFRO #19589.

468. PBS.

469. GCBRO.

470. PBS.

471. Ibid.; BFRO #12034.

472. BFRO #13714.

473. PBS.

474. BFRO #15306.

475. PBS.

476. BFRO #17981.

477. PBS.

478. Ibid.

479. Ibid.

480. GCBRO.

481. "Bigfoot Images Captured By Local Hunter," WPXI-TV, Channel 11 (Pittsburgh), October 29, 2007.

482. PBS.

483. BFRO #21962.

484. BFRO #25085.

485. PBS.

486. Ibid.

487. BFRO #24731.

488. Nick Redfern, "There's Something in the Woods...," http://monsterusa.blogspot. com/2009_06_01_archive.html.

489. Ibid.

490. Ibid.

491. Ibid.

492. Ibid.

493. PBS.

494. Stan Gordon, "Motorist Has Near Collision With Bigfoot In Pennsylvania," Paranormal News, http://www.paranormalnews.com/article.asp?articleID=1384.

495. Stan Gordon, "Pennsylvanians Report Close Encounters With UFOs and Bigfoot During 2009," Phantoms & Monsters, http://naturalplane.blogspot.com/2010/01/report-close-encounters-

bigfoot.html.

496. Ibid.

497. PBS.

498. Stan Gordon, "Pennsylvanians Report Close Encounters With UFOs and Bigfoot During 2009."

499. Zuchowski; PBS.

500. Zuchowski.

501. "Primate," http://en.wikipedia.org/wiki/Primate; "Doma people," http://en.wikipedia.org/wiki/Vadoma.

502. "*Gigantopithecus,*" http://en.wikipedia.org/wiki/Gigantopithecus.

503. Jane Christmas, "Giant ape lived alongside humans," McMaster University *Daily News* (November 7, 2005), http://dailynews.mcmaster.ca/story.cfm?id=3637.

Chapter 8

1. Giant Skeletons?, http://www.spanishhill.com/skeletons/default.shtml.

2. Ibid.

3. "The grave of a giant," *Towanda Daily Review,* October 25, 1897.

4. "Part 1: Aaron Wright, Solomon Spalding, and the riants of Conneaut," The Spalding Research Project, http://solomonspalding.com/SRP/saga2/sagawt0a.htm.

5. Ibid.

6. "Giant Skeleton in Pennsylvania Mound," American Antiquarian, 7 (1885): 52.

7. Giant Skeletons?; Giant Bones Discoveries, http://www.returnofthenephilim.com/GiantBonesDiscoveries.html.

8. Giant Skeletons?

9. Giant Bones Discoveries; 1973 Humanoid Reports, http://www.ufoinfo.com/humanoid/humanoid1973.shtml.

10. 1977 Humanoid Reports, http://www.ufoinfo.com/humanoid/humanoid1977.shtml.

11. Eberhart, p. 522; "Lenape Stone," http://en.wikipedia.org/wiki/Lenape_Stone.

12. "Lenape Stone."

13. Henry Mercer, *The Lenape Stone or the Indian and the Mammoth* (New York: G.P. Putnam's Sons, 1885; Eberhart, p. 522.

14. Coghlan, *Further Cryptozoology,* p. 206.

15. Giant Skeletons

16. Clark, *Unnatural Phenomena,* p. 280.

17. Ibid.

18. Ibid., p. 286.

19. "Creepy Things in the Woods," Paranormal News, http://www.paranormalnews.com/article.asp?articleID=755.

20. Stan Gordon, "More Huge Flying Creature Sightings In Pennsylvania," Paranormal News, http://www.paranormalnews.com/article.asp?articleID=1271.

21. Arment, *Cryptozoology and the Investigation of Lesser Known Mystery Animals,* pp. 217-18.

22. Ibid., p. 218; "Seal found inland near Delaware River," Associated Press, June 5, 2007.

23. Clark, *Unnatural Phenomena*, p. 284.

24. Ibid., pp. 282-3.

25. Arment, "Dinos in the USA," pp. 33-4; Guilley, p. 148.

26. Stan Gordon, "Mysterious Segmenting Snake-Like Creature Reported On Pennsylvania Roadway," Paranormal News, http://www.paranormalnews.com/article.asp?articleID=1396.

27. Arment, *Cryptozoology and the Investigation of Lesser Known Mystery Animals*, pp. 216-17.

28. Jersey Devil Sightings, http://www.castleofspirits.com/stories03/jersey.html.

29. Ibid.

30. McCloy and Miller, p. 143.

31. Ibid., pp. 144-6; Loren Coleman and Bruce Hallenbeck, *Monsters of New Jersey* (Mechanicsburg, PA: Stackpole Books, 2010), pp. 116, 118.

32. Arment, *Historical Bigfoot*, p. 281.

33. Arment, *Varmints*, pp. 538-9.

34. Rife, p. 15.

35. PBS.

36. Arment, *Varmints*, p. 589.

37. Berry, p. 107; PBS.

38. "Creepy Things in the Woods," Paranormal News, http://www.paranormalnews.com/article.asp?articleID=755.

39. 1935-1939 Humanoid Reports, http://www.ufoinfo.com/humanoid/humanoid1935.shtml.

40. Rife, pp. 15-16.

41. 1973 Humanoid Reports, http://www.ufoinfo.com/humanoid/humanoid1973.shtml.

42. Rife, p. 17.

43. Coghlan, *Further Cryptozoology*, p. 54; GCBRO.

44. "Creepy Things in the Woods."

45. "Pennsylvania koala bear/fisher type animal," Cryptozoology.com, http://www.cryptozoology.com/sightings/sightings_show.php?id=2606.

46. Danger Under Dixonville, http://www.angelfire.com/ut/branton/dixonville.html; "Pennsylvania's Underground," Think About It, http://www.think-aboutit.com/underground/PENNSYLVA-NIAUNDERGROUND.htm.

47. Historic Coal Mine Disasters in Pennsylvania 1900-1976, http://www.easternusresearch.com/easternusresearch/minelink1.html.

48. "Paranormal Phenomen," About.com, http://forums.about.com/ab-paranormal/messages?lgnF=y&msg=2360.1.

49. 2005 Humanoid Reports, http://www.ufoinfo.com/humanoid/humanoid2005.shtml.

50. 2007 Humanoid Reports, http://www.ufoinfo.com/humanoid/humanoid2007.shtml.

51. Unexplained-Mysteries.com, http://www.unexplained-mysteries.com/forum/index.php?showtopic=30092.

52. "More Beastly Legends!" Philadelphia Weirdness, http://phillyist.com/2008/07/30/philadel-phia_weirdness_6.php.

53. 1975 Humanoid Reports, http://www.ufoinfo.com/humanoid/humanoid1975.shtml.

54. Godfrey, pp. 188-9.
55. Ibid.
56. Ibid., pp. 187-8.
57. 1973 Humanoid Reports.
58. Monstropedia, http://www.monstropedia.org/index.php?title=Albawitch&redirect=no.
59. Godfrey, pp. 183-4.
60. Ibid.; Monstropedia.
61. The Humanoid Contact Database: Humanoid Reports—1999, http://www.iraap.org/rosales/1999. htm.
62. "Yet Another Strange Sighting in Pennsylvania," Paranormal News, http://www.paranormalnews. com/article.asp?articleID=1391.
63. "Creepy Things in the Woods," Paranormal News, http://www.paranormalnews.com/article. asp?articleID=755.
64. Craig Woolheater, "The Yardley Yeti," Ctyptomundo, http://www.cryptomundo.com/bigfoot- report/yardley-yeti.
65. Craig Woolheater, "Exclusive Photos of the Yardley Yeti," Cryptomundo, http://www.crypto- mundo.com/bigfoot-report/yardley-yeti3.
66. Stan Gordon, "Strange Giant Insects Seen In Pennsylvania," Paranormal News, http://www. paranormalnews.com/article.asp?articleID=1380.
67. Ibid.

Bibliography

"Alligator found in downtown Pittsburgh fountain," WTAE-TV, Channel 4 (Pittsburgh), August 23, 2007.

"Alligator found in Homewood," WTAE-TV, Channel 4 (Pittsburgh), August 2, 2007.

"Alligator found in Pennsylvania hasn't been claimed yet," The Croc Press (August 20, 2007). http://www.crocodopolis.net/newsarch081907.htm.

"Alligator on the lam in Philadelphia pond," Earth Times, http://www.earthtimes.org/articles/news/66656.html.

Amidon, Dan. "'Mountain lion' causes concern." *Towanda* (PA) *Daily & Sunday Review*, April 9, 2004.

Arment, Chad. "Black Panthers in North America: Examining the Published Explanations." *North American BioFortean Review* 2 (2000): 38-56.

—. *Boss Snakes: Stories and Sightings of Giant Snakes in North America.* Landisville, PA: Coachwhip, 2008.

—. *Cryptozoology and the Investigation of Lesser-Known Mystery Animals.* Landisville, PA: Coachwhip, 2006.

—. *Cryptozoology: Science and Speculation.* Landisville, PA: Coachwhip, 2004.

—. "Dinos in the USA." *North American BioFortean Review* 2 (2000): 32-39.

—. "Giant Snakes in Pennsylvania." *North American BioFortean Review* 2 (December 2000): 36-43.

—. *The Historical Bigfoot: Early Reports of Wild Men, Hairy Giants, and Wandering Gorillas in North America.* Landisville, PA: Coachwhip, 2006.

—. "A Pennsylvania Primate." *North American BioFortean Review* 3 (May 2001): 67-69.

—. *Varmints: Mystery Carnivores of North America.* Landisville, PA: Coachwhip, 2010.

Arnold, Stephanie. "Cougars again making tracks, residents say." *Philadelphia Inquirer*, December 3, 2003.

Ayad, Moustafa. "Bigfoot aficionados relay beastly tales, insight" *Pittsburgh Post-Gazette*, September 25, 2005.

Becker, Peter. "Mountain lion on the loose?" Wayne Independent (Honesdale, PA), October 21, 2003.

—. "Mystery Cat Passes Up BBQ After Man Yells Out." Wayne Independent (Honesdale, PA), May 20, 2004.

—. "Mystery Cat's Eyes Glowed In The Night." Wayne Independent (Honesdale, PA), May 11, 2004.

Berg, Christian. "Despite lack of proof, many believe cougars lurk in Penn's Woods." *Morning Call* (Allentown, PA), January 5, 2006.

—. "In search of the elusive Pennsylvania mountain lions." *Morning Call* (Allentown, PA), October 17, 2006.

Berry, Rick. *Bigfoot on the East Coast.* The Author: Stuarts Draft, VA: 1993.

"Big on Bigfoot." *Steubenville* (OH) *Herald-Star*, September 18, 2005.

"Bigfoot and UFOs! Kecksburg has it all." *Post-Tribune* (Merrillville, IN), October 23, 2003.

"Bigfoot makes appearance in Levittown." *Bucks County* (PA) *Courier Times*, March 2, 2004.

Bolgiano, Chris, and Jerry Roberts (eds.). *The Eastern Cougar: Historic Accounts, Scientific Investigations, and New Evidence*. Mechanicsburg, PA: Stackpole Books, 2005.

Bord, Janet, and Colin Bord. *Alien Animals*

—. *Bigfoot Casebook Updated*. Enumclaw, WA: Pine Winds Press, 2006.

—. *Unexplained Mysteries of the 20th Century*. Chicago: Contemporary Books, 1989.

Bresswein, Kurt. "Snakeheads slithering closer to area waters," *Express Times* (Easton, PA), August 1, 2004.

Bruger, T.W. "Woman reports seeing mountain lion near her house." *Patriot-News* (Harrisburg, PA), August 4, 2006.

Butz, Bob. *Beast of Never, Cat of God: The Search for the Eastern Puma*. Guilford, CT: Lyons Press, 2005.

"Cayman Found in DelCo.," WPVI-TV, Channel 6 (Philadelphia), September 20, 2005.

Clark, Jerome. *Unexplained!* Farmington Hills, MI: Visible Ink Press, 1999.

—. *Unnatural Phenomena: A Guide to the Bizarre Wonders of North America*. Santa Barbara, CA: ABC-CLIO, 2005.

Clark, Jerome, and Loren Coleman. *Creatures of the Outer Edge*. New York: Warner Books, 1978.

Coghlan, Ronan. *Cryptosup: A Supplement to A Dictionary of Cryptozoology*. Bangor: Northern Ireland: Xiphos Books, 2005.

—. *A Dictionary of Cryptozoology*. Bangor: Northern Ireland: Xiphos Books, 2004.

—. *Further Cryptozoology*. Bangor: Northern Ireland: Xiphos Books, 2007.

Coleman, Loren. *Mothman and Other Curious Encounters*. New York: Paraview Press, 2002.

—. *Mysterious America,* Revised edition. New York: Paraview Press, 2001.

Collins, Jim. "Do mountain lions exist in Pa.?" *Daily Review* (Towanda, PA), April 25, 2004.

Crable, Ad. "Our very own Hogzilla." *Lancaster* (PA) *New Era,* August 11, 2004.

"Creepy things in woods." *Bucks County* (NJ) *Courier Times,* October 21, 2003.

"Crocodile found in Pennsylvania," WJXX-TV, Channel 25 (Philadelphia), July 18, 2007.

"Dad, Son Catch 3-Foot Gator While Fishing." ABC News, September 26, 2005.

Donlin, Patrick. "Officials: Canine made paw prints." *Williamsport* (PA) *Sun-Gazette,* August 2, 2007.

—. "Paw prints on road has local man asking: Could cougars be here? *Williamsport* (PA) *Sun-Gazette,* August 1, 2007.

Downing, Robert. "The search for cougars in the eastern United States." *Cryptozoology* 3 (1984): 31-49.

Dyer, Ervin. "Piranhas are biting in the Ohio." Pittsburgh Post-Gazette, September 8, 2001.

Eberhart, George. *Mysterious Creatures.* Santa Barbara, CA: ABC-CLIO, 2002.

Einsig, Bill. "More tales about lions." *York* (PA) *Daily Record,* September 25, 2005.

Fontana, Erica. "Pennsylvania one of top states for Bigfoot sightings." *Indiana* (PA) *Gazette,* March 26, 2007.

"4-year-old pulls piranha from Lancaster County river." WBAL-TV, Channel 11 (Baltimore, MD), June 26, 2005.

Francis, Scott. *Monster Spotter's Guide to North America*. Cincinnati: HOW Books, 2007.

Frederick, Robb. "Stories abound at Bigfoot conference." *Pittsburgh Tribune-Review*, September 22, 2002.

Frye, Bob. "Five counties in Pennsylvania are home to wild hogs." *Pittsburgh Tribune-Review*, May 6, 2007.

—. "Mountain lions coming home." *Pittsburgh Tribune-Review*, January 15, 2006.

—. "Wild hogs join exotic species in Pa." *Pittsburgh Tribune-Review*, August 28, 20.

"Giant snakes on loose have people in uproar." WEWS-TV, Channel 5 (Cleveland, OH), June 15, 2007.

Godfrey, Linda. *Hunting the American Werewolf.* Madison, WI: Trails Books, 2006.

Gorden, Joe. "Task force focusing on invasive pig population." *Tribune-Democrat* (Johnstown, PA), November 12, 2006.

Griffith, Randy. "Does Bigfoot Lurk In Pa. Mountains?" *Tribune-Democrat* (Johnstown, PA), September 8, 2002.

Guilley, Rosemary. *Atlas of the Mysterious in North America.* New York: Facts on File, 1995.

Gwin, Harold. "Fans of Bigfoot, investigators plan conference." *Youngstown* (OH) *Vindicator*, September 14, 2003. Hall, Mark. "More giant snakes alive." *Wonders* 4 (September 1995): 80-89.

—. *Thunderbirds: America's Living Legends of Giant Birds.* New York: Paraview Press, 2004.

Hayes, John. "Authorities say alleged cougar attack a hoax." *Pittsburgh Post-Gazette*, October 26, 2008.

Heishman, Debby. "Tracking a mystery." Public Opinion (Chambersburg, PA), November 12, 2005.

Jennings, John. "Bigfoot returns." *Blairsville* (PA) *Dispatch*, January 31, 2003.

—. "Bigfoot strikes in Derry Township." Blairsville (PA) Dispatch, January 23, 2004.

Klement, Jan [pseud.]. The Creature: Personal Experiences with Bigfoot. Elgin, PA: Allegheny Press, 1976.

Kuhns, Mike. "Does the mountain lion roam Pa?" Pocono Record, October 14, 2009.

—. "Pocono readers 'swear' they've seen elusive mountain lion." *Pocono Record*, October 15, 2009. "Lake City firefighters capture alligator in Elk Creek." Erie Times-News, May 18, 2010.

Levin, Steve. "Mountain lion spotted in Beaver County." *Pittsburgh Post-Gazette*, February 19, 2004.

Lewerenz, Dan. "Despite recent reports, experts say no mountain lions in Pa." Associated Press, January 23, 2004.

"Lions, tigers and bears, oh boy!" *Clarion* (PA) *News*, December 7, 2006.

"Local Residents Report Mountain Lion Sightings." WGAL-TV, Channel 8 (Lancaster, PA), October 22, 2003.

Long, Eric. "A mountain lion near Montoursville?" *Williamsport* (PA) *Sun-Gazette*, February 20, 2007.

—. "Game Commission disputes mountain lion sighting." *Williamsport* (PA) *Sun-Gazette*, February 21, 2007.

—. "Here kitty, kitty ..." *Williamsport* (PA) *Sun-Gazette*, August 8, 2005.

Lutz, John, and Linda Lutz. "Century-old mystery rises from the shadows," *North American Bio-Fortean Review* 3 (October 2001): 30-50.

Lyman, Robert Sr. Amazing Indeed: Strange Events in the Black Forest, Volume II. Coudersport, PA: The Potter Enterprise, 1973.

Machosky, Michael. "Bigfoot researchers weed through hoaxes." Pittsburgh Tribune-Review, September 20, 2005.

McCloy, Robert, and Ray Miller Jr. Phantom of the Pines: More Tales of the Jersey Devil. Moorestown, NJ: Middle Atlantic Press, 1998.

McKee, Jason. "Authorities can't find evasive emu." Pottstown (PA) Mercury, March 5, 2004.

McKeever, Megan. "Reported cougar sightings increase." Daily Collegian (Penn State University), October 27, 2006.

Milford, Phil, and Jerry Byrd. "Pennsylvania fishermen urged to clear snakeheads from river. Bloomberg (February 20, 2006), http://www.bloomberg.com/apps/news?pid=newsarchive&sid=aaAE9X0umuQ4&refer=us.

Miller, George. "House cat or cougar?" *Erie* (PA) *Times-News*, October 30, 2003.

Miller, Todd. "Experts: Snake not attacking cats, birds." *Bucks County* (PA) *Courier Times*, June 16, 2007.

Montgomery, Robert. "Snakehead fish survives a winter in Pennsylvania." *Bass Times* (July 2005), http://sports.espn.go.com/outdoors/bassmaster/news/story?page=b_fea_bt_0507_exotic_species_snakehead_survives.

"Mountain Lion On The Loose?" KYW-TV, Channel 3 (Philadelphia), October 15, 2003.

Moyer, Ben. "Don't believe rumors that wolves have been reintroduced into Pennsylvania and New York forests." *Pittsburgh Post-Gazette*, March 5, 2006.

—. "Game Commission to track mountain lion sighting amid flood of reports." *Pittsburgh Post-Gazette*, November 5, 2006.

—. "Those lion sightings could have some teeth." *Pittsburgh Post-Gazette*, May 30, 2004.

Mueller, Gene. "Here we go again about mountain lion sightings." *Washington* (DC) *Times*, November 5, 2008.

Mullane, J.D. "Bigfoot meets the Yardley Yeti." *Bucks County* (PA) *Courier Times*, September 26, 2006.

—. "Bigfoot's on a tear through the state." *Bucks County* (PA) *Courier Times*, March 4, 2004.

—. "Creature related to Yardley Yeti?" *Bucks County* (PA) *Courier Times*, September 19, 2006.

—. "Yardley Yeti sightings rolling in." *Bucks County* (PA) *Courier Times*, September 21, 2006.

"Mystery gator spotted in central Pa. lake." *Harrisburg Patriot News*, July 18, 2003.

Nale, Mark. "Experts weigh in on possible mountain lion track sighting." *Centre Daily* (State College, PA), February 12, 2006.

"Northern Snakehead," Pennsylvania Fish & Boat Commission, http://fishandboat.com/water/fish/snakehead/snakehead.htm.

"Officials say wild boar problems continue." *Pittsburgh Post-Gazette*, November 3, 2003.

"Pacu, Not Piranha," Pennsylvania Fish & Boat Commission, http://www.fish.state.pa.us/images/pages/qa/fish/pacu.htm.

Patton, Judith. "Large animal attacks Lancaster County man." *Patriot-News* (Harrisburg, PA), October 10, 2008.

—. "Traffic-tying emu tasered, dies, on turnpike near New Stanton exit." *Patriot-News* (Harrisburg, PA), September 3, 2008.

"Pennsylvania," Bigfoot Field Researchers. Organization, http://www.bfro.net/GDB/state_listing.asp?state=pa.

"Pennsylvania," Gulf Coast Bigfoot Research Organization, http://gcbro.com/padb1.htm.

Pennsylvania Bigfoot Society, http://www.pabigfootsociety.com.

"Pennsylvania no stranger to Bigfoot sightings." *Waynesboro Record Herald*, February 18, 2002.

Pennsylvania Research Organization, http://www.paresearchers.com/index.html.

Peyre-Ferry, Marcella. "Is that a mountain lion?" *Daily Local News* (West Chester, PA), February 24, 2004.

Phillips, John. "Strange sightings reported." *Indiana* (PA) *Gazette*, February 13, 2003.

"Possible mountain lion footprint discovered in Centre County." *Centre Daily* (State College, PA), January 22, 2006.

Quann, Peg. "The mystery of the Mount Laurel lizards solved." *Burlington County* (NJ) *Times*, July 11, 2010.

Raystown Ray, http://www.raystownray.com.

Rife, Philip. *America's Nightmare Monsters*. Bloomington, IN: iUniverse, 2001.

Robinson, George. "Will the real puma stand up?" *Yardley* (PA) *News*, February 12, 2004.

Schneck, Marcus. "Bigfoot in Pennsylvania: Is he running with mountain lions?" *Patriot-News* (Harrisburg, PA), January 24, 2010.

—. "Pennsylvania coyotes have a bit of the wolf in their background." *Patriot-News* (Harrisburg, PA), January 24, 2010.

—. "Pennsylvania protects wild hogs in five counties." *Patriot-News* (Harrisburg, PA), January 23, 2009.

"Search for Carrick mountain lion called off." *Pittsburgh Tribune-Review*, February 16, 2007.

Serrao, John. "Hoax photo doesn't help believability of mountain lions in Poconos." *Pocono Record*, October 25, 2009.

Shalaway, Scott. "Mountain Lions moving in." Pittsburgh Post-Gazette, April 25, 2004.

Sherman, Rodney. "Have you seen Bigfoot?" *Clarion* (PA) *News*, April 6, 2006.

Shoemaker, Henry. *Allegheny Episodes*. Altoona, PA: Altoona Tribune, 1922.

—. "The Courage of Peter Pentz" (1912). Reprinted in *North American BioFortean Review* 2 (2000): 23-6.

—. *Extinct Pennsylvania Animals*. Altoona, PA: Altoona Tribune, 1917.

—. *Felis Catus in Pennsylvania?* Altoona, PA: Times Tribune, 1922. Reprinted in *North American BioFortean Review* 2 (2000): 27-8.

—. *Juniata Memories: Legends Collected in Central Pennsylvania*. Philadelphia: John Joseph McVey, 1916.

—. *More Pennsylvania Mountain Stories*. Reading, PA: Bright Publishing, 1912.

—. "The Panther in Pennsylvania." *Pennsylvania Game News* 31 (1943): 7, 28, 32.

—. *Stories of Pennsylvania Animals*. Altoona, PA: Altoona Tribune, 1913. http://www.altoonalibrary.org/books/stories%20of%20pa%20animals/stories%20of%20pa%20animals-html.htm.

Shuker, Karl. *Mystery Cats of the World*. London: Robert Hale, 1989.

"State Police tase loose emu on Pa. Turnpike." KDKA-TV, Channel 2 (Pittsburgh), September 3, 2008. Todd, Jennifer, and P.J. Reilly. "Sadsbury neighbors say man attacked by mountain lion." *Intelligencer Journal* (Lancaster, PA), October 10, 2008.

"Tracking mountain lion sightings." *Pittsburgh Tribune-Review*, November 26, 2006.

Warco, Kathie. "Baddest cat in town has some residents on edge." *Observer-Reporter* (Washington County, PA), September 11, 2003.

Weisberg, Deborah. "Alligator found near dam." *Pittsburgh Post-Gazette*, June 13, 2004.

—. "Fishers are making a comeback." *Pittsburgh Post-Gazette*, January 10, 2010.

—. "Local fisherman reels in a piranha." *Pittsburgh Post-Gazette*, August 1, 2006.

Wertz, Marjorie. "Group plans expedition in search for Bigfoot." *Pittsburgh Tribune-Review*, April 11, 2004.

Westcott, Scott. "Does Bigfoot live in Pennsylvania's woods?" *Erie Times News*, November 16, 2003.

Western Pennsylvania Conservancy. "The Eradication and Prevention of Feral Swine in Pennsylvania" (January 2008), http://www.paconserve. org/assets/feral-swine.pdf.

Rita Zeidner, "Genetic Profiling of Northern Snakehead Fish May Help Scientists Track Their Spread in U.S. Waters," Smithsonian National Zoological Park, http://nationalzoo.si.edu/Animals/NorthAmerica/ News/default.cfm.

Zagofsky, Al. "Elusive and adaptable, coyotes thrive in Pa." *Pocono Record*, June 17, 2007.

Zimmerman, Phyllis. "Some suspect mountain lion in horse attack." *Patriot-News* (Harrisburg, PA), July 30, 2006.

Zuchowski, Dave. "New rash of Bigfoot sightings reported across Fayette County." *Herald-Standard* (Uniontown, PA), March 17, 2010.